Scottish Baronial Families, 1250-1750

By
David Dobson

CLEARFIELD

Copyright © 2024
by David Dobson
All Rights Reserved

Published for Clearfield Company by
Genealogical Publishing Company
Baltimore, Maryland
2024

ISBN: 9780806359748

INTRODUCTION

From the eleventh century onwards, Scottish kings increasingly favoured the feudal system as a method of ruling and controlling the kingdom. To achieve this the Scots kings would encourage the immigration and settlement of Anglo-Norman and Flemish families, such as Bruce, Lindsay, and Somerville.

About this time, the kings established administrative units known as baronies. These baronies were supervised by lords known as barons, whose function included ensuring that the king's laws operated within the baronies, collecting taxes, maintaining a Barony Court where local justice was administered, and, importantly, providing the king with several knights and men when required. In fact, barons had the power to demand that their tenants fight for their overlord, a right which the Jacobite lords enforced, thereby strengthening their military power. By the late seventeenth century there were hundreds of baronies in Scotland; however, in the aftermath of the Jacobite rising of 1745-1746, the British government enacted the Heritable Jurisdiction Act of 1747, which reduced the powers of barons and the nobility in general.

In Scotland a baron was a vassal who held lands directly from the Crown. Strictly speaking, his lands must have been erected, or at least confirmed, by the king in *liberam baroniam*. A barony was granted to an individual and was normally inherited by his eldest son and heir. A barony could be forfeited to the Crown if the baron became rebellious, was incapable of running his estate, or resigned his charge. If a baron were found to be seriously in debt, the barony could be sold to pay his creditors. The barony would be returned to the Crown and then re-issued. Most baronies, on the death of a baron, would go to his heir, thus maintaining the family's link with the barony. Though baronies still exist, the power of the barons was severely diminished by the Heritable Jurisdiction Act in 1747. (See above.)

Before a barony was transferred from the deceased baron to his heir an inquest would be conducted, as in the following example:

'The Retour of Inquest serving Archibald Hamilton of Dalziel, advocate, eldest lawful son of the late James Hamilton of Dalziel, and of his wife, the late Margaret Hamilton, eldest daughter of the deceased Sir Archibald Hamilton and Benthill, of Rosehall, baronet, as nearest and lawful heir of tailzie and provision of the late Sir Hugh Hamilton of Rosehall, baronet, his uncle, in the barony of Rosehall, comprising Haggs, Kirkwood and Kirkshaw, Reyden and Gartmillan, Kipps, Brewlands, Easter Garturk, Grianletts, Blacklands, Haggsmuir, and Palace with manor-place, Dundyven, and its pertinents, Blairmeadow, and Benthill, in the parishes of Old and New Monkland, sheriffdom of Lanark; which have been in the hands of the king, as superior since September 1755.'

In the hierarchy of Scottish nobility, barons were just below viscounts. A barony should not be confused with a baronetcy.[1] King James VI created the noble rank of baronet in 1611, partly to raise funds and partly to sponsor the economic development of Ulster and later Nova Scotia. Baronets of Nova Scotia were generally granted 16,000 acres, on which they were required to settle colonists and develop the estates; however, King Charles I returned Nova Scotia to the French in 1631 as part of a peace treaty between England and France. Since the political union of Scotland and England in 1707 all new baronets have been established under the United Kingdom.

A baron had jurisdiction both civil and criminal. Every barony had a 'caput' or centre, usually where the baron lived or the barony court was held. The records of the barony courts, where they have survived, provide a unique insight into the social and economic life of the barony.

Records of barony courts provide exclusive insights to life of early modern Scotland. Every baron should have maintained a record of the activities of the barony court. Some can be found in local or national archives. Take the Guthrie family, for example. The Guthries were Barons of Guthrie in Angus from the medieval period and were generally Royalists – supporters of the House of Stuart. As Barons of Guthrie they were required to support the kings; so, for example, the Guthries checked on the loyalties of their tenants, according to the Baron Court Book of Guthrie, in 1686, where it was recorded that one Charles Air in Heughheid undertook not to become a 'fanatic (i.e., a Covenanter or militant Presbyterian).

Most surviving barony court books are unpublished; however, at least two Barony Court Books *have* been published; one is 'The Records of the Baron Court of Stitchill, 1655 to 1807' [C. Gunn, Edinburgh, 1905], and the other is 'The Court Book of the Barony of Urie, 1604 to 1747' [R. G. Barron, Edinburgh, 1892]. Occasionally, a printed source contains extracts from a Barony Court Book; for example, William Fraser's 'Cartulary of the Colquhouns of Luss' [Edinburgh 1873] includes part of the Court Book of the Barony of Luss between 1663 and 1792. The Forbes Barony Court Book, dating between 1659 and 1678, was published in Volume XIX of the *Scottish History Society Publications* in 1919. The Spalding Club published extracts from the Court Book of the Barony of Skene and Leyes in 1852.

Many barony court records and other documents dealing with the baronies remain in the archives of the landowners. However, there are some available for consultation in the National Records of Scotland in Edinburgh. These include those of the barony of Courthill from 1666 until 1719; Abercairney from 1689 until 1762; Drummond from 1712 until 1717; Lude from 1621 until 1908; Broxmouth and Pinkerton from 1620 until 1764; Abernethy, Cromdale, and Urquhart from

1617 until 1683; Monymusk from 1710 until 1771; Edinbellie from 1623 until 1793; Skene from 1613 until 1655; Logie Wishart from 1681 until 1738; Guthrie from 1666 until 1719; Leckie and Culbeg from 1687 until 1724; Thurso in 1719; and Argyll in 1747. The National Library of Scotland has the Barony Court of Calder from 1584 to 1601, The Ballikinrain Court Book, and the Barony Court Book of Corshill. Aberdeen University has the Barony Court Book of Philorth from 1653 until 1676; Dumfries and Galloway Archives has the Barony Court Book of Logan and Clanyard from 1739 until 1806; Angus Archives has the Barony Court Book of Balmadies from 1600 to 1629; while Glasgow City Archives has the Barony Court Book of Gorbals from 1700 until 1716.

The Barony Court Book of Stitchill, in Roxburghshire, reveals that a Thomas Whyte represented the barony in the Scottish army at the Battle of Dunbaron 3 September 1650. Thomas, though wounded, survived the battle and returned to Stitchill where the barony court provided him with an annual pension of ten Scottish pounds. These court records generally contain more mundane events, such as disputes between neighbours; for example, on 8 May 1694, 'the quhilk day Robert Hoggart in Stitchill is decerned and unlawed in ten pounds Scots money for breaking up of Andro Wilson's door under cloud and silence of night and assaulting and invading the said Andro threatening to kill him in his own house. The said Andro Wilson is unlawed and amerciat in ten pounds for his contumacie in not compeiring to hear and see Decreit pronounced against him for scandalizing the said Robert Hoggart in his good name and reputation by saying that he was a knave and unhonest man and many other opprobrious words and expressions he being lawfully sumond oft tymes called and not compeired.' The Scottish History Society published 'The Melrose Regality Records from 1547 to 1706' and 'The Court Book of the Barony of Carnwath, from 1523 to 1542'.

'The Atlas of Scottish History to 1707' [Edinburgh, 1996] provides excellent insight into baronies within a section entitled 'Baronies, Lordships and Earldoms in the early 15th century' which includes several maps showing what baronies existed and their locations. Another relevant source is 'Domination and Lordship, Scotland 1070-1230' [Edinburgh, 2011], which provides an insight into the pre-feudal social structure.

----

[1]The Kings of Scotland to encourage the growth of towns and development of the economy devised the idea of 'burghs of Barony' which were not under the control of particular families. For example, on 24 March 1459, King James II created Kirriemuir, Abernethy, and Douglas as 'burghs of barony' which enabled them to have merchant and craftsmen, such as bakers and brewers, a market cross, and weekly markets. These individuals have not been included in the list of baronial families.

TRANSCRIPTION OF A CHARTER, IN LATIN, BY KING ROBERT BRUCE GRANTING THE THANAGE OF DOWNIE IN ANGUS TO WALTER BICKERTON IN 1309– Robert, by the grace of God king of Scots greetings to all honorable men of the whole of his land. Know that we have given, granted and confirmed by this our present charter to Walter of Bickerton, for his homage and service, our whole thanage of Downie, with pertinents; to be held and had by the same Walter and his heirs of us and our heirs, in fee and heritage and in free barony, with *tol* and *tem*, with gallows and pit and *infangandthef*, by its correct bounds, in meadows and pastures, in moors and marshes, in roads and paths, in woods and plains, in stanks and mills, in waters and fishings, and with all liberties and easements and rightful pertinents; performing therefrom for us the service of one knight. In witness whereof we have caused our seal to be appended to our present chapter. Witnesses; Sir Bernard, our chancellor, William Earl of Ross, James the steward of Scotland, John of Menteith, Gilbert de la Hay, Robert of Keith, Robert Boyd and William Wiseman, knights. At Dunfermline, the twentieth day of March in the third year of our reign. [1309]

****

AN ABSTRACT OF A DEED BY THE EARL OF CRAWFORD SELLING LAND TO WALTER BARTRAHAM, A BURGESS OF EDINBURGH, AND HIS WIFE ELIZABETH, DATED 14 AUGUST 1478. [written in Medieval Scots]

"Be it kende till men, & - we David, Earl of Crawford, oure ayris baith of lyne and of talze and assignais, to be oblist to Walter Bartraham, burgess of Edinburgh, and Elisabeth, his spouse, and to that ayris and assignais, that for alsmekle as we have saulde to the sais Walter and Elisabeth and the langare Crawford-Lindesay within the scheRegalegill in our barony of liffande off thaim twa and to the ayris lauchfully gotten betwixt thaim, quhilkis failyeande to the nerrast and lauchfull ayris and assignis of the said Walter quhatsomevir the landis of Normangileis,]outhwood and Regalegill in our barony of Crawford Lindesay within the schireffdom of Lanark."

[Source – the Register of the Great Seal of Scotland, volume II, ms.1391]

Bibliography

Scottish Family Histories, Edinburgh, 1986.

The Atlas of Scottish History to 1707, [Edinburgh 1996]

The Register of the Great Seal of Scotland, [alias Registrum Magni Sigilli Regum Scotorum]

Surnames of Scotland, [New York, 1946]

The Jacobite Peerage, [Edinburgh, 1904]

NLS National Library of Scotland

NRS National Records of Scotland

See Margaret Stuart's *Scottish Family History*, repr. Genealogical Publishing Co., Inc., Baltimore 1979, for an almost comprehensive list of publications dealing with specific families.

The Register of the Great Seal of Scotland is the main source of information re property transactions from around 1320. Throughout the source the information is in Latin and from 1650 in English, very occasionally there is a deed written in Scots, viz.- on 25 May 1433 Andrew Ostler, a burgess of Forres, wrote stating 'Til al men that thir lettrez herys or seis Thom of Dolas, Lord of Tulyglenys, gretyng in God ayle-stand :- Wyt yhe me in my strenye and myster til haf put in wede til my lowyt and tender Baronet of Athlumney mark of the usuale mone of Scotland beforehand till me payit........'

Ancient sculptured stones at Kinkell

Castlerock Castle. View of entrance to castle.

Ruthven Castle. View from the north-east.

Rosslyn Castle. View from the south-east.

Castle Fraser. View from the north.

Fernieherst Castle. View of entrance to castle.

SCOTTISH BARONIAL FAMILIES, 1250-1750

ABERCROMBY OF MURTHLY IN PERTHSHIRE. King James III granted Alexander Abercromby, son of Sir Robert Abercromby of that Ilk, the lands and Barony of Murthly, also the lands of Abercromby in Fife, on 26 February 1481. [Abercrombies of Fife, Banff, etc, Stirling, 1890]

ABERCROMBY OF PITMEDDAN IN ABERDEENSHIRE. On 18 February 1513, King James IV confirmed George Abercromby in the lands of Pitmeddan with its mill, the lands of Pitmauchly, Harthills, Cardene,Newtoun, part of Haltoun of Ardune, Andie's croft, and Pete's croft, in Aberdeenshire, now incorporated into the Barony of Pitmeddan.

ABERCROMBY OF BIRKINBOG. Alexander Abercromby was created a Baronet of Nova Scotia on 18 June 1636. [Abercrombie, as a surname, is derived from a location in Fife, examples date from the late 13th century] [Bobby Abercrombie from Dysart, emigrated to Philadelphia in 1775]

ABERCROMBIE OF ABERCROMBY IN FIFE. On 19 August 1513, King James IV granted the lands of Abercromby in the Barony of Abercromby to Thomas Abercromby.

ABERCROMBIE. James Abercromby, an army officer from 1696 until his death in 1724, was created a Baronet by Queen Anne on 21 May 1709, as he died unmarried the baronetcy became extinct.

ABERNETHY OF ABERNETHY. Margaret Abernethy, Countess of Angus, was granted the barony of Abernethy ca1340 by King David II. [Abernethy is a surname of territorial origin, examples of the surname date from the thirteenth century] [Robert Abernethy was in Charles City, Virginia, by 1652]

ABERNETHY OF 'RETHY KINALTHUY' IN ANGUS. King Robert III granted the Barony of Rethy Kinalthuy to William Abernethy on 21 August 1404.

ABERNETHY OF ROTHIEMAY IN BANFFSHIRE. King James III granted Lord William Abernethy the Barony of Abernethy, the Barony of Concarne in Banffshire, the Barony of Redy in Angus, the Barony of Glencorse in Midlothian, the Barony of Plenderleith in Roxburghshire, and the lands of Dalgetty in Fife, the lands of Daldres in Stirlingshire, the lands of Saltoun in East Lothian, the lands of Lyelstoun and Uggistoun in Lauderdale, Berwickshire, on 5 August 1464., on 10 January 1483, King James III granted him the lands and Barony of Rothiemay, and the Barony of Corncarne in Banffshire, the Barony of Redy in Angus, also the lands of Dalgetty in Fife, the lands of Daldress in Stirlingshire, the lands and Barony of Glencorse in

Midlothian, the Barony of Saltoun in East Lothian, the lands of Lyallstoun and Ugstoun in Berwickshire, and the lands and Barony of Plenderleith in Roxburghshire, formed into the Barony of Abernethy; on 9 March 1492, King James IV granted Alexander Abernethy, son and heir apparent of James Abernethy of Rothiemay, the lands and Barony of Saltounwith its castle and mill, the lands and Barony of Glencorse with its mill, in Midlothian, also, the lands of Ugston and Lyalstoun in Berwickshire, the land and Barony of Ledy in Angus, the lands and Barony of Rothiemay and Cornecarne with castle and mill also the lands of Maschle and Edintoir in Banffshire. [see NRS.GD1.413.27][Court Book of Abernethy, Cromdale and Urquhart, 1617-1683, NRS.GD248.76.2]

ABERNETHY OF NATERDULL IN BANFFSHIRE. On 25 June 1549, Queen Mary confirmed Alexander Abernethy in the lands and Barony of Naterdull; on 21 May 1588, King James VI granted Alexander Abernethy, son of George Abernethy of Naterdull, the lands and Barony of Naterdull.

ACHISON, Sir ARCHIBALD, of Clancairny, was created as a baronet of Nova Scotia on 1 January 1628. [The surname means son of Adam, examples date from the fourteenth century] [Alexander Acheson, was a Second Lieutenant of the Royal Fencibles American Regiment in 1775]

ADAIR OF KINHILT IN WIGTONSHIRE. On 30 March 1596, King James VI confirmed Ninian Adair of Kinhilt in the lands and Barony of Kinhilt.

AGNEW OF LOCHNAW. Sir Patrick Agnew of Lochnaw, was created a baronet of Nova Scotia, on 28 July 1629. He married Margaret, daughter of Sir Thomas Kennedy of Culzean, their eldest son Sir Andrew Kennedy inherited the title, as 2nd baronet, married Anne Stewart, daughter of the Earl throughout of Galloway. Lochnaw remained as a barony held by the Agnews the period. [The family is of Norman-French origin, specifically from the Baronie d'Agneaux in Normandy; examples date from the fourteenth century][Niven Agnew, a prisoner from the Battle of Dunbar was transported to Boston in 1650][The Agnews of Lochnaw, Edinburgh, 1864]

ALEXANDER OF MENSTRIE IN STIRLINGSHIRE. Sir William Alexander, attempted to settle Scots in Nova Scotia in 1620s, King Charles I created hm as Baronet of Lochend in Nova Scotia, on 12 July 1625, he sold it to Sir Thomas Nicolson of Carnock on 31 December 1636. [A name from the Greek Alexander, common in Scotland since the medieval period] [Sir William Alexander founded Nova Scotia in the 1620s; Patrick Alexander, emigrated to East New Jersey in 1684] [Memorials of the Earl of Stirling and the House of Alexander, Edinburgh, 1877]

ALEXANDER OF TULLIBODY IN CLACKMANNANSHIRE. On 2 September 1641, King Charles I confirmed Charles Alexander, son of Sir William Alexander the Earl of Stirling and Viscount of Canada, the lands and Barony of Tullibody and the lands and Barony of Tillicoultrie, etc.

ALLARDYCE OF ALLERDYCE IN KINCARDINESHIRE. Sir John Allardyce resigned the barony in favour of his nephew Thomas Allardyce on 15 December 1426. [A surname derived from a site in Kincardineshire, examples of the surname date from the late thirteenth century] [John Allardyce was in Boston, New England, by 1684; James Allardyce, settled in St Vincent by 1796][The Pedigree of Robert Barclay-Allardice, [Edinburgh, 1892]

ANDERSON OF PAISLEY IN RENFREWSHIRE. William Anderson, a portioner of Newton, on 30 November 1652, was granted the lands, lordship, barony and regality and the abbey of Paisley, with its tower, fortalice, the town of Paisley, various lands, mills, mill-lands, fishing rights, coal, tenants, formerly in the hands of the Earl of Abercorn. [A common surname in Scotland meaning 'son of Andrew', examples date from the late thirteenth century] [Captain John Anderson,1665-1736, master of the Unicorn and Governor of New Jersey, while Dr James Anderson, died in Trinidad in 1826]

ANDORNES OF TEALING IN ANGUS. King James III granted to Anselm Andornes of Cortachy, the Barony of Tealing, including the lands of Polcak, the Kirkton of Telyn part of the land of Pittarmo, the lands of Balkello, Schielhill, with the mill of Tealing in Angus, also the lands of Polgavy in Perthshire on 18 April 1472; these lands and barony were granted to Thomas Ogilvy on 12 May 1473. [Anselm Adornes was a knight from Burgundy]

ANSTRUTHER OF ANSTRUTHER IN FIFE. William Candela was Baron of Anstruther before 1153, his grandson Henry assumed the surname Anstruther before 1200. Andrew Anstruther was killed at the Battle of Flodden on 9 September 1513. On 3 February 1602, King James VI granted the Barony of Anstruther to William Douglas the Earl of Angus; on 12 March 1631 King Charles I granted the lands, Lordship, and Barony of Anstruther to Lady Anne Stewart, wife of Lord Archibald Douglas. On 21 April 1649, the Barony of Anstruther was granted to Sir Philip Anstruther of that Ilk, when he died on 25 July 1679 his son succeeded to the Barony, and on his death on 24 November 1711, his son succeeded to the lands and title of Sir John Anstruther Baron of Anstruther, he died on 28 August 1754. [Anstruther is a surname of territorial origin from a village in Fife.][History of the family of Anstruther, Edinburgh, 1923]

ARBUTHNOTT OF ARBUTHNOTT IN KINCARDINESHIRE. On 29 January 1507, King James IV granted James Arbuthnott of that Ilk, the lands and Barony of Arbuthnott with its castle and fort, mill, also Miltoun, Pethill, Elpete, Drumyochir, Aldkayak, Cauldcotts, Broungarishill, Garrattismyre, Brigend, Lednaskeyne, Mongowdrum, Pitquhorthe, Meikle Fiddes with its mill and mill-land, Collistoun, Mutelaw, Threipland, Layis, Piterris, Dunrabbyn, Whitfield, Banff with its fulling-mill, and Bardisland with tenantries, also Portertoun and Orchardtoun in Kincardineshire, and the lands of Arduthy, Auchinzoich, Greencastle, Portarehalch, Portarecroft, part of Inverbervie and Benholm, formed into the Barony of Arbuthnott; on 21 April 1512, King James IV confirmed James Arbuthnott of that Ilk, in the lands and Barony of Arbuthnott, including the above properties, plus fishing rights at Bervie; on 16 May 1542, King James V confirmed Robert Arbuthnott in the lands and Barony of Arbuthnott; on 26 June 1553, Queen Mary granted Andrew Arbuthnott, son and heir apparent of Robert Arbuthnott of that Ilk, the lands and Barony of Arbuthnott, etc.; on 25 December 1582, King James VI confirmed Robert Arbuthnott, son of Andrew Arbuthnott in the lands and Barony of Arbuthnott; on 5 March 1588, King James VI granted Robert Arbuthnott of that Ilk, the lands and Barony of Arbuthnott. [a surname derived from a location in Kincardineshire, examples of the surname date from the twelfth century][John Arbuthnott, a Jacobite, was transported to the Chesapeake in 1747, while James Arbuthnott, a clergyman settled in the Leeward Islands in 1705][Memories of the Arbuthnotts of Kincardineshire and Aberdeenshire, London, 1920]

ARNOTT OF ARNOTT IN FIFE. On 6 March 1507, King James IV granted Walter Arnott, son and heir apparent of John Arnot of that Ilk, the lands and Barony of Arnott including the manor, the tower and fort, Faill, Little Arnot with its grain mill and fulling mill in Fife; Arnott of Woodmill, was killed at the Battle of Flodden on 9 September 1513. [a surname based on a location in Kinross-shire, with examples recorded since the thirteenth century]. [John Arnot, a Covenanter was banished to the West Indies in 1678, while Andrew Arnot, a clergyman settled in Pennsylvania in 1753][The House of Arnot, Edinburgh, 1918]

ARNOTT OF NOVA SCOTIA. Michael Arnot, was created a Baronet of Nova Scotia on 27 July 1629. He died before 1680 when his grandson Sir David Arnot became the second Baronet of Arnot. Sir David died on 1 January 1711.

AUCHENLECK OF AUCHENLECK IN AYRSHIRE ALSO IN ANGUS. Sir James Auchinleck, was granted the Barony of Auchenleck, incorporating the lands of Auchenleck, Rogerstoun, Kethstoun, Crakistoune, la Bannachtinis Yards, and Templeland in Kyle-Stewart, with castle, fortalice, tenants tenantries, and free servants, on 26 March 1446. [Also, a placename of Gaelic origin in Angus; examples of the surname date from the late thirteenth century, sometimes abbreviated into AFFLECK. King James III granted some lands in Panmure to be incorporated into the Barony of Auchenleck on 12 July 1470. [Joseph Auchenleck, a Jacobite, was transported to Antigua in 1716; Thomas Auchenleck, master of the <u>Golden Lion of Dundee</u> bound for Virginia in 1627.][A saga of the early Auchenleck and Afflecks, East Linton, 2021]

AUCHENLECK OF SCHETIN IN ABERDEENSHIRE. On 22 October 1574, King James VI confirmed George Auchenleck of Balmanno in the Barony of Schetin.

AUCHTERLONIE OF AUCHTERLONIE IN ANGUS. On 7 December 1547, Mary, Queen of Scots, granted James Ouchterlonie, son and heir of Alexander Ouchterlonie of that Ilk, the lands and Barony of Auchterlonie alias Kelly, with its manor, gardens, orchards, mills, and tenantries in Angus; on 23 November 1591, King James VI confirmed William Auchterlonie of that Ilk in the lands and Barony of Auchterlonie or Kelly. [The surname is one of Gaelic origin, the prefix 'Auch means 'field'. The Auchterlonie surname is derived from a location near Forfar in Angus, there since at least the mid thirteenth century when John de Othirlony exchanged his lands for those of Kelly in Fife] [Patrick Oucherlonie, from Angus, died in Maryland in 1753, while John Auchterlonie, settled in Kingston, Jamaica, before 1826][The Ochterloney family of Scotland and Boston, Boston, 1902]

BAILLIE OF LAMBERTOUN, LANARKSHIRE. King David II granted the barony Lambertoun to William Baillie around 1345. [Baillie is an occupational surname which is derived from 'ballie' or 'bailiff, meaning a minor magistrate, examples date from the early fourteenth century in Scotland] [in 1682 several Baillies, gypsies, were transported to New York, while Robert Baillie, a planter in Georgia, died in Florida in 1782][Lives of the Baillies, Edinburgh, 1872]

BAILLIE OF CORSANORDLY IN BANFFSHIRE. On 9 August 1452 King James II granted Thomas Baillie the Barony of Corsanordly.

BAILLIE OF LOCHEND. Gideon Baillie was created as a Baronet of Nova Scotia on 21 November 1636.

BAILYTH OF LAMMYTON IN LANARKSHIRE. On 2 January 1493, King James IV granted William Bailyth the lands and Barony of Lammytoun in Lanarkshire with its tower, manor and orchard.

BAIRD OF CAMBUSNETHAN IN LANARKSHIRE. King Robert the Bruce granted Robert Baird the Barony of Cambusnethan around 1320. [RGS.I.79]. The Barony of Cambusnethan was granted to Thomas Somerville and his wife Janet by King Robert III 1390. [RGS.I.828] [The surname is probably one of territorial origins from a location in Lanarkshire, Examples of the surname date from around 1200] [William Baird, a Jacobite was transported to Virginia in 1747] [An account of the surname of Baird, Edinburgh, 1857]

BAIRD OF NEWBYTH IN EAST LOTHIAN. John Baird was created a Baronet by King Charles II in 1660, he died on 27 April 1698 in Edinburgh, and was succeeded by his son Sir William Baird, born 1654, died in Edinburgh in 1737. His son Sir John Baird then inherited the barony, but as he died childless in 1745 the barony became extinct. [The families of Auchmeddan, New Byth, and Sauchtonhall, London, 1870]

BAIRD OF SAUGHTON HALL IN MIDLOTHIAN. Sir Robert Baird was created as a Baronet of Nova Scotia on 28 February 1696, married Elizabeth Fleming, daughter of Michael Fleming of Ratho Byres, their son James Baird became the second baronet on the death of his father in 1697. James Baird married [1] Margaret Hamilton, and [2] Elizabeth Gordon. Sir Robert Baird, son of the first marriage, became 3rd baronet. Sir Robert married [1] Janet Baikie [2] Helen Hope, his eldest son, Sir David born 1728, duly became the 4th baronet. Sir David was a Lieutenant of the 1st Royal Regiment died on 1 July 1745 from wounds received at the Battle of Fontenoy. As he had no children his brother Sir William Baird, a Captain of the Royal Navy, became the 5th Baronet of Saughtonhall. The Bairds have remained baronets there. [Alexander Baird, son of Sir Robert Baird and Elizabeth Fleming, married Magdalena van Fleck in New York in 1700, while Richard Frederick Baird, son of Sir James Gardiner Baird, died in Bermuda in 1819]

BALFOUR OF MONTQUHANNY IN FIFE. On 1 April 1493, King James IV granted Michael Balfour, son and heir apparent of Michael Balfour of Montquhanny, the lands of Montquhanny and Strathore, with the mill of Montquhanny, to be united into the Barony of Montquhanny on 1 April 1493; on 23 March 1548, Queen Mary granted Michael Balfour, son and heir apparent of Andrew Balfour of Balquhany, the lands and Barony of Montquhanny. [The surname is based on a Gaelic placename – *Baile Phir* meaning 'pasture farm.'][The Balfours of Pilrig, Edinburgh, 1907]

BALFOUR OF DENMILNE IN FIFE. John Balfour of Denmilne was killed at the Battle of Flodden on 9 September 1513. Sir James Balfour, the Lyon King of Arms, was created a baronet of Nova Scotia on 22 December 1633. [The surname is derived from a place in Fife, examples date from 1300]. [William Balfour died in Virginia before 1686, while Henry Balfour, died in Charleston in 1794] [The Denmiln mss in NLS, Edinburgh, 1928]

BALFOUR OF BURLIEGH IN FIFE. On 19 November 1600, King James VI confirmed Sir Michael Balfour of Balgarvie, the lands and Barony of Burliegh.

BALLENDEN OF OCHILTREE IN AYRSHIRE. On 9 August 1586, King James VI granted Sir Ludovic Ballenden of Auchnoule in the lands, Lordship and Barony of Ochiltree; on 28 July 1587, King James VI granted Sir Ludovic Ballenden the lands and Barony of Broughtoun in Midlothian.

BANNERMAN OF ELSICK IN KINCARDINESHIRE. On 28 December 1682 Alexander Bannerman was created as a Baronet, on his death on 11 April 1711, his son became the 2nd Baronet of Elsick, the next Baronet of Elsick was Sir Alexander Bannerman in 1745 fled to Rome. [The surname may mean one who carried the banner or standard of the family into battle] [several Bannermans emigrated to Hudson Bay in 1815] [The Bannermans of Elsick and Watertown, Aberdeen,1900]

BARCLAY OF BELHELVIE IN ABERDEENSHIRE. King Robert I granted Walter Barclay, the Thanage of Belhelvie around 1320.

BARCLAY OF CRAIMBETH AND CLEISH IN FIFE. Robert, Duke of Albany, the Regent, granted the Baronies of Craimbeth and Cleish to David Barclay around 1413. [A surname probably derived from Berkeley in England, examples in Scotland date from the twelfth century] [Ninian Barclay, master of the Eagle bound from Dunbarton to Nova Scotia in 1628, while Alexander Barclay died in Philadelphia in 1770][History of the Scottish Barclays, Folkestone, 1915]

BARCLAY OF DRUMBLATE IN ABERDEENSHIRE. On 30 May 1493 King James IV confirmed Patrick Barclay of Grantully, in the Barony of Drumblate; on 26 February 1517, King James V granted Walter Barclay of Grantully, the lands of Grantully, with its tower, fort, etc, including Haltoun of Grantully, Reishouse, with its mill, Ailhouse with crofts, Feauchill, Kirkhill, Birkhill, Sanquhar, Cornecathro, Wolfshaw, Milnschaw, Studefald and Broomhill, the woods of Corsky and Ramslaid in Banffshire, also parts of the Barony of Drumblate, including the lands of Sleach, Newtoun, part of Garry, part of Kirktoun of Drumblate with mill, lands of Adamstoun and Broomhill , plus Lossindrum, in Aberdeenshire, lands of Castletoun of Kinedward and Golkhall, Kinarrochy with fishing on the Ithan River, part of Montcoffer, fishing rights on the Deveron, etc, incorporated into the Barony of Barclay.

BARCLAY OF TOLLIE IN ABERDEENSHIRE. On 24 July 1594, King James VI granted Patrick Barclay of Tollie, the lands and Barony of Tollie-Barclay; on 4 July 1601, King James VI granted Patrick Barclay, son of Patrick Barclay of Tollie-Barclay, the lands and Barony of Tollie-Barclay etc

BARCLAY OF URY IN KINCARDINESHIRE. Colonel David Barclay had a charter from James VII creating the barony of Ury in 1679. [Ancestry of the Barclays of Mathers and Ury][The Barclays of Ury, London,1881]

BARTOUN OF OVER BARTOUN IN MIDLOTHIAN. Robert Barton of Over Bartoun, the Royal Treasurer, was granted the lands of Over Barntoun with its fort, manor-house, the lands of Bewlaws, the lands of Foulford, in Midlothian, now created into the Barony of Bartoun. [possibly Anglian, meaning a farm settlement, a surname recorded in Scotland since the thirteenth century][Walter Barton, was in Boston by 1686, while Lewis Barton, a Jacobite, was transported to the colonies in 1+747]

BARR, ROBERT, was created as a baronet of Nova Scotia on 29 September 1628. [A surname of territorial origin from Barr in Renfrewshire, or Barr in Ayrshire; examples date from the fourteenth century] [William Barr emigrated to Maryland in 1674, while John Barr died in Tobago in 1808]

BAYNES OF KINNEIL IN WEST LOTHIAN. On 11 June 1658, Oliver Cromwell, the Lord Protector, granted John Baynes, the Receiver General of Revenue in Scotland, was granted the lands, lordship and barony of Kinneil with its towers, fortalices, manor places, mills, mill-lands, salmon and other fishings, coals, saltpans, tenandries, services of free tenants, feu duties, and others. [Probably from the Gaelic word *ban* for white or fair, examples date from the fourteenth century] [Alexander Baine in Boston, New England, in 1697, while Donald Bain died in Jamaica in 1801][Genealogical chart of the family of Bain in Haddington, Edinburgh, 1871]

BEATOUN OF BALFOUR IN FIFE. Originated by Robert of Bethune who settled here around 1180 from Flanders. On 9 August 1507, King James IV confirmed John Beaton of Balfour in the lands of Balfour and the Newtoun of Kettle, and Hole Kettle with its mill, in Fife, now incorporated into the Barony of Balfour. [Perhaps from Bethune in the Pas de Calais, France, examples of the surname date from the late twelfth century] [Alison Beaton, from Edinburgh, was transported to the American Plantations in 1695, while John Bethune, an American Loyalist, died in Upper Canada in 1815][The Beatons, Edinburgh, 1986]

BEATOUN OF CARNTOUN IN KINCARDINESHIRE. On 10 February 1507, King James IV granted James Beaton, son of David Beaton of Creich, the lands of Carntoun alias Fordoun, including the lands of Convaly, Fordounflat with its mill, the mill of Baltryne, now incorporated in the Barony of Carntoun; on Edinburgh, 14 May 1563, Queen Mary granted David Beatoun, son and heir apparent of Robert Beatoun of Creich, the lands and Barony of Dunbog in Fife, also the lands and Barony or Carntoun alias Fordoun in Kincardineshire.

BEATOUN OF LUNDY IN ANGUS. On 9 May 1513, King James IV granted Griselle Beatoun, daughter of David Beatoun of Creich, the lands and Barony of Lundy.

BEATOUN OF DUNBUG IN FIFE. On 7 August 1586, King James VI confirmed James Beatoun of Creich, in the lands and Barony of Dunbug and Contrahills, etc.

BEATOUN OF BANYENOCHE IN INVERNESS-SHIRE. On 27 December 1639, King Charles I granted Andrew Beatoun, son of Lord Balfour, the lands and Lordship of Banynoche, the Barony of Ugstoun in Moray, the lands of Fochabers in Moray, the lands and Barony of Strathaven in Banffshire, the lands and Barony of Huntly in Aberdeenshire.

BENNETT OF GRUBETT IN ROXBURGHSHIRE. On 10 October 1639, King Charles I granted William Bennett, rector of Ancrum, the lnds and Barony of Grubett.

BENNETT FROM FIFE. George Bennett, son of Reverend William Bennett, was in the Service of Casimir, King of Poland, and became a nobleman there, he was created as a Baronet on 28 July 1671, he died childless about 1700 when the Baronetcy ended.

BICKERTON OF LUFNESS IN EAST LOTHIAN. King David II granted Walter Bickerton the Barony of Wistoun around 1320. [The surname is derived from a place in north-east England, as a surname it appears in Scotland from 1200]

BLACKADDER OF TULLIALLAN IN PERTHSHIRE. On 21 March 1530, King James V, granted John Blackadder, son and heir apparent of John Blackadder of Tulliannan, the land and Barony of Tulliallan with fort, mills, fishing, etc in Strathearn, Perthshire; Sir John Blackadder of Tulliallan was created as a baronet of Nova Scotia on 18 July 1626. [the Blackadders of Tulliallan were disposed in 1632] [A territorial surname from Berwickshire; examples date from the fifteenth century] [Thomas Blackadder, born 1660s in Troqueer, was a merchant in New England][The life and diary of Colonel John Blackader, Edinburgh, 1824]

BLAIR OF ARDLER IN ANGUS. On 10 June 1542, King James V granted Thomas Blair of Balthayock, the lands of Ardler and Baldowrie in Angus, also, the lands and Barony of Cults in Fife, and the lands and house of Goddings in Perthshire, incorporated into the Barony of Ardler. [a surname of territorial origin, from Gaelic for 'field', examples date from the thirteen century] [James Blair founded the College of William and Mary in 1693, while Reverend John Blair emigrated to the West Indies in 1702][Blair of Balthayock, 1150-1850, Baltimore, 2001]

BLAIR OF INVERKEILLOUR IN ANGUS. On 2 March 1608, King James VI granted William Blair of Balgillo the Barony of Inverkeillour. [Five generations of the family of Blair. Exeter.1895]

BLAIR OF KINFAUNS IN PERTHSHIRE. On 18 September 1666, William Blair of Kinfauns was created as a Baronet.

BONAR OF KELTIE IN PERTHSHIRE. On 5 March 1526, King James V granted Walter Bonar, the land and mill of Keltie in Strathearn, now incorporated into the Barony of Keltie; on 26 January 1587, King James VI granted Niian Bonar, son and heir apparent of William Bonar of Keltie, the lands and Barony of Keltie. [a surname probably from the French 'bonair' meaning courteous, examples date from the thirteenth century]

BONAR OF CARNEBADDIE IN PERTHSHIRE. On 9 December 1585, King James VI confirmed William Bonar of Rossie in the lands and Barony of Carnebaddie.

BORTHWICK OF DALHOUSIE IN MIDLOTHIAN. On 5 November 1484, King James III granted John Borthwick of Cruikstoun, the lands of Cruikstoun and the Barony of Dalhousie on 5 November 1484. [The surname comes from a place in Roxburghshire, examples date from the fourteenth century] [James Borthwick settled in Virginia before 1733, while William Borthwick, a bank manager, absconded to America in 1822]

BORTHWICK OF BORTHWICK IN MIDLOTHIAN. On 21 August 1538, King James V granted Lord William Borthwick, the lands of Lochwhorat, and castle, the castle at Borthwick, parts of Buteland, in Midlothian, lands of Borthwick in Selkirkshire, the lands of Ligartwood in Berwickshire, lands of Heriot etc in Peebles-shire, the lands of Hyndland in Lanarkshire, the lands and Barony of Aberdour in Aberdeenshire, the lands of Little Ormstoun in Peebles-shire, the lands of Nantharne, etc, in Berwickshire, now forming the Barony of Borthwick; on 15 January 1544, Queen Mary confirmed a grant by Lord John Borthwick to Gavin Borthwick of Fentoun of the lands and Barony of Borthwick; on 23 October 1571, King James VI confirmed William Borthwick, son of William Borthwick, in the lands, Barony and Lordship of Borthwick. [The Pedigree of Lords Borthwick, London, 1869]

BOSWELL OF GLASMONT IN FIFE. King James II granted David Boswell, son of David Boswell of Balmulto, the Barony of Glasmont, comprising of the lands of Glasmont, of Cragincat, Balglalee, Balmulto, Balgregy, Strruthy, Muretoun, Dundonald, Cartmor, Pitkenny, Capildra and Balbethy, on 4 November 1458. Sir Alexander Boswell of Balmulto was killed at the Battle of Flodden on 9 September 1513; on 13 March 1576, King James VI granted John Boswell, heir of David Boswell of Glasmount, the Barony of Glasmount; on 29 September 1587, King James VI confirmed John Boswell in the Barony of Glasmont. [a surname derived from a place in Normandy, examples in Scotland date from the twelfth century] [Dr James Boswell died in Montserrat in 1767, while David Boswell died in Jamaica in 1790][History of the Boswells, London, 1906]

BOSWELL, OF AUCHENLECK IN AYRSHIRE. On 20 November 1504, King James IV granted Thomas Boswell, the lands and Barony of Auchenleck with its castle, fort, mill, and tenantries to Thomas Boswell. [The treasures of Auchenleck, London, 1975]

BOTHWELL OF ETHAY IN ORKNEY. On 6 April 1649, King Charles II granted Alexander Bothwell of Glencorse the lands and Barony of Ethay.

BOYD OF STEWARTON IN AYRSHIRE. King James III granted Thomas Boyd, Earl of Arran, the lands of Stewartoun, the lands of Trarinzean with tower and tenantries, the lands of Turnberry, the lands of Risdalemuir, in Ayrshire, also the lands of Meikle Cumrae in Bute all united into the Barony of Stewarton, on 26 April 1467. On the same day Thomas Boyd was granted the lands of Cavertoun in Roxburghshire, the lands and Barony of Tealing in Angus, and the lands of Polgavy in Perthshire. Also, the Island of Arran which became the Barony of Arran on 26 April 1467. [The surname may come from the Gaelic word for Bute, i.e. *bod*; examples date from the early thirteenth century] [Thomas Boyd, settled in North Carolina by 1694, while Reverend John Boyd settled in New Jersey, died there in 1708]

BOYD OF KILMARNOCK IN AYRSHIRE. King James II granted Thomas Boyd, Earl of Arran, the lands and Barony of Kilmarnock with its castle, the lands of Hartshawmuir, the lands of Ralstone, and part of the lands of Gaveleich in Ayrshire, the Barony of Dalry, Kilbride, and Nodisdale, and the lands of Monfode in Ayrshire, all incorporated and united into the Barony of Kilmarnock, on 26 April 1467; on 6 September 1545, Queen Mary granted Robert Boyd, son and heir apparent of Robert Boyd of Kilmarnock, the lands, Lordship and Barony of Kilmarnock, also with the lands and Baronies of Dalry and Kilbryde, etc. in Ayrshire; on 12 January 1592, King James VI granted Lord Thomas Boyd the lands, Lordship and Barony of Kilmarnock. [The Boyds of Kilmarnock, Kilmarnock, 1980]

BOYD OF TEMPLE IN MIDLOTHIAN. On 26 February 1642, King Charles I confirmed James Boyd in the lands and Barony of Temple

BRODIE OF BRODIE IN MORAY. On 15 February 1577, King James VI confirmed Alexander Hay, the Royal Chancellor, in the lands and Barony of Brodie; on 4 March 1577, the king confirmed George Brodie, son of Alexander Hay of that Ilk, in the lands and Barony of Brodie. [The genealogy of the Brodie family, from Malcolm, Thane of Brodie, 1249-1285, to 1862. Eastbourne, 1862]

BROWN. On 17 February 1664, King Charles II created James Brown in Barbados as a Baronet.

BROWN. Robert Brown, Lord Provost of Edinburgh, was created a Baronet on 24 February 1710. [A common surname in Scotland, earlier was Broun possibly from the French 'Le Brun', examples date from the twelfth century in Scotland] [Alexander Brown emigrated to Virginia in 1666, while Jean Brown, from Aberdeenshire, emigrated to Philadelphia, moved to Barbados, died in St Croix in 1758]

BRUCE OF DUN IN ANGUS. King Robert I granted Alexander Bruce the barony of Dun around 1320. [A surname of territorial origin based on Brix in Normandy, examples of the surname in Scotland date from the twelfth century.] [Alexander Bruce was transported from Leith to Virginia in 1666, while Michael Bruce was transported to Barbados or Virginia in 1668][Genealogical descent of the royal line of Bruce, Edinburgh, 1860]

BRUCE OF CLACKMANNAN. King James III granted David Bruce, son John Bruce, the lands and Barony of Clackmannan in Clackmannanshire, also the lands and Barony of Raitt in Perthshire, on 26 March 1472; King James IV confirmed the grant of the lands and Barony of Clackmannan and the lands and Barony of Raitt in Perthshire by David Bruce to his son David Bruce on 11 September 1497; on 3 February 1507, King James IV confirmed Sir David

Bruce, son of David Bruce of Clackmannan, the lands and Barony of Clackmannan with its castle, fort mill, tofts, crofts, and the lands of Halhill, Hillend, Carrishill, Girmanstoun, Gartlaw, Birkhill, Lynmill, Tullygarth, Mortimerside, Cragory, Camelin, East Park, and Wester Kennet in Clackmannanshire, also the lands and Barony of Rait in Perthshire; on 12 February 1551, Queen Mary granted Robert Bruce of Rait, nephew and heir apparent of Sir David Bruce of Clackmannan, the Barony of Clackmannan.

BRUCE OF BRIGHAM IN BERWICKSHIRE. On 1 July 1495 Sir Andrew Bruce of Brigham, was granted the lands and barony of Leuchars-Moneypenny in Fife formerly held by Alexander Monypenny.; on 28 March 1497 Sir Alexander Bruce was granted the lands of Earlshall and Prusk in the Barony of Leuchars in Fife.

BRUCE OF LIVINGSTONE IN WEST LOTHIAN. On 1 February 1592, King James VI confirmed Sir Alexander Bruce of Airth in the lands and Barony of Livingstone.

BRUCE OF EARLSHALL IN FIFE. On 26 July 1597, King James VI confirmed Andrew Bruce of Earlshall, in the lands and Barony of Earlshall.

BRUCE OF LEUCHARS-MONEYPENNY IN FIFE. On 22 March 1599, King James VI granted William Bruce, son and heir apparent of Alexander Bruce of Earlshall, the lands and Barony of Leuchars-Moneypenny etc incorporated into the Barony of Earlshall.

BRUCE OF DURIE IN FIFE. On 17 July 1600, King James VI granted Edward Bruce, Commandator of Kinloss and a Senator of the College of Justice, the lands and Barony of Durie.

BRUCE OF KINLOSS IN MORAY. On 2 February 1601, King James VI granted Edward Bruce, the commandator of Kinross, the lands and Barony of Kinloss.

BRUCE OF AIRTH OF STENHOUSE. Sir William Bruce was created 1st Baronet of Stenhouse in 1628. [A History of the Stenhouse Family, Edinburgh, 1999]

BRUCE OF STANEHOUSE IN LANARKSHIRE. William Bruce was created a baronet of Nova Scotia on 26 June 1629; a sasine 11 August 1629.

BRUCE OF ALVA IN STIRLINGSHIRE. On 6 October 1641, King Charles I granted Alexander Bruce, son of George Bruce of Carnock, the lands and Barony of Alva.

BRYSSIE OF DOLPHINGTOUN IN EAST LOTHIAN. Oliver Cromwell, the Lord Protector, granted Captain Benjamin Brissie, a merchant in Leith, the lands and Barony of Dolphingtoun with its tower, manor place, coal heughs, and others, on 28 July 1654. [Possibly a variant of 'Bryce', examples of which date from the late twelfth century] [Malcolm Bryce, a Covenanter, was transported to the colonies in 1685, while Archibald Bryce was a factor in Richmond, Virginia, by 1776]

BUCHANAN OF STRATHYRE IN PERTHSHIRE. On 21 May 1474 King James III granted Walter Buchanan, son and heir of Patrick Buchanan of that Ilk, the lands of Strathyre, the lands of Glenguile, now merged into the Barony of Strathyre. [A surname derived from a district in Stirlingshire, examples date from the thirteenth century][George Buchanan, a physician from Dunbartonshire, settled in Baltimore before 1739 while John Buchanan, a Jacobite, was transported to Maryland in 1747][History of Clan Buchanan and its Septs, Toronto, 2002]

BURNETT OF TULLYBOYLL IN KINCARDINESHIRE. King Robert I granted the Barony of Tullyboyll to Alexander Burnett in 1324.

BURNET OF LEYS IN ABERDEENSHIRE. On 10 January 1596, King James VI confirmed Alexander Burnet of Leys, in the lands and Barony of Leyis; on 21 April 1626 Sir Thomas Burnett of Leyis was created as a baronet of Nova Scotia, a sasine dated 14 June 1626, he died on 27 June 1653, and was succeeded by the 2nd Baronet Sir Alexander Burnet who died in 1663. Next came Sir Thomas Burnet as 3rd baronet, he died in 1714, and was succeeded by Sir Alexander Burnet as the 4th Burnet who died in 1758. [The surname is derived from the Old English name 'Beornheard', and is recorded in the Borders from around 1200 and in Aberdeenshire since the 14th century. [John Burnett, a merchant from Aberdeen was bound for Virginia in 1635, while William Burnett, a physician from Dumfries, settled in West Florida by 1776] [The Family of Burnett of Leys, Aberdeen, 1901]

BURNETT........ Oliver Cromwell, the Lord Protector, granted the lands and Barony of Maner, the Barony of Lintoun, the lands and Barony of Newlands, the lands and Barony of Traquair with tower, manor-place, mills, mill-lands and others, the lands and Barony of Horsburgh, all in Peebles-shire, formerly held by the Earl of Traquair, to Alexander Burnett, son of Alexander Burnett of Carlips an advocate, on 27 November 1657.

BUTTERGASK OF TROUP IN BANFFSHIRE. King David II granted the Barony of Troup to Andrew Buttergask in 13..... [a surname derived from the village of that name in Perthshire, examples of the surname date from 1261.

CADELL , was created as a baronet of Nova Scotia on 21 May 1628. [a possibly variant of the surname Calder, examples date from the sixteenth century] [Christian Cadell was transported to Barbados in 1663, while George Caddell emigrated to New York in 1774][The Cadells of Banton, Grange, Tranent and Cockenzie, 1668-1890, Edinburgh, 1890]

CALDER OF CALDER IN INVERNESS-SHIRE. On 29 May 1476, King James III granted William Calder, the lands and Thanage of Calder, the lands and baronies of Clunes and of Boith, the lands of Balmakaith, Rate, in Nairnshire, the lands of Moy, the lands of Dunmaglass, Kinkellis in the Tanage and Barony of Calder Invermarky, Mulquhaiche and Drumwourny in Inverness-shire, now united as the Barony of Calder; on 22 January 1639, King Charles I confirmed Colin Campbell, son of John Campbell, the younger, of Calder, in the Thanage and Barony of Calder. [Possibly from the place of Cawdor in Nairnshire, examples date from the twelfth century] [Alexander Calder from Caithness, settled in Georgia in 1775, while Margaret Calder, from Strathspey, emigrated to New York in 1774]

CAMERON OF LOCHIEL IN INVERNESS-SHIRE. On 9 January 1528, King James V confirmed Ewan Alansoun Cameron of Locheil, in many lands in Inverness-shire, now formed into the Barony of Locheil. [The Camerons, Stirling, 1974]

CAMPBELL OF 'RUBEI' IN ANGUS. In 1321 King Robert Bruce created Donald Campbell the Baron of 'Rubei' in Angus. [a surname from the Gaelic *Caimbeul* meaning crooked mouth, examples date from the thirteenth century][James Campbell, a prisoner of war captured at the Siege of Worcester, was transported to Boston in 1652, while John Campbell was a tavern-keeper in Boston by 1699][A History of Clan Campbell, 3 vols, Edinburgh, 2002][The Clan Campbell, 8 vols., Edinburgh, 1913]

CAMPBELL OF MELFORD IN ARGYLL. King David II granted the barony of Melfirth to Gillespie Campbell on 2 May 1343.

CAMPBELL OF KINLOCH-ROWEL IN ARGYLL. On 19 June 1452, King James II granted lands in Argyll now united into the Barony of Kinloch-Rowell to Lord Duncan Campbell.

CAMPBELL OF INNERMETH IN PERTHSHIRE. On 20 June 1452, King James II granted John Campbell of Lorne the Barony of Innermeth with other lands in Perthshire, Fife and Kinross-shire, now incorporated in the Barony of Innermeth.

CAMPBELL OF INVERARAY IN ARGYLL. King James III granted Colin Campbell, Earl of Argyll, Inveraray as a burgh of Barony on 8 May 1474; on 18 January 1526, King James V confirmed Archibald Campbell, son and heir apparent of Colin Campbell, the Earl of Argyll, the Lordship of Lorne, the Barony of Kilmun, the Barony of Lochaw, the Barony of Orchy, Over Cowal, , the lands of Strathachie, the lands of Orchard and Ardmernok, the Barony of Ottir, the lands of Achnagarry, the lands of Glassary, the lands of Concraw, Kildalwin, Inverneil, Glak, the lands of Camys and Achtyewin, the lands of Melfort, the lands of Eddirling, the lands of Tausnach and Stelag, the lands of Bordland with the castle at Dunoon, the lands of Ardschodinch, the lands of Tollart Fleming, the lands of Loyng, the lands of Suna, the lands of Glen Sora and Lettir, the lands of Glenary, the lands of Lochstrewinheid, in Argyll, the lands of South Knapdale, the castle of Tarbert, the lands of Kintyre, the lands of North Knapdale, in Argyll, the lands and Barony of Menstrie with its mill in Clackmannanshire, the lands of Pannell, the lands of Nether Glenny, the lands of Drumlane and Blairbeuok, also the lands of Gloome with Castle Campbell, in Perthshire, and Pinkertoun in East Lothian; on 27 September 1580, King James VI granted Archibald Campbell, son and heir apparent of Colin Campbell the Earl of Argyll, the lands, Lordship and Barony of Lorne, the lands and Barony of Kilmun, the lands and Barony of Kilmichael, the lands and Barony of Skipinch, etc.; on 27 September 1580, King James VI granted Archibald Campbell, the Earl of Argyll, the lands and Barony of , the lands and Barony of Tarbert, in Argyll, also the lands and Barony of Pinkerton in East Lothian, and the lands and Barony of Boquhen in Stirlingshire, etc; on 26 February 1642, King Charles I confirmed Archibald Campbell, the Earl of Argyll, in the lands and Baronies of Lochaw, Ardskeodneiche, Glenaray, Glenscherow, Inveraray,, Craigneish, Kilmichael, Tarbert,Skipnes, Cowal,Strathquhyre, kilmond, Strathauchie, Bordland, Glenarrould, Ardmernok, Lorne, Torresay, Lesmore, Glencoan, Rosneth, the Baronie of Ardnamurchan, the lands, and the Lordship and Barony of Kintyre.

CAMPBELL OF KILMICHAEL IN ARGYLL. On 26 February 1481, King James III granted Colin Campbell the Earl of Argyll, land in Knapdale, various islands, merged into the Barony of Kilmichael.

CAMPBELL OF PINKERTON IN EAST LOTHIAN. King James III granted Colin Campbell, Earl of Argyll, the lands of Meikle Pinkertoun and the lands of Little Pinkertoun in East Lothian, now united into the Barony of Pinkertoun on 29 April 1483.

CAMPBELL OF AUCHINTWERELY IN DUNBARTONSHIRE. King James IV granted Archibald Campbell, son and heir apparent of Colin Campbell the Earl of Argyll, the lands of Auchintwerely and Dunnerlock with their mills and fishing rights on the River Clyde, also, the lands of Nethermains of Duchell with its mill in Renfrewshire, formed into the Barony of Auchintwerely on 3 July 1489.

CAMPBELL OF SKIPINCH IN ARGYLL. On 19 September 1502, Archibald Campbell, Earl of Argyll, was granted by King James IV the lands of Skipinch with its castle, fort etc, also the lands of Lathourling, Kilpenny, Colintre, Altgallorcas, Ariwoware, Glenskipale, Glenrestill, Clynaig, Orgaig, Sronerestill, Garweile, Laganerowok, and the lands of Arymore in Knapdale, now incorporated into the Barony of Skipinch; on 13 August 1511, King James IV granted Archibald Campbell, the Earl of Argyll, various properties in the Barony of Strachan and Kilmun in Argyll.

CAMPBELL OF GLEN LYON IN PERTHSHIRE. On 7 September 1502, King James IV granted Duncan Campbell of Glen Orchy, the lands of Glen Lyon, including parts of Gallyn, Meggarne, Milltoun, Brandvoy, Keroclauchy, Cragilk, Invwemuke, Glenmarane, Glencallich, Regill, Crageny, Slattish, Laganecassy, Ruskich, Inverbarris, Carnbayne, Inveringlass, Sestill, Derrycammys, now incorporated into the Barony of Glenlyon; On 1 March 1648, King Charles I granted John Campbell, son of Colin Campbell of Aberurquill, the lands and Barony of Glen Lyon in the Lordship of Dunkeld, Perthshire.

CAMPBELL OF GLENORCHY IN ARGYLL. On 26 April 1503, King James IV granted Duncan Campbell of Glenorchy the lands and Barony of Finlarig with its mill, in the lordship of Glen Dochart in Perthshire; on 16 May 1513, King James IV granted Sir Duncan Campbell of Glenorchy the land and Barony of Finlarig with its mill, the lands of Crandych with its mill, the lands of Scheane, Balloch, and Auchacharne with their mills, part of Murlagan with its mill, the lands of Ladcarre and Eddirfameneauch with its mill in Perthshire now incorporated into the Barony of Finlarig. Sir Duncan Campbell was killed at the Battle of Flodden on 9 September 1513; on 15 June 1551, Queen Mary confirmed Colin Campbell of Glen Orchy, in the lands and Barony of Finlarg, and other lands in Perthshire, now incorporated into the Barony of Finlarig; on 17 February 1599, King James VI granted Sir Duncan Campbell of Glen Orchy, the lands and Barony of Glen Falloch in Perthshire; Sir Duncan Campbell of Glenorchy, born 1550, died 1631, was created a baronet of Nova Scotia with 16,000 acres there by King Charles I on 29 May 1625. He was a politician and Hereditary Sheriff of Perthshire for life. He married Jean Stewart, daughter of the Earl of Atholl, their son went to his brother Sir Robert Campbell [1580-1648] as Third Baronet of Glenorchy, he was a Member of Parliament and husband of Isabel MacIntosh of Torcastle, their son John, became the 4th Baronet of Glenorchy on the death of his father. Sir John Campbell, Baronet of Glenorchy, born 1615, died by 1677, husband of Mary Graham, daughter of the Earl of Airth. their son became 5th Baronet of Glenorchy about 1670. He was a supporter of King Charles II. He married Mary Rich, daughter of the Earl of Holland in 1657, on 13 August 1631. On 13 August 1681 he was created Earl of Breadalbane and Holland at which point the baronetcy merged with the peerage. [The Campbells, 1250-1513, Edinburgh, 2006]

CAMPBELL OF GLEN LYON IN PERTHSHIRE. On 7 September 1502, King James IV granted Duncan Campbell of Glen Orchy, the lands of Glen Lyon, including parts of Gallyn, Meggarne, Milltoun, Brandvoy, Keroclauchy, Cragilk, Invwemuke, Glenmarane, Glencallich, Regill, Crageny, Slattish, Laganecassy, Ruskich, Inverbarris, Carnbayne, Inveringlass, Sestill, Derrycammys, now incorporated into the Barony of Glenlyon; On 1 March 1648, King Charles I granted John Campbell, son of Colin Campbell of Aberurquill, the lands and Barony of Glen Lyon in the Lordship of Dunkeld, Perthshire.

CAMPBELL OF MERTNEM IN AYRSHIRE. On 22 April 1505, King James IV granted Sir Hugh Campbell of Lowdoun, the lands and Barony of Mertnem, with its tenantries.

CAMPBELL OF ROSNEATH IN DUNBARTONSHIRE. On 24 April 1509, King James IV granted Archibald Campbell, the Earl of Argyll, the lands of Rosneath incorporated into the Barony of Rosneath; on 5 October 1545, Queen Mary granted the Earl of Argyll, the lands and Baronies of Glenfruin and of Rosneath.

CAMPBELL OF KIRKTOUN IN INVERNESS-SHIRE. On 14 October 1510, King James IV granted Archibald Campbell, the Duke of Argyll, the lands of Kirktoun and Inchbare, now incorporated into the Barony of Kirktoun.

CAMPBELL OF CALDOR IN MORAYSHIRE. On 22 February 1512, King James IV granted Sir John Campbell the lands of the Thanage of Caldor, the lands of the Barony of Clunes and Boith, lands of Balmakaith, part of Rait in Nairnshire; the lands of Moy in Morayshire, and also the lands of Dunmaglas, Kindeis, Invermerky, Mulquhaich and Drumworny in Inverness-shire, together with the castle and fort of Caldor, now incorporated into the Barony of Caldor; on 8 February 1522, King James V granted John Campbell, the Thane of Caldor, the lands of Easter Ard, Corbett's lands, lands of

Fetterty in Inverness-shire, also the lands of Balgem in Nairnshire; on 6 December 1535, King James V corfirmed the sale by Lord Lindsay of the lands and Barony of Strathnairn, with the fort at Castledavy to John Campbell of Caldor.

CAMPBELL OF LAWERS IN PERTHSHIRE. On 16 June 1525, King James V granted James Campbell of Lawers, including Lawer-moir, Lawer-manach, and Clene-lawers in Perthshire, now incorporated into the -Barony of Lawers, which was confirmed by the king on 4 June 1540, he was also granted the Barony of Auchinreoch, on 14 February 1544, Queen Mary confirmed James Campbell of Lawers in the Barony of Wouchtertiry in Perthshire; on 16 September 1546, Queen Mary granted Duncan Campbell, son and heir of James Campbell of Lawers, the Barony of Auchenreoch, also other lands incorporated into the Barony of Lawers

CAMPBELL OF LOUDOUN IN AYRSHIRE. On 20 August 1533, King James V granted Hugh Campbell of Loudoun the lands and Barony of Wester Loudoun, with its castle, fort, mills, etc.

CAMPBELL OF BUTE. On 27 August 1534, King James V granted Colin Campbell of Ardkinglas the Lordship of Bute.

CAMPBELL OF ABERNETHY IN PERTHSHIRE. On 9 June 1537, King James V granted Archibald Campbell, Earl of Argyll, the lands, Barony, Regality, and Lordship of Abernethy, with mills, fishing rights, etc.; on 9 February 1541, King James V granted Archibald Campbell, Earl of Argyll the lands, Barony, Regality and Lordship of Abernethy, with mills and fishing rights, also the lands of Mylnecroft in Aberargy in Perthshire; on 23332 October 1542, King James V granted Archibald Campbell, son and heir apparent of Archibald Campbell, Earl of Argyll, the lands, Barony, Regality, and Lordship of Abernethy, etc.

CAMPBELL OF MENSTRIE IN CLACKMANNANSHIRE. On 22 October 1542, King James V granted Archibald Campbell, son and heir apparent of the Earl of Argyll, the lands and Barony of Pinkerton in Midlothian, land in East Lothian, land in Perthshire, also in Fife, together with Menstrie, now incorporated into the Barony of Menstrie.

CAMPBELL OF LUNDIE IN ANGUS. On 12 October 1545, Queen Mary confirmed Sir John Campbell in the lands and Barony of Lundy etc; on 13 December 1627, Colin Campbell of Lundie, was created as a Baronet of Nova Scotia. A Colinwas Baronet of Lundie from around 1650 until 1696. Campbell [Campbell is from the Gaelic 'Caimbeul' or 'crooked mouth'.].

CAMPBELL OF LORNE IN ARGYLL. On 10 February 1572, King James VI granted Colin Campbell of Bothquan, brother german of the Earl of Argyll, the lands, Lordship and Barony of Lorne, also the lands and Barony of Pinkertoun in East Lothian, and the Barony of Menstrie in Stirlingshire, the lands and Barony of Lochawe, the lands and Barony of Glen Orchy, the Barony of Cowal, the lands and Barony of Tarbert, the lands and Lordship of Knapdale and Kintyre, etc.

CAMPBELL OF FINLAYSTOUN IN RENFREWSHIRE. On 27 May 1574, King James VI confirmed Margaret Campbell in the lands and Barony of Finlaystoun and Ramfourlie-Cunningham.

CAMPBELL OF ABERUCHILL. James Campbell of Aberuchill was created as a baronet of Nova Scotia on 13 December 1627.

CAMPBELL OF ARDNAMURCHAN IN ARGYLL. Donald Campbell was created as a Baronet of Nova Scotia with a grant of 16000 acres there on 1 January 1628, he died in 1651 with no heir when the Baronetcy became extinct.

CAMPBELL, OF AUCHENBRECK IN ARGYLL. Dugald Campbell, of Auchinbreck, Argyll, was created as a Baronet of Nova Scotia with a grant of 16000 acres there on 12 January 1628, on his death in 1641 his son, Sir Duncan Campbell became the second Baronet of Auchenbreck, he fought against the Royal forces in Ireland, later he was killed at the Battle of Inverlochy in 1645.

CAMPBELL OF GLEN FALLOCH IN ARGYLL. On 19 February 1642, King Charles I granted John Campbell son and heir of Campbell of Glen Orchy, was granted the lands and Barony of Glen Falloch.

CAMPBELL OF RICCARTOUN IN AYRSHIRE. On 20 March 1649, King Charles II granted Sir Hugh Campbell of Cesnock the Barony of Riccartoun.

CAMPBELL OF MUGDOCK IN STIRLINGSHIRE. On 13 March 1650, King Charles II granted Lord Neil Campbell, son of the Marquis of Argyll, the Barony of Mugdock incorporated into the Barony of Neilstoun.

CAMPBELL OF ARDKINGLASS IN ARGYLL. On 23 March 1679 Colin Campbell of Ardkinglass was created as a Baronet, on his death in April 1709, the title was inherited by his son Sir James Campbell who died, childless, on 5 July 1752 when the baronetcy became extinct.

CARDYNE OF FOSS IN PERTHSHIRE. King James III granted Andrew Cardyne, son of Duncan Cardyne, the lands of Foss in the Barony of Apnadul, as a Barony in 1483. [possibly a version of Gardyne, a territorial surname from Angus, examples date from the thirteenth century]

CARGILL OF KINLOCH IN PERTHSHIRE. King James IV granted Walter Cargill of Lasingtoun, the lands and Barony of Kinloch in Perthshire, including Easter Kinloch and Wester Kinloch with its mill, on 16 January 1500. [a surname derived from a place in Perthshire, examples date from the thirteenth century][John Cargill emigrated to North Carolina in 1754, while Richard Cargill, a Jacobite, was transported to Maryland in 1747][Cargill of Haltoun of Rattray, ms, 1930]

CARLISLE OF CARLISLE IN DUMFRIES-SHIRE. On 12 June 1478, King James III, granted Lord John Carlisle the lands of Drumcoll in Dumfries-shire now united into the Barony of Carlisle; on 24 December 1529, King James V granted Janet Scrymgeour, widow of Lord James Carlisle, the lands and Barony of Carlisle with its castle and fort in Dumfries-shire, the Barony of Kinmund with the tower and fort of Kelhead, Lochirwood, Murhouse, Cummertrees, Bridekirk, Dalebank with its fishery, the lands of Dornock with its mill and fishing, etc in Dumfries-shire, also part of Pitinanne with its mills in Lanarkshire; on 4 March 1581, and on 7 March 1581, King James VI confirmed Michael Carlisle, son of Lord William Carlisle, in the lands and Barony of Carlyle incorporating several lands in Dumfries-shire and Lanarkshire. [the name of Carlisle comes from Carlisle in Cumberland, examples date from the twelfth century][William Carlyle settled in South Carolina in 1688, while Adam Carlyle settled in Virginia by 1750][History of the Paisley branch of the Carlisle family, Winchester, 1909]

CARMICHAEL OF CARMICHAEL IN LANARKSHIRE On 8 March 1529, King James V granted William Carmichael of that Ilk the lands of Carmichael in Lanark with manor house, mill, castle, fort, etc, now incorporated into the Barony of Carmichael; on 15 August 1540, King James V granted John Carmichael, son and heir apparent of William Carmichael of that Ilk, the lands of Carmichael, as above; on 14 July 1599, King James VI granted Sir John Carmichael of that Ilk, the lands and Barony of Wiston in Lanarkshire [A name derived from a place in Lanarkshire, examples date from the thirteenth century] [John Carmichael, was captured at the Siege of Worcester and transported to Boston in 1652, while several Carmichaels emigrated to the Carolinas during the eighteenth century].

CARMICHAEL OF CRAWFORD-LINDESAY IN LANARKSHIRE. On 11 August 1542, King James V confirmed John Carmichael in the lands and Barony of Crawford – Lindsay.

CARMICHAEL OF WESTERRAW IN LANARKSHIRE. James Carmichael of Westerraw and Hyndford was created as Baronet of Carmichael in Nova Scotia on 17 July 1627.

CARMICHAEL OF BONINGTON IN LANARKSHIRE. Around 1676 Sir James Carmichael was created as a Baronet, on his death around 1680 the Baronetcy was held by his son Sir John Carmichael who died in 1691.

CARNEGIE OF KINNAIRD IN ANGUS. John Carnegie of Kinnaird was killed at the Battle of Flodden on 9 September 1513. On 17 July 1542, King James V confirmed Robert Carnegie of Kinnaird, in the lands of Kinnaird and Little Carcary, with the manor of Kinnaird, and salmon fishing in the River South Esk, and the community on Montreathmont Muir in Angus, now incorporated into the Barony of Kinnaird; on 18 February 1552, Queen Mary confirmed Robert Carnegie of Kinnaird, in the lands and Barony of Carriden in West Lothian; on 8 December 1552, Queen Mary, confirmed Robert Carnegie of Kinnaird in the lands and Barony of Panbride in Angus; on 25 January 1557, Queen Mary confirmed John Carnegie, son of Robert Carnegie of Kinnaird, in the Barony of Mennie in Aberdeenshire; on 25 March 1565, Queen Mary, granted John Carnegie, son and heir apparent of Sir Robert Carnegie of Kinnaird, the Barony of Kinnaird, and on 6 April 1565, the lands and Barony of Ethie; on 14 October 1591, King James VI granted Sir John Carnegie of Kinnaird, the lands and Barony of Kinnaird; on 2 November 1591, King James VI granted David Carnegie of Kinnaird, the lands and Barony of Eassie in Angus, and other ands now incorporated in the Barony of Cookstoun. [The Carnegys of Lour, Angus, 2000]

CARNEGIE OF ETHIE IN ANGUS. On 1 March 1596, King James VI granted John Carnegie, son of David Carnegie of Cullothy, the lands and Barony of Ethie and other lands in Angus; on 8 January 1639, King Charles I granted David Carnegie, the heir apparent of Ethie, many lands in Angus and Kincardineshire, forming the Barony of Craigs.

CARNEGIE OF PITTARROW IN KINCARDINESHIRE. David Carnegie of Pittarrow, son of Sir Alexander Carnegie was created a Baronet by King Charles II on 22 June 1633 he died in November 1708, when the title devolved to his son Sir John Carnegie as 2nd Baronet, on his death on 3 April 1729 the title went to his son Sir James Carnegie who died in 1765. [a territorial surname from Angus, examples date from the fourteenth century][Andrew Carnegie, born in Dunfermline in 1837, emigrated to USA where he became a multi-millionaire][Skibo, its lairds and history, Edinburgh, 1906][History of the Carnegies, Earls of Southesk, Edinburgh, 1867]

CARNEGIE-ARBUTHNOTT OF BÁLNAMOON IN ANGUS. James Carnegie the younger of Balnamoon, later known as James Carnegie-Arbuthnott was granted the Barony of Balnamoon on 23 February 1758.

CARRUTHERS OF HOLMENDIS IN DUMFRIES-SHIRE. On 1 April 1542, King James V confirmed John Carruthers in various properties in Dumfries-shire, incorporated into the Barony of Carruthers. [a name from a place in Dumfries-shire][John Carruthers died in Antigua in 1700, while James Carruthers, from Edinburgh, was in Boston by 1761][Records of the Carruthers family, London, 1934]

CARSTAIRS OF KILCONQUHAR IN FIFE. On 21 April 1649, King Charles II granted the lands and Barony of Kilconquhar to John Carstairs, eldest son of Sir John Carstairs of Kilconquhar. [A territorial name originally Castle Tarres, examples date from the twelfth century][Thomas Carstairs from Fife, emigrated to Pennsylvania in 1784]

CASSILLIS OF THAT ILK IN AYRSHIRE. On 20 July 1536, King James V granted Gilbert Cassillis, Lord Kennedy, many properties in Ayrshire now formed into the lands and Barony of Cassillis, which was confirmed on 6 February 1541. [a territorial surname from Ayrshire, examples date from the seventeenth century[[John Cassels died on the Darien Expedition of 1698, while John and Isobel Cassels, servants from Edinburgh, emigrated to Philadelphia in 1775][Records of the family of Cassells, Edinburgh, 1870]

CATHCART OF DUNDONALD IN AYRSHIRE. On 13 December 1482, King James III granted Lord Alan Cathcart, the custody of Dundonald Castle with its lands, also Balrasse, Parkthorne, Auchinynche, Bogside, Galrigs, Gudelands in Kyle Stewart in Ayrshire as a Barony; on 21 March 1512, King James IV granted Lord John Cathcart the lands and Barony of Sundrum, including its castle, fort, orchards and mills, the lands of Bardarroch, Drumsmoden, Drumjowene, Welleis, Trevinax, Drumfarne, Dalmakaw with its mill, Auchhinwetyn, Strobanach, Kilmanach with its mill, Clochharnane, Berngor, Threipland, Gallowyhill, Lochend, Barcleuch, Maxweltoun, in Ayrshie, now incorporated into the Barony of Sundrum, which was confirmed on 8 July 1541. Alan Cathcart, the Master of Cathcart, was killed at the Battle of Flodden on 9 September 1513. [a name derived from a place in Renfrewshire, a surname recorded in Scotland by the twelfth century] [Andrew Cathcart was in Boston in 1691, while William Cathcart, a physician, settled in South Carolina in 1737]

CATHCART OF CARLETON IN AYRSHIRE. On 20 January 1704, Hugh Cathcart of Carleton was created as a Baronet, he died in March 1728 and was succeeded by his son Sir John Cathcart as second Baronet of Cathcart who died before 1765. [The Cathcarts of Carleton and Killochan, Ayr, 1955]

CHALMER OF STRATHECHIN IN ABERDEENSHIRE. On 8 November 1528, King James V granted Andrew Chalmer, son and heir apparent of John Chalmer of Strathechin, the lands of Strathechin with its grain mill, fulling will and part of Rosseviot in Aberdeenshire, now incorporated into the Barony of Strathechin.

CHALMER OF SEGGYDEN IN PERTHSHIRE. On 10 August 1531, King James V granted Thomas Chalmer, son and heir apparent of David Chalmer of Stathy, the lands of Seggyden, Bin, North Leyis, the mill of Kinfauns, with fishing rights on the River Tay, in Perthshire, as a Barony.

CHALMER OF DRUMLOCHY IN PERTHSHIRE. On 18 December 1559, King Francis and Queen Mary, confirmed William Chalmer, son and heir of William Chalmer of Drumlochy, in the Barony of Drumlochy.

CHALMERS. On 24 November 1664, King Charles II created Sir James Chalmers, son of Gilbert Chalmers of Cults in Aberdeenshire, as a Baronet. [the name comes from Old French meaning chamber, a surname in Scotland since the twelfth century][Margaret Chambers settled in Pennsylvania in 1696, while Marion Chalmers emigrated to East New Jersey in 1685]

CHARTERS OF CUTHILGURDY IN PERTHSHIRE. On 14 December 1495 King James IV granted John Charters, son and heir apparent, the lands and Barony of Cuthillgurdy; on 6 August 1508, King James IV confirmed John Charteris in the lands and Barony of Cuthilgurdy. [A territorial surname derived from Chartres in France, a surname recorded in Scotland since the thirteenth century] [Henry Charteris died in 1698 bound for Darien, while Laurence Charteris, a Jacobite, was transported to St Kitts in 1715][Charters of Amisfield, Dumfries, 1938]

CHEYNE OF MIDDLE CREICHY IN ABERDEENSHIRE. On 15 February 1528, King James V granted Alexander Cheyne, Creichy and Creich-malaid in Aberdeenshire with mills, incorporated into the Barony of Middle Creichy. [A name derived from Quesney in Normandy, examples in Scotland date from 1200][John Cheyne emigrated to East New Jersey as an indentured servant in 1685, while a Miss

Cheyne died in Lunenburg, Nova Scotia, in 1821]
[The Cheyne family in Scotland, Eastbourne, 1931]

CHEYNE OF ESSILMONT IN ABERDEENSHIRE. On 5 December 1541, King James V granted Thomas Cheyne, son and heir apparent of Patrick Cheyne of Essilmont, the lands of Essilmont, with fort and manor, the lands of Craghead, Carnehill, Corstane, the Auld Mylnetoun with the Mill of Essilmont, parts of Chapeltoun of Essilmont, and the land of Forthry, now incorporated in the Barony of Essilmont; on 29 July 1587 King James VI confirmed Patrick Cheyne in the Barony of Essilmont, also various lands in Shetland and the Orkney Islands, and on 15 August 1587, the lands and Barony of Aberdour in Aberdeenshire; on 2 October 1588, King James VI confirmed Patrick Cheyne in the lands and Barony of Essilmont; on 27 October 1600, King James V confirmed John Cheyne of Pitrichie, heir of Patrick Cheyne of Essilmont, the lands and Barony of Essilmont including lands in Aberdeenshire, Shetland and Orkney.

CHISHOLM OF COMERMORE IN INVERNESS-SHIRE. On 13 March 1539, King James V granted John Chisholm various lands in Strathglass incorporated into the Barony of Comermore. [a name from Lanarkshire, examples date from the thirteenth century][Colin Chisholm from Inverness was a doctor on Grenada in 1793], while some Chisholms settled in Upper Canada in 1826] [The Clan Chisholm, Edinburgh, 1953] [History of the Chisholms, Inverness, 1891] [The Ancient family of Chisholm, London, 1905]

CLAYHILLS OF INVERGOWRIE IN ANGUS. On 3 March 1642, King Charles I confirmed Robert Clayhills, son and heir apparent of Robert Clayhills of Baldovie, a merchant burgess of Dundee, various lands now incorporated into the Barony of Invergowrie. [A territorial surname from Perthshire, examples date from the sixteenth century]

CLELAND OF PAISLEY IN RENFREWSHIRE. On 1 November 1652 George Cleland, brother of the late Sir James Cleland of Monkland was granted the lands and barony of Paisley with castles, towers, mills, mill-lands, woods, marshes and mosses, coals and coal heughs, fishing, manor places, corn houses, orchards, and the abbey of Paisley, which formerly belonged to the Earl of Abercorn and Sir William Hamilton. [The surname Cleland is probably derived from Cleland in Lanarkshire, examples date from the fourteenth century] [James Cleland, a surgeon from Lanarkshire, settled in Jamaica in 1735, while William Cleland, a merchant from Edinburgh, died in Barbados in 1719]

CLERK OF BOYNE IN MORAY. On 21 April 1649, King Charles II granted John Clerk, a merchant in Edinburgh, the lands, Barony and Thanage of Boyne. [originally *clericus* meaning a monk or priest, later a scholar, examples date from the twelfth century][Mary Clerk, a Covenanter from Kirkcudbright was transported to Jamaica in 1685, while John Clark, a farmer, settled in New Hampshire in 1774]

CLERK OF PENICUIK IN MIDLOTHIAN. John Clerk a merchant burgess of Edinburgh, was granted the lands and barony of Penicuik together with other nearby properties such as the barony of Glencorse, in the Sheriffdom of Edinburgh, now included in the barony of Penicuik, with the tower and manor place of Reglis as its principle messuage on 14 July 1654. [Andrew Clerk, a schoolmaster was bound for New York in 1705][Alexander Clerk, a Scots sailor, from Sweden to the Delaware in 1638] [NRS.Penicuik mss 3141/3214/ 5897]

COCHRANE OF OCHILTREE IN AYRSHIRE. In 1673 Sir John Cochrane of Ochiltree was created as a Baronet. [A surname derived from a place in Renfrewshire, examples date from the thirteenth century, [David Cochrane, a merchant from Glasgow, settled in Richmond, Virginia, by 1776, while James Cochrane, a soldier, settled in Georgia by 1737.] [Inventory of the charter chest of the Earldom of Dundonald, 1219-1672, Edinburgh, 1910]

COCKBURN OF CARRIDEN IN MIDLOTHIAN. On 10 November 1366, King David II granted Alexander Cockburn the Barony of Carriden.

COCKBURN OF LANGTOUN IN BERWICKSHIRE. King James III granted Alexander Cockburn of Langtoun, the lands and Barony of Carriden with its tenants and tenantries in West Lothian on 15 March 1474; on 23 February 1510, King James IV granted the lands and Barony of Langtoun with it mill and tenantries, in Berwickshire, also the lands and Barony of James Cockburn of Carriden with its mill, also the Loch-mill of Linlithgow in West Lothian, now incorporated into the Barony of Langtoun; Sir William Cockburn of Langtoun was killed at the Battle of Flodden on 9 September 1513. On 9 January 1542, King James V granted Alexander Cockburn, son and heir apparent of James Langtoun of Langtoun, the lands and Barony of Langtoun etc in Berwickshire, also the lands and Barony of Carriden in West Lothian, now incorporated into the Barony of Langtoun; on 11 November 1595, King James VI confirmed William Cockburn of Langtoun in the lands and Barony of Langtoun; Cockburn of Langtoun was created a baronet of Nova Scotia on 21 November 1627, the 2nd baronet was Sir William Cockburn from 1628 until 1650, followed by another Sir William Cockburn,

3rd baronet from 1650 until 1657, next came Sir Archibald Cockburn as 4th baronet from 1657 until 1705, then came another Sir Archibald Cockburn, the 5th baronet from 1705 until 1710, Sir Alexander Cockburn was 6th baronet from 1710 until 1739, the 7th baronet was Sir Alexander Cockburn from 1739 until 1745, he had a career as a soldier, being an Ensign of the 1st Regiment of Guards who fought at the Battle of Fontenoy. [The surname is derived from a place in the Merse, examples date from 1200] [Alexander Cockburn, a physician in Grenada, died in 1815, while, John Cockburn, a mason from Kelso, settled in New Jersey in 1684.] [Records of the Cockburn Family, Edinburgh, 19...]

COCKBURN OF INVERARITY IN ANGUS. On 15 April 1527, King James V confirmed Alexander Cockburn, son and heir apparent of William Cockburn of Cockburn, in the lands and Barony of Inverarity.

COCKBURN OF SKIRLING IN LANARKSHIRE, ALSO OF LETHAM IN EAST LOTHIAN. On 13 July 1586, King James VI granted William Cockburn, eldest son of Sir James Cockburn of Skirling, the lands and Barony of Skirling; and King James VI granted William Cockburn the lands and barony of Skirling, also lands in Robertoun and Newholme, with the fort, mills fishing rights, and tenantries, incorporated into the free tenantry of Letham on 19 January 1615.

COCKBURN OF FYVIE IN ABERDEENSHIRE. On 3 October 1591, King James VI granted Richard Cockburn of Clarkingtoun, the lands and Barony of Fyvie, etc.

COCKBURN OF THAT ILK. On 24 May 1671, James Cockburn of that Ilk, a merchant burgess of Edinburgh, was created as a Baronet, on his death on 1 January 1704, he was succeeded by his son Sir William Cockburn, an Advocate, as the 2nd Baronet, he died on 4 January 1751.

COLLACE OF MENMUIR IN ANGUS. On 3 November 1507, King James IV granted Walter Culles of Balnamoon, the lands and Barony of Menmuir with its tower, mansion, fort, grain millll, and fulling-mill, the lands of Auchfarsy, the house and lands of Balfour, Pitmedy, Chapeltoun and Woodland. [Possibly derived from Collace, in Perthshire, examples date from the fourteenth century][Killis Collis was a planter in Virginia in 1654]

COLQUHOUN OF LUSS IN DUNBARTONSHRE. On 6 January 1542, King James V granted John Colquhoun of Luss the lands and Barony of Luss, with castle, tower, of Rosneath, islands in Loch Lomond, forests, fishing rights, the lands and Barony of Colquhoun, the lands of Gartscrub, etc. in

Dunbartonshire, the lands of Sauchie in Stirlingshire, and the mill of Saline in Fife, now incorporated into the Barony of Luss. John Colquhoun of Luss was created as a Baronet by King Charles I on 30 August 1625 with 16,000 acres in Nova Scotia, later called Tilliquhoun. He married Lillias Graham, daughter of the Earl of Montrose, and died around 1650. Their son Sir John Colquhoun became the Second Baronet of Luss. Between 1650 and 1674 he was, intermittingly in the 1680s, a Member of Parliament for Dunbartonshire, he married Margaret Baillie. He died on 11 April 1676 and was succeeded by his son. Sir James Colquhoun the Second of Luss who died unmarried in 1680. The land and title then went to his uncle Sir James Colquhoun of Corcagh, County Donegal, Ireland. He died in 1688. He was followed by his son Sir Humphrey Colquhoun who was an MP, Militia Colonel, and civil servant. He died in 1718 when the Barony of Luss became a property of a branch of the Clan. [A territorial surname from Dunbartonshire, examples date from the thirteenth century] [a Walter Colquhoun from Dunbartonshire, settled in Antigua in 1775, and died there in 1802, while, Alexander Colquhoun, a surgeon, settled in New York before 1749] [Cartulary of the Colquhouns of Luss, Edinburgh, 1873]

COLVILLE OF CLEISH IN FIFE. King James IV granted Robert Colville of Hiltoun, the lands of Middle Cleish, Dolyland, Hattoun of Cleish with its tower, fort, and parkland, Bordland of Cleish, Nevinstoun Easter and Wester, the Brewland of Cleish with its tenantries, the lands of Blair Cramby, the lands of Blacksauling with its woods and lakes in Fife, now incorporated into the Barony of Cleish; on 21 July 1537, King James V confirmed the grant by Sir James Colville of East Wemyss of the lands and Barony of Cleish to Robert Colville. [The Ancestry of Lord Colville of Culross, London, 1887]

COLVILLE OF OCHILTREE, AYRSHIRE. King James II granted the lands and Barony of Ochiltree, also the Barony of Oxnam in Roxburghshire, to Robert Colvill on 16 February 1450; on 3 September 1511, King James IV granted Robert Colville of Ochiltree, with the lands and Barony of Tillicoutry, including the lands of Balharty, Drummy, Schannach, Coscnachtane, Colinsdavach with its grain mill, Carntoun with its fulling mill, Ellisdavoch and Harvisdavoch, in Clackmannanshire. Sir Robert Colville of Ochiltree was killed at the Battle of Flodden on 9 September 1513. [It is a surname derived from a place in Normandy; examples of the surname in Scotland date from the mid twelfth century][Archibald Colville, a planter, died in Barbados in 1647, while John Cooper was bound for Darien on the Isthmus of Panama in 1699.]

COLVILLE OF EAST WEMYSS IN FIFE. On 20 August 1533 King James V confirmed James Colville in the lands, Lordship and Barony of East Wemyss;

on 15 June 1581, King James VI granted James Colville, son and heir apparent of James Colville of East Wemyss, the lands and Barony of Tillicoultry in Clackmannanshire; on 19 December 1598, King James VI confirmed Robert Colville, son and heir apparent of James Colville of East Wemyss, in the lands and Barony of East Wemyss; on 8 January 1599, King James VI confirmed Robert Colville, son of James Colville of East Wemyss, in the lands and Barony of Tillicoutry.

CONGILTOUN OF TARBET IN EAST LOTHIAN. On 8 May 1509, King James IV granted Henry Congiltoun of that Ilk, the island and lands of Fetheray, Tarbet, and the islands of Craigleith in the Firth of Forth, incorporated into the Barony of Tarbet. [a territorial surname derived from a location in East Lothian, examples date from the twelfth century][John Congilton, from Edinburgh, was transported to Barbados in 1663]

COOPER OF GOGAR IN MIDLOTHIAN. King Charles I created John Coopar as a Baronet in 1638, he died on 30 August 1640 at the blowing up of Douglas Castle, his son John Cooper then became the second Baronet, who died after 1686. [a surname which may come from the trade of cooper, or from the burgh of Cupar in Fife, examples date from the thirteenth century] [Alexander Cooper, a prisoner of war, was transported to New England in 1650, while Ann Cooper, from Wick, settled in New York in 1774]

CORRIE OF KELDWOOD IN DUMFRIES-SHIRE. On 1 August 1529, King James V granted George Corrie, son and heir of Thomas Corrie of Keldwood, the lands of Newby with its tower, fort, manor house and fishing rights, the lands of Barmkirk, Crofthead with its mill, Milfield, the lands of Stableton,, Robgill with its fishing, Cummertrees, Ellerbeck, Middleby, Gallzeanleys, Hidewood, Priestswoodside, Saltcoats, Ryvell, Nether Keldwood with its manor-house, Bourlands with its fishing, in Dumfries-shire, also, the lands of Thomastoun with its mill, Craigincalye, Auld Cragach, Myntoch, Little Challauch and Anean in Ayrshire, now incorporated into the Barony of Keldwood. [from the lands of that name in Dumfries-shire, examples of the surname date from the twelfth century][Joseph Corrie, a merchant, settled in St Thomas in the West Indies by 1783, while Archibald Corrie, a forger, was transported to the colonies in 1747][Records of the Corrie family, 802-1899, London, 1899]

CRAIG OF COLDINGHAM IN BERWICKSHIRE. On 15 January 1642, King Charles I granted Thomas Craig, son and heir of Robert Craig an advocate, the lands, Lordship and Barony of Coldingham. [a surname from one of several sites, examples date from the thirteenth century][Patrick Craig from

Orkney, died on the Darien Expedition in 1698, while George Craig from Elgin settled in Pennsylvania around 1751]

CRAIGIE OF GAIRSAY IN ORKNEY. In 1707 Sir William Craigie was created a Baronet, on his death on 9 April 1712 the baronetcy was inherited by his son David Craigie of Gairsay. [a territorial surname from 4 possibles locations, examples date from the fourteenth century][Margaret Craigie, settled in Georgia in 1774, while John Craigie, a merchant from Kilgraston, died in Quebec in 1813]

CRAMOND OF MELGUND IN ANGUS. On 18 August 1540, King James V granted William Cramond, son and heir apparent of James Cramond of Auldbar, the Barony of Melgund, including South Melgund, Calakschaw, Woodend, Baberhill and its mill, domestic lands of Auldbar, the salmonry, land of Clatterbane, lands of Bullion, in Angus, confirmed by the king on 9 January 1542. [a surname derived from a place in West Lothian, examples date from the thirteenth century][John Cramond, from Glasgow, emigrated to Virginia in 1759, moved to Jamaica in 1777]

CRANSTOUN OF GREENLAW IN BERWICKSHIRE. On 2 March 1452, King James II granted Thomas Cranstoun the lands of Greenlaw incorporated into the Barony of Greenlaw; on 29 July 1573, King James VI granted George Cranstoun of Corsby, son and heir apparent of John Cranstoun of Cranstoun, the lands and Barony of Bowne in Berwickshire. [a territorial name from a location in Midlothian, examples of the surname date from the thirteenth century][Dr James Cranstoun settled in Rhode Island in 1638][Cranston MSS]

CRAWFORD OF SANQUHAR IN DUMPHRIES-SHIRE. King David II granted the Barony of Sanquhar to John Crawford around 1345. [A placename from Upper Lanarkshire, possibly an early Flemish settlement, examples of the surname date from the twelfth century][Gideon Crawford, a Covenanter, was transported to Carolina in 1684; while Matthew Crawford, from Glasgow, was in Boston by 1700.]

CRAWFORD OF CRAWFORD-LINDSAY IN LANARKSHIRE. King James IV granted Archibald Douglas the Earl of Angus and Lord Douglas, the lands and Barony of Crawford-Lindsay on 25 January 1496; he also granted him the lands and Barony of Braidwood with its tower and fort, also the tenantries of Hewedes, with the patronage of the Hospital of St Leonards in Lanark on 8 May 1497. [The Crawford peerage, Edinburgh, 1829]

CRAWFORD OF KILBIRNY IN AYRSHIRE. Malcolm Crawford of Greenock granted Robert Crawford, his son and heir apparent, the lands of Kilbirny in

Ayrshire, also the lands and Barony of Crawford-John by King James IV on 4 May 1499; on 1 April 1600, King James VI confirmed John Crawford of Kilbirny, in the Barony of Kilbirny. John Crawford, was also created as a baronet of Nova Scotia on 14 May 1628.

CRAWFORD OF PITFOUR IN PERTHSHIRE. On 24 May 1510, King James IV granted John the Earl of Crawford the lands of Pitfour with its mill and fishing, the lands of Pitcowock and Drumgreen in Perthshire, now incorporated into the Barony of Pitfour.

CRAWFORD OF FEDERAT IN ABERDEENSHIRE. On 19 March 1530, King James V confirmed George Crawford of Federat, the lands of Federat with its mill, the lands of Auldquhat, Whitestones, Balmakelly, Ironside, Auchquhaich, Auchyoch, Borrokloch, Showaldy, Atenford, Culche, Pundercroft, Corbyhill, Allauthane with mills, Corsgeicht, Crecy, Bruntbrea, Annauchy, Broomhill, and Whitecairns, in Aberdeenshire, also the lands of Dragy, Glenbeget Gaich with its mill, in Inverness-shire, now incorporated into the Barony of Federat.

CRICHTOUN OF CRICHTOUN IN MIDLOTHIAN. King Robert III granted John Crichtoun the barony of Crichtoun around 1400; King James II granted the Barony of Crichtoun to Sir Wiliam Crichtoun on 27 April 1440. [a name with several variants, derived from a site in Midlothian, examples of the surname date from the twelfth century][Elizabeth Crichtoun, from Edinburgh, was transported to the American colonies in 1697, while John Crichtoun, a Covenanter, was transported to East New Jersey in 1685]

CRICHTOUN OF SANQUHAR IN DUMFRIES-SHIRE. On 27 April 1440 King James II granted Sir Robert Crawford the Barony of Sanquhar; on 23 April 1464 King James III granted Sir Robert Crichtoun the Barony of Sanquhar. [Sanquhar and the Crichtons, Dumfries, 1907]

CRICHTOUN OF KIRKMICHAEL IN DUMFRIES-SHIRE. Sir William Crichtoun was granted the Barony of Kirkmichael, which included the town, lands and mill of Dalfubil-Garvald, Garvald, Mikkelholme, Achinskeoch, le Knokkis, Molyne, Rahillis, Monygep, Cronyantou, with tenants and their free servants, formerly held by Sir James Douglas of Dalkeith, on 2 May 1439, confirmed by King James II on 11 June 1450.

CRICHTON OF TYBBRIS IN DUMFRIES-SHIRE. On 27 February 1450, King Robert II granted the lands and Barony of Tybbris to Sir George Crichtoun.

CRICHTOUN OF CAITHNESS. King James II granted Admiral George Crichtoun, Earl of Caithness, the Barony of Blackness, the Barony of Strathmount, the Barony of Whitburn, the Barony of Tybbris, Aumornesse and the Monches in Dumfries-shire, together with lands in West Lothian, Wigtonshire, Clackmannanshire, Renfrewshire, and Peebles-shire, united into a Regality, on 8 July 1452.

CRICHTON OF CLUNY IN PERTHSHIRE. On 17 December 1475 King James III granted the lands and Barony of Cluny to David Crichton of Cranstoun; on 24 January 1592, King James VI confirmed Robert Crichton of Cluny, son and heir of Robert Crichton of Eliok the Royal Advocate, the lands of Cluny and others now incorporated into the Barony of Cluny; on 16 March 1597, King James VI confirmed Sir Robert Crichton of Cluny, in the Barony of Cluny.

CRICHTON OF CRANSTOUN-RIDDALE IN MIDLOTHIAN. King James III granted David Crichtoun, the lands of Crichtoun-Riddale with its tenants and tenantries, the lands of Nesbit with its tower in East Lothian, united into the Barony of Cranstoun-Riddale; and the lands of Davidstoun in West Lothian, on 20 October 1491; on 27 December 1494 King James IV granted Patrick Crichtoun of Cranstoun-Riddel the lands and Barony of Oures in Kincardineshire, which he sold to William Keith the Earl Marischal on 16 October 1495; on 2 February 1572, King James VI confirmed Robert Crichtoun in the lands and Barony of Cranstoun-Riddell.

CRICHTON OF RAGARTOUN IN PERTHSHIRE. On 20 October 1491 King James IV granted Sir James Crichton of Carnys, the land and Barony of Ragartoun with its mill, manor house, and fort in Strathaird in Perthshire, also lands and Barony of Whitburn

CRICHTOUN OF RUTHVENDAVY IN ANGUS. King James IV granted Adam Crichtoun, son and heir apparent of James Crichtoun of Ruthvendavy, the lands and Barony of Ruthvendavy, on 28 March 1493; on 14 October 1504, King James IV granted the lands of Ruthvendavy, also those of Brigtoun, Mintoun, Earlsruthven, with woods, mill, etc, to Adam Crichtoun created into the Barony of Ruthvendavy; on 27 November 1506, King James IV confirmed James Crichtoun, son and heir apparent of Sir Adam Crichtoun of Ruthvennys, as Baron of Craggs in Angus, including Kelery, Easter Derry, Easter Crag, Over Crag with its mills, Mill-land, etc.; on 8 January 1563, Queen Mary granted John Crichtoun of Ruthvenis, the lands and Barony of Craggs; on 16 December 1573, King James VI granted Adam Creichtoun, son and heir apparent of John Creichtoun of Ruthven, the lands and Barony of Craggs.

CRICHTOUN OF PANBRIDE IN ANGUS. On 18 June 1507, King James IV, granted Lord Robert Crichtoun of Sanquhar the lands and Barony of Panbride with its mill, port and fishing.

CRICHTOUN OF INVERNITY IN PERTHSHIRE. On 5 July 1510, King James IV granted John Crichtoun of Blackburn the lands of Invernity and Tullybelton, with fishing rights on the River Tay, now incorporated into the Barony of Invernyty; on 6 June 1581, King James VI confirmed John Crichtoun, Robert Crichtoun of Inner son and heir apparent of Invernyty, the lands and Barony of Invernity, also Tullybeltane, Redgorton, etc incorporated into the said Barony.

CRICHTOUN OF STRATHURD IN PERTHSHIRE. On 31 August 1529, King James V granted Sir John Crichtoun of Strathurd, the lands of Nethertoun, the Mains of Tullibody with its mill, tower, orchard and brewery in Clackmannan, now part of the Barony of Strathurd;

CRICHTOUN OF FENDRAUGHT IN ABERDEENSHIRE. On 19 November 1535, King James V granted James Crichtoun the lands and Barony of Fendraught, with castle, fort, mill etc, also the lands and Barony of Inverkeithny, with mill, fishing rights, etc, in Banffshire, and the lands and Barony of Mailherb and Forgandenny with mill, fishing rights, etc. in Perthshire; on 15 August 1539, King James V confirmed William Crichtoun of Fendraught in the lands and Barony of Inverkeithny [alias Conveth] in Banffshire; on 11 August 1546, Queen Mary granted James Crichtoun, son and heir apparent of William Crichtoun of Fendraught, the lands and Barony of Fendraught, also the lands and Barony of Conveth, in Banffshire, and Newtoun of Forgan, etc in Perthshire; on 29 April 1599, King James VI confirmed George Crichtoun, son of Sir James Crichtoun of Fendraught, in the lands and Barony of Fendraught, also the lands and Barony of Conveth; on 10 August 1599, King James VI granted James Crichtoun, son of James Crichtoun of Auchingowell, the lands and Barony of Fendraught etc; on 21 September 1641, King Charles I granted James Crichtoun of Fendraught the younger the lands and Barony of Fendraught, the lands and Barony of Kinnardie, the lands and Barony of Netherdale, the lands and Barony of Pittendreich, etc;

CRICHTOUN OF NAUGHTAN IN FIFE. On 16 December 1574, King James VI granted Alexander Crichtoun, the apparent of Drylaw, the lands and Barony of Nauchtan; on 1 October 1580, King James VI confirmed Alexander Crichtoun of Drylaw, in the Barony of Naughtan.

CRICHTOUN OF LUGTOUN IN MIDLOTHIAN. On 29 July 1581, King James VI confirmed Patrick Crichtoun in the lands and Barony of Lugtoun;

CUMING OF CULTER-CUMING IN ABERDEENSHIRE. On 24 February 1513, King James IV confirmed Alexander Cuming of Culter, the lands and Barony of Culter with its mill, woods, and fishing rights, also the land and Barony of Tulliboy, with its mill, woods, lochs, and fishing rights, now incorporated into the Barony of Culter-Cuming, this was confirmed by the king on 24 February 1513; on 9 December 1564, Queen Mary, granted Alexander Cumming, son and heir apparent of Alexander Cumming of Culter, the lands and Barony of Culter-Cumming; on 16 December 1598, King James VI confirmed Alexander Cuming of Culter in the lands and Barony of Tullieboy now incorporated into the Barony of Culter-Cuming; [The surname may come from Comines in Flanders; as a surname it exists from the twelfth century] [Ralph Cumming, a surgeon, died in Antigua in 1808, while Thomas Jones Cumine, from Aberdeenshire, died in Demerara in 1820] [Family records of the Bruces and the Cumyns, Edinburgh, 1870]

CUMING OF ALTYRE IN MORAY. On 16 May 1553, Queen Mary granted Thomas Cumming, nephew of Alexander Cumming of Altyre, the lands and Barony of Altyre.

CUMING OF ERNSIDE IN MORAY. On 2 February 1601, King James VI confirmed William Cuming, son of John Cuming of Ernside, in the Barony of Ernside.

CUNNINGHAM OF REIDHALL IN MIDLOTHIAN. William Cunningham was granted the Barony of Reidhall by King Robert III in 1396, formerly held by Murdo Stewart. [A surname derived from a location in Ayrshire, examples date from the twelfth century] [John Cunningham, an explorer in Greenland and Labrador in 1606, while Janet Cunningham emigrated to East New Jersey in 1685]

CUNNINGHAM OF POLMAIS-CUNNINGHAM IN STIRLINGSHIRE. King James III granted Alexander Cunningham of Polmais, the lands of Polmais Marshall, Polmais-Sinclair, Auchinbowie, and part of the lands of Leylands, Erthbeg, Airthmalar, Slamannan in Stirlingshire, fishing rights on the Firth of Forth, and Eschelis and Spittalfield in Peebles-shire, also part of the lands of Cleghorn with its mill, in Lanarkshire, the lands of Boithaldy, part of the lands of Ardargy, and Over-Auchinlesky, Elchquhok and Ballabraham, Inchmartin, Cragdaly, Straithardill, Sulzery and Kinnaird in Perthshire, part of the lands of Balmuto, Pitconnochy, West Wemyss and Bogtoun in Fife, now united into the Barony of Polmais-Cunningham, on 19 February 1484; On 14 May 1491, King James IV confirmed the grant by Sir Alexander Cunningham to his son and heir apparent, of the lands and Barony of Polmais-Cunningham; on 9 July 1512, King James IV granted James Cunningham, son and heir apparent of Robert Cunningham of Polmais, land of Airth-Malare, Polknaif, Slammanan, part of Hallis of Airth, also the lands and Barony of Polmais-Cunningham, the lands of Polmais-Sinclair, part of Levilands, part of Airthbeg, Airth-Malare, Pitfoulis, and others in Stirlingshire.

CUNNINGHAM OF KILMAURS IN AYRSHIRE. King James IV granted William Cunningham, son and heir apparent of Lord Cuthbert Cunningham of Kilmaurs, the lands and Barony of Kilmaurs with it castle and fort, the lands of Skermorley, the lands of Polquharn and Clune in Kyle, the lands and Barony of Finlaystoun- Cunningham, Ranfurele and Waterstoun in Renfrewshire, the lands and Barony of Kilmarranok, the lands of Crawmenan in Stirlingshire, the lands of Dripps in Lanarkshire, the lands and Barony of Glencairn in Dumfries-shire, the lands and Barony of Redshaw in Midlothian, the Barony of Hassildean in Selkirkshire, and the lands and Barony of Hiltoun in Berwickshire, on 6 June 1498; King James IV granted William Cunningham, son and heir apparent of Cuthbert Cunningham the Lord of Kilmaurs, the lands and Barony of Reidhall with its mill in Midlothian, also, the lands of Langlands in the Barony of Kilmaurs the castle, fort and manor-house of Kilmaurs on 10 July 1509; on 27 February 1511, King James IV granted Cuthbert Cunningham the Earl of Glencairn the lands and Barony of Haseldean in Roxburghshire incorporated as the Barony of Haseldean; On 24 July 1511, King James IV granted Cuthbert Cunningham, the Earl of Glencairn, the county and Barony of Glencairn, including Auchincane, Lochwhir, Darangill. Mawhirnane,Kirkcubre, Glen Corse, Craigneston, Powrane, Conrait, Mynnisgrill, etc, now incorporated into the County and Barony of Glencairn; on 22 January 1528, King James V granted Sir William Cunningham, baron of Glencairn, son and heir apparent of Cuthbert Cunningham the Earl of Glencairn, the lands and Barony of Wester Loudoun with its castle, fort, mill, the Barony of Stevenstoun with its castle, fort, mill, fishing etc, in Cunningham, Ayrshire; on 20 July 1551, Queen Mary granted Alexander Cunningham, the Earl of Glencairn various properties in the Barony of Renfrew; on 5 June 1581, King James VI granted James Cunningham, Lord Glencairne, the lands and Barony of Stevenstoun.

CUNNINGHAM OF AUCHTERMACHNY AND KILDYNNY IN PERTHSHIRE. On 27 August 1505, King James IV granted the lands and Barony of Auchtermachny and Kildynny, with the lands of Polgaris, Kilfassatis and Baldaloch in Dunbartonshire, to Sir Humphrey Cunningham of Glengarnock.

CUNNINGHAM OF GLEN GARNOCK IN AYRSHIRE. On 30 December 1539, King James V, confirmed William Cunningham in the Barony of Glen Garnock, including its castle, mill and lake, and several properties, now incorporated into the Barony of Glen Garnock; on 16 March 1559, King Francis and Queen Mary confirmed John Cunningham of Glen Garnock, the lands and Barony of Auchtermacanye and Kyldlynne in Perthshire; on 21 April 1599, King James VI granted James Cunningham, nephew and heir apparent of John Cunningham of Glen Garnock, the lands and Barony of Auchtermachny and Kildynny, the lands and Barony of Glen Garnock, and the Barony of Ballindalloch.

CUNNINGHAM OF CUNNINGHAMHEAD. On 10 March 1512, King James IV granted William Cunningham, son and heir apparent of Robert Cunningham of Cunninghamhead, the lands and Barony of Polkelly, including the lands of Polkelly, Darclavoch, Clonherb with its mill, Gre, Drumboy, the lands of Balgray with its tower, manor house, and mill, etc., in Ayrshire, also the lands of Limflare in Lanarkshire, now incorporated into the Barony of Polkell; William Cunningham of Cunninghamhead was created as a Baronet of Nova Scotia on 4 July 1627.

CUNNINGHAM OF STEVENSTOUN IN AYRSHIRE. On 1 March 1550, Queen Mary confirmed Janet Cunningham, daughter of John Cunningham of Caprintoun, in the lands and Barony of Stevenstoun.

CUNNINGHAM OF ROBERTSLANDS. On 25 November 1630, David Cunningham of Robertslands was created as a Baronet of Nova Scotia.

CUNNINGHAM OF AUCHINHERVIE. David Cunnynghame of Auchinhervie was created a baronet of Nova Scotia on 23 December 1633. On 3 August 1673 Robert Cuningham of Auchenharvie was created as a Baronet, when he died in March 1674 his son Sir Robert Cuningham became the 2nd Baronet of Auchenharvie in Ayrshire but as he died childless that year the baronetcy became extinct.

CUNNINGHAM OF CORSHILL IN AYRSHIRE. On 26 February 1672, Alexander Cunningham of Corshill was created as a Baronet, he died in March 1685, when his son Sir Alexander Cunningham became the 2nd Baronet, he died in 1730 when his son Sir David Cunningham succeeded to the Baronetcy.

CUNNINGHAM OF MILNCRAIG IN AYRSHIRE. On 3rd February 1702, David Cunningham an Advocate, was created as a Baronet, in January 1708 on his ham, death he was succeeded by his son Sir James Cunningham as 2nd Baronet of Milncraig.

CURROUR OF LOGIE-MEIGLE IN PERTHSHIRE. On 28 July 1543, Queen Mary, granted Alexander Currour, son and heir apparent of Andrew Currour of Logie Meigle, the lands and Barony of Logie Meigle etc in Perthshire now incorporated into the Barony of Logie Meigle. [a surname of occupational origin meaning 'courier', examples date from the thirteenth century]

DALMAHOY OF DALMAHOY AND OVER LIBERTOUN IN MIDLOTHIAN. On 8 March 1476 King James III granted the lands and Baronies of Dalmahoy and Upper Libertoun to Alexander Dalmahoy; on 28 May 1556, Queen Mary granted Alexander Dalmahoy, son and heir apparent of William Dalmahoy of that Ilk, the lands and Barony of Dalmahoy; on 10 August 1598, King James VI confirmed Alexander Dalmahoy of that Ilk, in the lands and Barony of Dalmahoy and Over Libertoun. [A surname derived from a place in Midlothian, examples date from the thirteenth century] [Thomas Dalmahoy, a Jacobite, was transported to St Kitts in 1716][The Family of Dalmahoy of Dalmahoy, London, 1870]

DALMAHOY OF DALMAHOY IN MIDLOTHIAN. On 17 December 1679 John Dalmahoy of that Ilk was created as a Baronet. In 1700 Sir Alexander Dalmahoy became the 2nd Baronet, next came his son Sir Alexander Dalmahoy as 3rd Baronet.

DALRYMPLE OF STAIR IN AYRSHIRE. Sir James Dalrymple of Stair, born in May 1619, a lawyer, was created a Baronet on 2 June 1664 by King Charles II, and by King William III as Viscount Stair on 21 April 1690 when the Baronetcy merged with the peerage. [a placename in Ayrshire, examples as a surname date from the fourteenth century][Charles Dalrymple emigrated to Maryland in 1670; John Hamilton Dalrymple, died in Jamaica in 1804]

DALRYMPLE, JAMES, of Killoch, son of Viscount Stair, was an Advocate and Clerk of Session, he was created a Baronet on 28 April 1698, when he died in May 1719, he was succeeded as the 2nd Baronet by his son Sir John Dalrymple who died on 24 May 1743.

DALRYMPLE OF NORTH BERWICK IN EAST LOTHIAN. Hew Dalrymple, 3rd son of Viscount Stair, was created a Baronet on29 April 1698, he was Lord President of the Court of Session until his death on 1 February 1737, the 2nd Baronet of North Berwick was his grandson Sir Hew Dalrymple, an Advocate and a Member of Parliament, he died in London in November 1790.

DALRYMPLE OF HAILES IN MIDLOTHIAN. On 8 May 1701 David Dalrymple, son of Viscount Stair, an Advocate and MP was created a Baronet, was Solicitor General to Queen Anne and Auditor of the Exchequer, he died on 3 December 1721, his son Sir James Dalrymple, born 24 July 1692 succeeded to the title of 2nd Baronet Hailes until his death on 24 February 1751.

DALZELL OF DALZELL IN LANARKSHIRE. King Robert III granted George Dalzell the Barony of Dalzell formerly held by James Sandilands around

1400. [a placename in Lanarkshire which appears as a surname in the thirteenth century][George Dalzell, a merchant, settled in Antigua before 1765, while Reverend Dalziel, settled in Bermuda in 1779][The Binns papers, J. Beveridge, 1938]

DALZELL OF GLENAE, DUMFRIES-SHIRE. Robert Dalyell of Glenae, Dumfries-shire was a MP for Dumfries-shire until his death in September 1685, his son Sir John Dalzell succeeded to the Baronetcy of Glenae, also was MP for Dumfries-shire, married Henrietta Murray, and died in March 1689, their son Sir Robert Dalzell, born 1687, then became the 3rd Baronet of Glenae, however on the death of his cousin the Earl of Cornwath he acquired that title while the baronetcy was merged into the peerage.

DARNLEY, Lord HENRY, son and heir apparent of the Earl of Lennox, was granted many lands in the Northern Highlands incorporated into the County, Lordship and Barony of Ross on 15 May 1565 by Queen Mary.

DAVIDSON OF CURRIEHILL IN MIDLOTHIAN. In 1661 Sir William Davidson, the Conservator of the Scots Privileges at Veere in the Netherlands, was created as a Baronet in 1661, as he died childless in 1680, the barony became extinct. [a patronymic name common in Scotland, examples date from the thirteenth century][Peter Davidson, from Dundee, emigrated to Maryland in 1684, while William Davidson emigrated to East New Jersey in 1684]

DAW OF WEST BARNS IN FIFE. On 20 March 1649, King Charles II granted, Andrew Daw, a burgess of Crail, the lands and Barony of West Barns. [A diminutive of David, examples date from the fifteenth century][Andrew Daw, a Jacobite, was transported to Maryland in 1716]

DEMPSTER OF CARESTOUN IN ANGUS. On 14 March 1539, King James V granted David Dempster, son and heir apparent of William Dempster of Carestoun, the lands and Barony of Careston, with mills, fishing rights, etc, also, the lands and Barony of Pitmouis, with mill, etc, the lands of Presach, Friock, Pitforth, and Breiklo in Angus. [Letters of George Dempster, 1756-1813, London, 1934]

DEMPSTER OF AUCHTERLESS IN ABERDEENSHIRE. On 6 June 1592, King James VI granted Robert Dempster, son and heir of Thomas Dempster of Auchterless, the lands and Barony of Auchterless. [an occupational surname from deemster or judge, examples date from the thirteenth century[Edward Dempster, a shipmaster, died in Jamaica in 1669, while William Dempster was in Virginia in 1654]

DICK OF SYMINGTON IN LANARKSHIRE. King Robert I granted Thomas Dick the Barony of Symington by 1320. [a diminutive of Richard, a surname recorded in Scotland by the fifteenth century][Jean Dick was transported to the American colonies in 1695, while John Dick, a Covenanter was banished to Carolina in 1684]

DICK OF BRAID IN MIDLOTHIAN. King Charles I created Sir William Dick, a merchant burgess of Edinburgh, born 1580 son of John Dick a merchant burgess of Edinburgh, Baronet of Braid, possibly in 1638, also the lands and Barony of Caerlaverock and Locherwod in Dumfries-shire, on13 September 1641, he died in Westminster on 19 December 1655. His grandson William Dick became the second Baronet of Braid,and was dead by 1695. Then followed William Dick, born 1679, an officer of militia in New York, he died in 1733 without a son, so the title went to his cousin Robert Dick in Shetland who died in 1743. Charles Dick of Frackafield then became the fifth Baronet.

DICK OF PRESTONFIELD IN MIDLOTHIAN. On 22 March 1707, Sir James Dick was created Baronet of Prestonfield, on his death on 15 November 1728 the Baronetcy went to Sir William Dick. [Curiosities of a Scots charter chest, 1600-1800, Edinburgh, 1897]

DISHINGTOUN OF BALGLASSY IN ABERLEMNO, ANGUS. King Robert Bruce granted the lands of Balglassy and the mill there to William Dishington on 1320s. [RGSS.I.App.1.78]; on 28 April 1477 King James III, granted John Dishington, son and heir apparent of John Dishington of Ardros, the lands and Barony of Balglassy in Angus; on 5 November 1510, King James IV granted George Dishingtoun, son and heir apparent of Sir John Dishington of Ardros, the lands and Barony of Claschedeugly with its mill in Kinross-shire. [Possibly derived from a place in Northumberland, examples date from the fourteenth century]

DISHINGTOUN OF ARDROS IN FIFE. On 7 December 1506, King James IV granted George Dishingtoun, son and heir apparent of John Dishingtoun of Ardros, in Fife, the lands and Baronies of Ardros and Kinbrachmont, with their mills, tenantries, etc., also, the lands and Barony of Balglassy, Balbany, Boghall, and Tullywhanlan, with mills etc , in Angus, and the lands and Barony of Curry with its mills in Midlothian; on 31 December 1529, King James V granted William Dishingtoun, son and heir apparent of George Dishington, the lands and Baronies of Ardross and Kinbrachmont with mills, also the lands and Baronies of Balglassy, Baldany, Boghall, Tullywhandland with mills, in Angus, the lands and Barony of Curry, and the

Langhirdmanstoun with mills in Midlothian, the lands and Barony of Clasheduigly with mills, and the lands and Lordship of Cullenachie, in Kinross-shire; on 10 March 1580, King James VI confirmed Thomas Dishington in the lands and Barony of Ardros; on 17 April 1600, King James VI confirmed Thomas Dishingtoun of Ardros, son and heir of Thomas Dishington of Ardros, the lands and Barony of Ardros.

DON OF NEWTON DON IN BERWICKSHIRE. On 7 June 1667, Alexander Don was created as a Baronet, he died in 1687, when his son Sir James Don became the 2nd Baronet, around 1710 his son Sir Alexander Don became the 3rd Baronet of Newton-Don, he died on 13 April 1749.

DONALDSON OF LUDE IN PERTHSHIRE. On 1 February 1508, King James IV granted John Donaldson, son and heir apparent of Donald Johnson of Lude, the lands and Barony of Lude. [A patronymic meaning 'son of Donald', examples date from the late thirteenth century][Barbara Donaldson was transported from Edinburgh to the American Plantations in 1697 while James Donaldson, a Jacobite, was transported to Maryland in 1747] [The Lords of the Isles, Clan Donald, London, 1984][The Barony Court Book of Lude 1621-1908, ms.NRS.GD50.169]

DONALDSON OF HILTOUN IN ABERDEENSHIRE. On 23 June 1638, King Charles I granted John Donaldson, a merchant burgess of Aberdeen, the Barony of Hiltoun.

DOUGLAS OF THE FOREST OF SELKIRK, ETTRICK AND TRAQUAIR. Were granted to Lord James Douglas, and formed into a free barony, by King Robert I around 1318. [The Douglas Book, Edinburgh, 1885]

DOUGLAS OF KILBOTHACK. King David II granted the lands and Barony of Kilbothock to William Douglas in 1341. [a place name derived from a site in Lanarkshire in Gaelic meaning 'dark stream', examples of the surname date from the twelfth century][William Douglas, a Covenanter, was transported to East New Jersey in 1685, while Isabella Douglas emigrated to Pennsylvania in 1698][History of the House and Race of Douglas and Angus, Edinburgh, 1808]

DOUGLAS OF DALKEITH IN MIDLOTHIAN. King David II granted the Barony of Dalkeith to William Douglas the younger on 6 January 1341; in 1370 Dalkeith and its castle was granted to Lod James Douglas, son of James Douglas, on 10 December 1507, King James IV granted James Douglas, son and heir apparent of John Douglas, the Earl of Mortoun, the lands and

Barony of Prestoun in Kirkcudbrightshire, now incorporated in the Barony and Regality of Dalkeith; on 22 April 1543, Queen Mary confirmed James Douglas in the lands, Lordship, Regality, and Barony of Dalkeith; on 2 June 1564, Queen Mary granted James Douglas the lands, Lordship Regality and Barony of Dalkeith, the lands and Barony of Garmiltoun-Dunning, the lands and Barony of Caldorcleir, the lands and Barony of Whittingham, the lands and Baronies of Newlands, Lintoun and Kilbucho, the lands and Barony of Eschels, the lands and Barony of Robertoun, the lands and Barony of Edmestoun, the lands and Barony of Aberdour, the lands and Barony of Mortoun, the lands and Barony of Mordingtoun, the lands and Baronies of Prestoun, Borg and Buthill, incorporated into the Barony of Dalkeith; on 5 June 1581, King James VI granted Lord John Maxwell, the lands, Barony and Regality of Mortoun, the lands and Barony of Prestoun, the lands and Barony of Hutton-sub-mora, the lands and Barony of Newlands, the lands and Barony of Robertoun, etc incorporated in the Barony of Mortoun.

DOUGLAS OF ABERNETHY, PERTHSHIRE, ALSO OF BUNKLE, BERWICKSHIRE. King Robert III granted George Douglas the Baronies of Abernethy and of Bunkle, around 1397.

DOUGLAS OF BOTHWELL IN LANARKSHIRE. On 26 April 1425, King James I granted Archibald, Lord Douglas, the lands and Barony of Bothwell.

DOUGLAS OF ABERCORN, EAST LOTHIAN. King James I granted James Douglas of Balvany, the Barony of Abercorn with its castle on 7 March 1425, also, the Barony of Aberdour and Rattray in Aberdeenshire, on 18 April 1426.

DOUGLAS OF MORTOUN IN DUMFRIES-SHIRE. King James II granted the Barony of Mortoun with its castle to James Douglas of Dalkeith on 28 February 1439.

DOUGLAS OF TEMPLETOUN IN EAST LOTHIAN. On 13 October 1479 King James III granted Archibald Douglas, the Earl of Angus and Lord Douglas, the Barony of Templetoun, including the castle of Templetoun, Castletoun, Boyntoun, Samiltoun, Redside, Halfplewland, and others united into the Barony of Templetoun.

DOUGLAS OF GLENQUHIM IN PEEBLES-SHIRE. On 20 September 1440, King James II granted the Barony of Glenquhim to James Douglas, Lord Avendale; on 7 July 1451, King James II granted William, Earl of Douglas the lands and Barony of Glenquhyme.

DOUGLAS OF LAUDERDALE IN BERWICKSHIRE. On 6 July 1451 King James II granted the lands, lordship and Regality of Lauderdale, and the Barony of Romanos in Peebles-shire, to William, the Earl of Douglas on 6 July 1451.

DOUGLAS OF RUTHERGLEN IN LANARKSHIRE. King James II granted to William, Earl of Douglas, the lands of Ferme of Lanarkshire, and the Barony of Abercorn in West Lothian, with its castle, annexed and incorporated, on 7 July 1451.

DOUGLAS OF BOLTON IN EAST LOTHIAN. On 7 July 1451 King James II granted the Barony of Bolton to William, Earl of Douglas.

DOUGLAS OF SPROSTOUN IN ROXBURGHSHIRE. On 7 July 1451, King James II incorporated the Baronies if Hawick, Bedrule, Smailholme, and Sprostoun into the Barony of Sprostoun which he granted to William, Earl of Douglas.

DOUGLAS OF ABERDOUR IN ABERDEENSHIRE. On 7 July 1451, King James II granted the Barony of Aberdour to Willliam, Earl of Douglas.

DOUGLAS OF BOTHWELL IN LANARKSHIRE. On 7 July 1451 King James II granted William, Earl of Douglas, the Lordship and Barony of Bothwell with its castle, also the lands and Barony of Carmunnock, also in Lanarkshire, formed into a free Regality; on 4 July 1492 King James IV granted Archibald Douglas the Earl of Angus the towns of Bothwell and Uddingston, also Scherrailles, Ricardystoun, Urcaswod, Knowhohble, Poffillis, Schawis, Meikle Hareshaw, the lands of Woodhead, Newlands, Aikenhead, Unthank, Alderstoun, Suynste, Gudelockhill, in the Barony of Bothwell, with its castle and the mill of Uddingstoun in Lanarkshire, the lands of Easter Dunsire with its mill and lands of Westoun, Todhills, lands of Trottandshaw, Byrecleugh, Handaxwood, Horshop, Hartshawmeadow, and Kettleshiel in the Forest of Dye in Berwickshire, united into the Barony of Bothwell; on 31 August 1547, Queen Mary granted James Douglas, son and heir apparent of Archibald Douglas, the Earl of Angus, the lands, Lordship and Barony of Douglas also the lands and Barony of Crawford-Douglas, and the lands, Lordship, Barony and Regality of Kirriemuir in Angus, etc; on 31 December 1574, King James VI granted Archibald Douglas, Earl of Angus, the lands and Lordship of Oxnam in Roxburghshire; on 3 February 1602, King James VI granted William Douglas the Earl of Angus, the lands, Lordship, Barony and Regality of Kirriemuir, the lands, Lordship and Barony of Abernethy, the lands, Lordship and Barony of Selkirk, the lands, Lordship and Barony of Jedburgh, the lands, Lordship and Barony of Buncle and Prestoun, the lands, Lordship, Barony and Regality of Bothwell, the lands, Lordship and Barony of Douglas, the Lordship of Crawford-Lindsay

DOUGLAS OF SUNDERLANDHALL IN SELKIRKSHIRE. On 16 January 1464, King James III granted the lands of Sunderlandhall, to William Douglas of Cluny together with the lands of Cranstoun in Midlothian, the lands of Traquair and Lethanehope in Peebles-shire, which with the lands of Cranstoun in Midlothian also Traquair and Lethanhope in Peebleshire, now formed the Barony of Sunderlandhall.

DOUGLAS OF TEMPLETOUN IN EAST LOTHIAN. On 13 October 1479 King James III granted Archibald Douglas, the Earl of Angus and Lord Douglas, the Barony of Templetoun, including the castle of Templetoun, Castletoun, Boyntoun, Samiltoun, Redside, Halfplewland, and others united into the Barony of Templetoun.

DOUGLAS OF TERREGLES IN DUMFRIES-SHIRE. King James IV granted Janet Douglas, daughter of Archibald Douglas the Earl of Angus, the lands and Baronies of Terregles and Kirkgunzeone, also lands in the Barony of Urr in Kirkcudbrightshire, and the lands of Hoddum, Tolligarth, Lockerbie, Huttoun, Avondale, Moffatdale, and Kirkandrews in Annandale, Dumfries-shire, the lands of Fewrule in Roxburghshire, the lands of Barnwell and Symington in Ayrshire on 22 December 1495.

DOUGLAS OF SELKIRK IN SELKIRKSHIRE. On 10 March 1508, King James IV confirmed George Douglas, son and heir of the Earl of Angus, in the lands and Lordhip of Selkirk, with the lands of Philiphaugh, etc, incorporated into the Barony of Selkirk.

DOUGLAS OF CRAWFORD-LINDSAY IN LANARKSHIRE. On 20 January 1511, King James IV granted George Douglas, son and heir apparent of the Earl of Angus, the lands, Lordship and Barony of Crawford-Lindsay including the castle and fort of Crawford, the lands of Howcleuch, Racleuch. Hardtop. Budhouse, Ellieshaw, Powtrale, Crookstone, Nether Newton, Little Clyde, Glaspane, Manys, Mudlaw, Cowhill, the lands of Westschaw, Whitecamp, Kirkhope, Southouse, Normangill, Blackhouse, Crymperamp, Harecleuch, Bonnytoun, and Halkshawis in Lanarkshire, now incorporated into the Barony of Crawford-Lindsay; on 25 February 1511, King James IV granted George Douglas, son and heir apparent of the Earl of Angus, the lands, Lordship, Barony and Regality of Abernethy in Perthshire.

DOUGLAS OF BRAIDWOOD IN LANARKSHIRE. On 25 February 1511, King James IV granted William Douglas, son of the Earl of Angus, the lands and Barony of Braidwood with its tower, fort and mill.

DOUGLAS OF HAWICK IN ROXBURGHSHIRE. On 15 June 1511, King James IV granted Sir William Douglas of Drumlanark, the lands and Barony of Hawick, including the house of Hawick with its mill, Mains, Crumhaugh, Mains of Kirktoun, Flekkis, Murinese, Ramsay-clowis, and Braidle, etc, incorporated into the Barony of Hawick. Sir William Douglas was killed at the Battle of Flodden on 9 September 1513.

DOUGLAS OF CAVERS IN ROXBURGHSHIRE. On 9 August 1511, King James IV granted James Douglas the lands and Barony of Cavers, with its castle, manor house and mill, Trowis, Eschebank, Yarlside, Cavilling, Langside, Blackbull, Synglie, Stanhope, Penerie, Colleford, Driloch, Elrechill, Mains of Denholm, and others in Roxburghshire, now incorporated into the Barony of Cavers; on 21 February 1577, King James VI granted James Douglas, son and heir apparent of William Douglas of Cavers, the lands and Barony of Cavers.

DOUGLAS OF KEIR IN PERTHSHIRE. On 22 November 1526, King James V granted George Douglas, brother of the Earl of Angus, the lands and Barony of Keir, with its fort, manor-house mills, fishing etc, the lands of Auchlochy in the Barony of Kippenross, the lands of Lochfield, Burnbank, Calyequhat and Annat in the Lordship of Menteith, the lands of Lanark, Fyve Coygis, Dallewhy with its mill, the lands of Lupnoch, Grenok, the lands of Bochaldy, in the Barony of Polmais, the lands of Pitcairn, the lands of Strowe with its mill, in Perthshire, the lands of Inverallan, the lands of Queenshall, in Stirlingshire.

DOUGLAS OF GLENBERVIE IN KINCARDINESHIRE. On 6 April 1538, King James V confirmed Archibald Douglas in the lands and Barony of Glenbervie, with its tower, fort, manor, mill, etc, also the lands and Barony of Kemnay in Aberdeenshire, with its mill, etc, this was confirmed on 14 April 1542; on 18 May 1552, Queen Mary granted William Douglas son and heir apparent of Archibald Douglas of Glenbervie, the lands and Barony of Kemnay; on 14 July 1592, King James VI granted Robert Douglas, brother german of William Douglas, the lands and Barony of Glenbervie and Kemnay; Sir William Douglas, son of Robert Douglas and his wife Elizabeth Auchinleck, was created Baron of Glenbervie in 1622 and Baronet of Douglas in Nova Scotia, by King Charles I, with 16,000 acres, on 18 August 1625. He died at Ferme on 14 April 1714. He married Janet Irvine of Drum, Aberdeenshire and died about 1660. Their son Sir William Douglas inherited the title of Glenbervie. His wife was Anne Douglas. He died on 12 April 1686 and was succeeded by his son Sir Robert Douglas. Sir Robert was a soldier and Colonel of the Scots Greys which he led at the Battle of Steinkirk, Flanders, in 1692. There being no children the baronetcy went to his cousin Sir Robert Douglas, born 1661, baronet of Ardit in Fife on 24 July 1692. He married twice, firstly to Mary Ruthven, and died anuary 1748 and was succeeded by his son Sir William Douglas.

DOUGLAS OF KINROSS IN KINROSS-SHIRE. On 20 January 1541, King James V granted William Douglas, son and heir apparent of Robert Douglas of Loch Leven, the lands and Barony of Kinross, with Loch Leven with its castle, the house and lands of Kinross with mills and fishing rights, the lands and Barony of Keillour with its fort and mill in Perthshire, the lands and Barony of Lugtoun and its fort in Midlothian, the lands and Barony of Longnewtoun with its tower, fort, mills, etc in Roxburghshire, now incorporated in the Barony of Keillour; on 26 July 1565, Queen Mary granted Robert Douglas, son and heir apparent of William Douglas of Loch Leven, the lands and Barony of Kinross, including Loch Leven and its castle, etc., the lands and Barony of Keillour, the lands and Barony of Lugtoun, and the lands and Barony of Longnewtoun.

DOUGLAS OF MOFFAT IN DUMFRIES-SHIRE. On 30 May 1542, King James V granted Patrick Douglas the Barony of Moffat including Moffat, Grantoun, Newtoun, Corhead in Dumfries-shire also, the lands of Borg in Kirkcudbrightshire, incorporated in the Barony of Moffat.

DOUGLAS OF COCKBURNSPARTH IN BERWICKSHIRE. On 4 April 1547, Queen Mary confirmed Sir George Douglas of Pitendreich in the lands, Lordship, and Barony of Cockburnspath.

DOUGLAS OF DRUMLANGRIG IN DUMFRIES-SHIRE. On 14 April 1547, Queen Mary granted William Douglas, son and heir apparent of James Douglas of Drumlanrig, the lands and Barony of Drumlanrig, the lands and Barony of Hawick, the lands and Barony of Tibberis in Roxburghshire; on 28 January 1592, King James VI confirmed Sir William Douglas of Drumlanrig, in the lands and Barony of Drumlanrig.

DOUGLAS OF NAUCHTANE IN FIFE. On 2 May 1572, Queen Mary granted George Douglas, the Commendator of Arbroath, the lands and Barony of Nauchtane.

DOUGLAS OF ECKFORD AND GRYNMSLAW IN ROXBURGHSHIRE. On 8 January 1575, King James VI confirmed Margaret Douglas in the lands and Baronies of Eckford and Grymslaw, in Roxburghshire, also the lands and Barony of Kirkurd in Peebles-shire.

DOUGLAS OF PLUSCARDIN IN MORAY. On 18 February 1578, King James VI granted Archibald Douglas the lands and Barony of Pluscardin.

DOUGLAS OF KIRKNESS IN FIFE. On 6 January 1587, King James VI confirmed Robert Douglas of Loch Leven, in the lands and Barony of Kirkness.

DOUGLAS OF ABERLADY IN EAST LOTHIAN. On 29 August 1589, Patrick Douglas of Kilspindy, was confirmed into the Barony of Aberlady

DOUGLAS, Lord JAMES, was granted the forests of Selkirk, Ettrick, also with a Baronetcy of 16000 acres in Nova Scotia in the 1620s.

DRUMMOND OF AUCHTERARDER IN PERTHSHIRE. King James IV granted Lord John Drummond, the lands of Dalchoneze, Gauchory, Craiginnech, Emarchlare, Auchery, Glasinwed, Dalchildra, Auchtirmuthill, Drummayne, Bordlands, Cultilchaldich, Barnaclis, Cammischenis, Glassingallis, Mewe and Corelundy, in Strathearn, Perthshire, now united and incorporated into the Barony of Auchterarder, on 25 July 1493; he was also granted the lands and Lordship of Drummond of Menteith in Stirlingshire as a free Barony on 31 January 1496; on 26 August 1498, King James IV granted Lord John Drummond the lands and Dominion of Drummond with its forest in Menteith in Stirlingshire; on 18 February 1509, King James IV granted to Lord John Drummond, the lands of Tulliquhrawne, Mewy, Dalquhonze, Garchory, Dalchillerane, Drumman with its castle, fort, manor house, and orchards, Bordlands, Cutichaldiche, Steruthill, Cragyneche, Emirchlare, Auchary, Clashinved and Corylundy , with their mills, in Strathearn, Perthshire, now united as the Barony of Auchterarder. [a surname probably derived from Drymen, a surname recorded since the thirteenth century] [William Drummond was executed as a rebel in Virginia in 1677, while, Robert Drummond settled in East New Jersey by 1689][Genealogical Memoirs of the House of Drummond, Edinburgh, 1808] [The Lords Madertie, Drummond family of Strathearn, Innerpeffray, 2006]

DRUMMOND OF HAMILTOUN IN LANARKSHIRE. On 11 May 1496, King James IV granted Beatrix Drummond, daughter of Lord John Drummond, the lands and Barony of Hamiltoun with its castle and fort, the lands and Barony of Mechanshire, Carmunnock, Druschagart, parts of Crawford-John, the lands of Stonehouse, Bothwell Forest in Lanarkshire, also the lands of Fynnart in Renfrewshire, the lands of Birkinside in Berwickshire, the Barony of Kinneill with its castle and fort in West Lothian.

DRUMMOND OF INNERPEFFREY IN PERTHSHIRE. On 4 March 1536, King James V granted John Drummond the Barny of Innerpeffery, with Dounfalls, mills, fishing rights on the River Earn, the lands of Easthill of Dounfalls, its mill, Fornocht, East Fordoun of Auchterarder, Dalpatrick, Bordland of Stragaith, Auchinglen, Quilt, Thomquhare, Kirktoun of Stragaith with mill, in

Perthshire; on 24 September 1543, Queen Mary confirmed John Drummond of Innerpeffery, in the lands and Barony of Innerpeffrey; on 4 February 1595, King James VI confirmed James Drummond of Innerpeffrey, in the Barony of Innerpeffrey including various lands in Perthshire.

DRUMMOND OF DRUMMOND IN PERTHSHIRE. On 5 March 1536, King James V granted Lord David Drummond, the Barony of Drummond, including the Barony of Cargill, including Kirktoun of Cargill, Balquhoy, Halton, Lysington, Gallowhill, Whitfield, Wolfhill, Woodhead, Reidstane, Brakywell, Stobhall, Whitleis, with Stobhall's manor, mills, orchards and fishing rights on the River Tay and Isla in Perthshire, also the lands of Ardgatht, Smithstoun, Laidcreuff, in Angus, the lands of Drymen with castle, mill, etc, the lands of Auchtermuthill and Cultobragan with orchards and mill, etc., the lands and Barony of Kincardine, etc, all incorporated intohe Barony of Drummond. This was confirmed on 23 May 1538 by King James V. On 7 December 1543. Queen Mary confirmed Lord David Drummond in the lands and Barony of Cargill.[The Drummond Court Book, 1712-1717, ms. NRS.GD24.1.781]

DRUMMOND OF PITCARNIS IN PERTHSHIRE. On 6 June 1556, Queen Mary confirmed William Drummond, heir of Henry Drummond of Ricartoun, in the lands and Barony of Pitcarnis.

DRUMMOND OF OLD MONTROSE IN ANGUS. On 10 February 1577, King James VI confirmed Jean Drummond, Lady Montrose, in the lands and Barony of Auld Montrose, also lands in the Barony of Dundaf in Stirlingshire; on 23 May 1581, King James VI granted John Graham, son and heir apparent of John Graham the Earl of Montrose, the lands and Barony of Auld Montrose, the lands and Barony of Aberuthven, etc incorporated in the Barony of Auld Montrose, also the lands and Barony of Kincardin, the lands and Barony of Athera in Stirlingshire, etc, now incorporated in the Barony of Kincardine.

DRUMMOND OF CARNOCK IN STIRLINGSHIRE. On 8 August 1584, King James VI granted Thomas Drummond of Corskaiplie, the lands and Barony of Carnock.

DRUMMOND OF ETHIE IN ANGUS. On 10 August 1601, King James VI granted John Drummond of Halthringdene the lands and Barony of Ethie.

DRUMMOND, OF CARNOCK. Sir John Drummond of Carnock was created a Baronet around 1640, he was son of Sir Alexander Drummond and his wife Elizabeth Hepburn. Sir John sold the lands of Carnock to Sir Thomas

Nicolson and died at the Battle of Alford in Aberdeenshire in 1645. He had married the daughter of Rollock of Duntreath, but with no known children the title became extinct.

DRUMMOND OF CONCRAIG IN PERTHSHIRE. James Drummond, born 1648, son of the Earl of Perth, was exiled as a Jacobite in 1687, joined the Court of exiled King James in Paris, died there on 11 May 1716. [The Jacobite Peerage, Edinburgh, 1904]

DUGUID OF AUCHINHUIFF IN ABERDEENSHIRE. On 15 March 1595, King James VI granted William Duguid, son and heir of Robert Duguid of Auchinhuiff, Auchinhuiff and other lands in Aberdeenshire now incorporated into the Barony of Auchinhuiff. [An Aberdeenshire surname, examples date from the fourteenth century][William Duguid, a Lieutenant of the Virginia Militia in 1745]

DUNBAR OF TIBRIS MORTOUN IN DUMFRIES-SHIRE. King David II granted George Dunbar the lands and Barony of Tibris and Mortoun in 1320s. [Dunbar pedigrees, Stratford, 1910]

DUNBAR OF WESTFIELD IN MORAY. King James III granted Sir Alexander Dunbar the lands of Westfield in Fochabers in Moray, also the lands of Auldcasch in Moray, now formed the Barony of Westfield. On 10 February 1468; and on 14 August 1472 the king granted him the lands of Balmuir, Tollirstoun, Cocklaw, Denside, Alehousehill, Buthlaw, in Aberdeenshire, as the Barony of Cluny. [A surname of territorial origin derived from Dunbar in East Lothian, examples date from the thirteenth century][Alexander Dunbar was in Nansemond County, Virginia by 1654, while Robert Dunbar, a prisoner of war captured at the Battle of Dunbar, was transported to New England in 1650, and died there in 1693]

DUNBAR OF CUMNOCK IN AYRSHIRE. King James III granted Cuthbert Dunbar, the lands and Barony of Cumnock also the lands and Barony of Mochrum in Wigtonshire, and the lands of Blantyre in Lanarkshire, on 11 August 1472; Also, the lands and Barony of Blantyre with its tenants and tenantries were granted to Cuthbert Dunbar, brother german of Patrick Dunbar of Cumnock on 31 March 1479; on 14 February, King James IV granted John Dunbar of Mochrum various lands in the Barony of Mochrum formerly held by Patrick Clugston of that Ilk; on 31 January 1503, King James IV granted John Dunbar, son and heir apparent of Cuthbert Dunbar of Blantyre, the lands and Barony of Blantyre in Lanarkshire; On 12 December 1507, King James IV granted James Dunbar, son and heir of Sir James

Dunbar of Cumnock, the lands and Barony of Cumnock. Sir John Dunbar was killed at the Battle of Flodden on 9 September 1513; on 14 June 1547, Queen Mary granted Patrick Dunbar, son and heir apparent of Alexander Dunbar of Cumnock, the lands and Barony of Cumnock; on 30 September 1563, Queen Mary granted William Dunbar, son and heir apparent of John Dunbar of Blantyre, the lands and Barony of Blantyre; on 3 November 1587, King James VI granted the lands and Barony of Glasgow to Walter [Dunbar?] the Commendator of Blantyre in Lanarkshire, also the lands and Baronies of Ancrum , Eskirk, Lilliesleif, and Carstairs; on 26 August 1591, King James VI granted Walter the Barony of Glasgow as a Lordship and Regality; on 18 January 1599, King James VI granted Walter, Lord Blantyre, the lands and Barony of Blantyre.

DUNBAR OF CLUGSTON IN WIGTONSHIRE. On 29 January 1509, King James IV granted Patrick Dunbar, son and heir of John Dunbar of Mochrum, the lands of Clugston and other lands in Wigtonshire, now incorporated into the Barony of Clugston.

DUNBAR OF CUNZE IN MORAY. On 30 January 1532, King James V granted James Dunbar of Cunze the lands and Barony of Sanquhar, Whitra, Newtoun, Chapeltoun, Auchinlese, Drum of Pluscardin, the forests of Tulloch and Drummyn, etc in Moray.

DUNBAR OF DARKLES IN MORAY. On 20 March 1544, Queen Mary confirmed Patrick Dunbar of Darkles, in the lands and Barony of Sanquhar etc, in Moray.

DUNBAR OF DORES IN INVERNESS-SHIRE. On 17 December 1569, King James VI granted David Dunbar, son and heir apparent of Robert Dunbar of Dores, the Barony of Dores.

DUNBAR OF BALDOON IN WIGTONSHIRE. On 13 October 1664, King Charles II created David Dunbar of Baldoon as a Baronet.

DUNBAR OF HEMPRIGGS IN CAITHNESS. On 10 December 1706, James Dunbar was created a Baronet, on his death in 1724, his son Sir William Dunbar became the second Baronet of Hempriggs. Sir William died on 12 June 1793.

DUNCAN OF RATHO IN MIDLOTHIAN. On 5 March 1642, King Charles I granted James Duncan, son of James Duncan of Ratho, the Barony of Ratho. [a name of Gaelic origin, examples date from the twelfth century][William

Duncan, a militiaman in Barbados in 1679, while John Duncan, a Jacobite, was transported to Maryland in 1747]

DUNCANSON OF STRUAN IN PERTHSHIRE. On 15 August 1451 King James II, incorporated the lands of Struan, of Rannoch, Glenerach, Carrie, Innyreadoune, Farna, Dysart, Faskell, Kilkeve, Banagard and Balenfart in Atholl, with Blair Atholl Castle into the free Barony of Struan. [a patronymic meaning son of Duncan, a Gaelic name, Willelmus filius Dunecan, in 1135] [James Duncan, a Covenanter, was transported to America in 1670, while Matilda Duncanson, from Inveraray, died in Washington in 1799][Duncan of Caputh, pp in Perth and Kinross library]

DUNDAS OF FINGASK IN PERTHSHIRE. King James I granted James Dundas of that Ilk, the Barony of Fingask on 24 May 1429; on 28 January 1583, King James VI granted William Dundas, son and heir apparent of Archibald Dundas, the lands and Barony of Fingask; on 14 August 1588, King James VI confirmed William Dundas, son of Archibald Dundas of Fingask, the lands and Barony of Fingask. [a territorial surname from Dundas in West Lothian, examples date from the twelfth century] [James Dundas was bound for East New Jersey in 1685, while William Dundas was in Boston in 1687][Dundas of Fingask, Edinburgh, 1891]

DUNDAS OF WINCHBURGH IN WEST LOTHIAN. King James III granted Archibald Dundas of that Ilk, the Barony of Winchburgh and the lands of Echeling in the Barony of Dummaning, on 22 November 1471.

DUNDAS OF BOTHKENAR IN STIRLINGSHIRE. On 17 January 1483, King James III granted John Dundas of that Ilk, now incorporated Barony of Bothkennar; on 11 January 1490 King James IV granted John Dundas of Dundas the lands of Blairmucks in Lanarkshire as the Barony of Harthill.

DURHAM OF KINNELL IN ANGUS. On 15 November 1641, King Charles I granted James Durham of Kinnell, the lands and Barony of Kinnell. [a territorial surname from north-east England, examples date from the thirteenth century][Mary Durham emigrated to Baltimore in 1775]

DURIE OF DURIE IN FIFE. On 26 February 1507, King James IV granted John Dury of that Ilk, the lands of Dury, also the lands of Balcrowy, with the lands of Hauch with its mill, also the lands of Lanerkin, Auchinbee, Ballinold and Auchloy in Strathearn, Perthshire, now incorporated in the Barony of Dury; on 3 February 1558, Queen Mary, granted David Durie, son and heir apparent of Henry Durie of that Ilk, the lands and Barony of Durie; on 1 February 1578, King James VI granted Robert Durie, son and heir apparent of David Durie of that Ilk, the lands of Durie with other lands in Fife and Perthshire incorporated into the Barony of Durie. [a territorial name derived from a place in Fife, examples of the surname date from the thirteenth century][Isobel Durie, a Covenanter, was transported to East New Jersey in 1685, while Dr John Durie died in Trinidad in 1811][Lands of the Barony of Durie, papers 1457-1699, NRS.RH9.4.3.16]

EDGAR OF KIRK-ANDREWS IN KIRKCUDBRIGHTSHIRE. King Robert I granted the Barony of Kirkandres to Richard Edgar by 1320. [an Old English name popularised by King Edgar of Scotland around 1200, examples date from the thirteenth century] [John Edgar, from Dumfries, was in Boston by 1694, while James Edgar was in Charleston in 1805] [The Scottish House of Edgar, London, 1873]

EDINGTON OF EDINGTON IN BERWICKSHIRE. On 27 September 1542, King James V granted David Edington, son and heir apparent of John Edington of that Ilk, the lands and Barony of Edington, with its tower, mill lands, the lands of Clarebald, land in Hutton, the house and land of Duns, fishing rights on the River Whitadder, etc. in Berwickshire, incorporated into the Barony of Edington; on 2 March 1594, Thomas Edington of that Ilk, sold the lands and Lordship of Dalhousie also the Barony of Edington to Gilbert Ramsay. [a territorial surname from Berwickshire, examples date from the twelfth century] [David Edington, an officer of the Black Watch, during the French and India Wars]

EDMONSTOUN OF BOYNE IN BANFFSHIRE. On 17 March 1369, King David II confirmed Sir John Edmonstoun in lands in the Thanage of Banffshire, now a Barony.

EDMONSTOUN OF BUCHWHADROCK IN STIRLINGSHIRE. King James IV granted James Edmondstoun the lands and Barony of Buchwhadrock on 27 April 1495. [Edmonstone Chronicles, Colorado, 2004]

EDMONDSTOUN OF EDNAM IN ROXBURGHSHIRE. On 31 July 1496, King James IV granted James Edmonstoun, son of John Edmonstoun of that Ilk, the lands and Barony of Ednam with its mill, the lands of Riselaw in Berwickshire, also parts of Hirsmanstoun, Currie, and Niddrie Marshal with mills and tenantries near Edinburgh; on 16 January 1544 Queen Mary granted John Edmonstoun of that Ilk the lands and Barony of Ednam, etc; on 2 February 1594, King James VI granted John Edmonstoun the lands and Barony of Ednam. [a surname derived from a location near Edinburgh, a surname recorded since1200][John Edmonstone, a prisoner of war, captured at the Siege of Worcester, was transported to Boston in 1652, while Charles Edmunston, from Lerwick, settled in Charleston in 1799]

ELLEM OF BUTTERDEAN IN BERWICKSHIRE. On 25 September 1541, King James V granted Peter Ellem, son and heir apparent of Butterdean, the lands of Butterdean, with towers, manor, and mill,the lands of West Borthwick, land in Mordington, and Cobrandspath, in Berwickshire, now incorporated in the Barony of Butterdean; on 15 December 1587, King James VI confirmed John Ellem, son of Peter Ellem of Butterdean, the lands and Barony of Butterdean. [A surname derived from a place in Berwickshire, examples date from the thirteenth century]

ELIOTT OF STOBBS. On 20 March 1649, King Charles II granted William Elliott of Stobbs the Barony of Halrule. Sir Gilbert Eliott was created Baronet of Stobbs in 1666, and died in 1677, he was succeeded by Sir Willian Eliott and died in 1699 next was Sir Gilbert, the 3rd Baronet of Stobbs who died in 1764. [The surname comes from the Old English name *Aefwald*, examples of the surname and its variants date from the sixteenth century] [George Elliot, born 1717 in Roxburghshire, fought in the French and Indian Wars, while Charles Elliot from Stobbs, was Attorney General of North Carolina before 1756]
[The Elliots, the story of a Border Clan, [1974]

ELLIOT OF HEADSHAW IN ROXBURGHSHIRE. On 19 April 1700, Sir Gilbert Elliot of Headshaw was created as a Baronet, later known as Lord Minto a Lord Justiciary, he died on 1 May 1718 and was succeeded by his son Sir Gilbert Elliot as 2nd Baronet, who was Lord Justice Clerk, he died on 16 Apil 1766.

ELPHINSTOUN OF AIRTH IN STIRLINGSHIRE. King James IV granted John Elphinstoun of Pittendreich the lands and Barony of Airth also the lands of Cragorth on 8 November 1497; on 27 August 1502, King James IV granted John Elphinstoun of Airth, the lands middlethird of Cragrossy in Perthshire, to be incorporated into the Barony of Airth-Chamberlain; this was confirmed by the king on 4 January 1504; William Elphinstoun, cupbearer to King Charles I, was created as a baronet of Nova Scotia on 1 January 1628; sasine dated 28 January 1630. [The surname is derived from land in the parish of Tranent, while examples date from 1235] [William Elphinstone, an apothecary emigrated to Georgia in 1733, while Captain Keith Elphinston, master of the Perseus in America in 1778][Sir William Fraser's 'The Elphinstone Family Book', 1897],

ELPHINSTOUN OF INVERNOCHTY IN ABERDEENSHIRE. On 8 August 1507, King James IV granted Alexander Elphinstoun, son and heir apparent of Sir John Elphinstone of that Ilk, the lands of Invernochty, Ballebeg with its mill, forests, also the Glens of Glennochty, Invernechty, Ledmakey, Culquhony, Culquhary, in Strathdon, Meikle Mygve, Easter Migve, Tullyprony, Blalock and Corriecreiff in Cromar, Aberdeenshire; on 10 December 1507, King James IV granted Andrew Elphinstoun, the lands of Sklater with the forest of Congarff, lands of Fennelost, Bolquhame, Balnaboith in Glenbuchat, Balnaboith in Kelbethock, Ballintamore, Tullyskeuch, Summeil, Culbalauche with the forest of Baddynyoun and Kilvalauch, Easter Clova with Corrykeyzane, Contelauche with Braidshaw, Auchmillan, with the east part of Glenlos, Kinclune with its new mill, together with the lands of Skaleter, now incorporated into the Barony of Invernochty. Lord Elphinstone was killed at the Battle of Flodden on 9 September 1513.

ELPHINSTOUN OF ELPHINSTOUN IN STIRLINGSHIRE. On 29 August 1512, King James IV granted Lord Alexander Elphinstoun, the lands of Quarrell in Stirlingshire, now united into the Barony of Elphinstoun; on 12 August 1513, King James IV granted Lord Alexander Elphinstoun the lands and Barony of Invernochty, Balbegy with its mill, the Glens of Glennochty, Ledmakey, Colquhony and Culquharry in the Lordship of Strathdon, also, the lands of Skalster with the forest of Corgarff, the lands of Fennelost, Balquhan, Balnaboith in Glenbichat, Balnaboith in Kilbethok, Ballintamore, Tulleskeuch, Summeill, Culbalach, the forst of Baddinyone and Kilbalauch, Easter Cova, Corriekinzean, Contelauch, with Braidshaw, Auchmillan, part of Glenlose, Kinclune, the mill of New Mylne, in Aberdeenshire, Kildrummy, Clova, Old Auchindore, Drumnahufe, Dosky, Cookshill, the mill of Inverburquhare, Argaith, Culqueich, Discory with its mill, Pitinlauch, Glencoy, Newton, with the castle of Kildrummy, now united into the Barony of Kildrummy in Aberdeenshire. On 24 September 1608, King James VI granted Lord James Elphinstone, Lord Balmerino, the lands and Barony of Dingwall in Easter Ross and on 21 June 1608 the lands and Barony of Delny in Easter Ross; on 26 March 1601, King James VI confirmed Lord Robert Elphinstoun the lands and Barony of Elphinstoun also the Barony and Regality of Kildrummie in Aberdeenshire

ELPHINSTOUN OF HENDERSTOUN IN PEEBLES-SHIRE. On 6 April 1513, King James IV granted George Elphinstoun, son and heir apparent, the lands of Henderstoun, Newby, Schelnes and Whithalch in Peebles-shire, also part of Smithfield, and of Corscuminfield, also part of Catterso, now incorporated into the Barony of Henderstoun, on 20 July 1528, King James V granted George Elphinstoun of Henderstoun, the lands of Kingsmuir in Peebles-shire, also the lands of Eddirstoun, Cademuir, Brigland, Whithauch, Bonnytoun and Foulmyre, and the River Tweed, united into the Barony of Henderstoun.

ELPHINSTOUN OF BARRY IN ANGUS. On 1 July 1600 King James VI granted Janes Ephinstone of Barntoun, the lands, Barony and Regality of Barry.

ELPHINSTONE OF LOGIE IN ABERDEENSHIRE. On 2 December 1701, James Ephinstone was created as Baronet of Logie. On his death on 10 March 1722 his only son Sir John Elphinstone became the 2nd Baronet of Logie.

ERSKINE OF INCHTURE IN PERTHSHIRE. On 2 October 1365, King David II granted Alan Erskine the Barony of Inchture.

ERSKINE OF KINNOULL IN PERTHSHIRE. King David II granted the Barony of Kinnoull to Lord Robert Erskine, around 1359; on 8 January 1367, King David II confirmed Nicholas Erskine in the Barony of Kinnoull;

ERSKINE OF DUN IN ANGUS. King Robert II granted the Barony of Dun to Thomas Erskine on 8 November 1376; on 28 January 1449 King James II granted John Erskine, eldest son of Alexander Erskine, the Barony of Dun; On 18 February 1537, King James V granted John Erskine, son and heir of John Erskine of Dun, the lands and Barony of Dun, with its castle, fort, mill, fishing rights, etc.; on 13 April 1542 King James V confirmed John Erskine the younger in the lands and Barony of Dun now incorporated with various lands near Montrose, fishing rights in the River Esk; on 29 February 1556, Queen Mary confirmed John Erskin of Dun in the lands and Barony of Easter Brechin alias Wester Morphy; on. 7 February 1563, Queen Mary confirmed John Erskine in the lands and Lordship of Erskine. [the name derived from a location in Renfrewshire, and as a surname dated from the thirteenth century,] [Henry Erskine, Lord Cardross, settled in South Carolina in 1684, Reverend Henry Erskine emigrated to the Leeward Islands in 1768][The Lairds of Dun, London, 1931]

ERSKINE OF DUNNOLTER IN DUNBARTONSHIRE. King James IV granted Alexander Erskine, son and heir apparent of Thomas Erskine, the lands and Barony of Dunnolter, also land at Ballhagate in Aberdeenshire, on 23 July 1489.

ERSKINE OF ALLOA IN CLACKMANNANSHIRE. King Robert III granted Thomas Erskine the Barony of Alloa and the forest of Clackmannan around 1404; on 12 August 1489 Alexander Erskine, son and heir apparent, was granted the lands and Regality of Alloa with its mill, also the forest of Clackmannan; the lands of Nesbit and Douglas in Roxburghshire, the lands of Coltinhouse and Tulchgorme and Middle third with their mills, in Stirlingshire, the lands of Pittarrow in Angus, the lands and Baronies of Balmacalye and lands of Newton in Kincardine, also the lands and Barony of Kelly; On April 1502, King James IV granted Lord Alexander Erskine the lands and Barony of Alloa, with its castle, fort and mill, also lands in Clackmannanshire including Ferrytoun, Little Dovan, as a Regality and Barony; Lord Erskine was killed at the Battle of Flodden on 9 September 1513; on 11 September 1529, King James, granted Lord John Erskine the lands and Barony of Tullibody, and the lands of Banchry, in Clackmannanshire; on 26 February 1642, King Charles I granted Lord John Erskine the lands, Lordship, Barony and Regality of Alloa, the lands and Barony of Kellie in Aberdeenshire, the Barony of Logieblair, the lands and Barony of Bothkenner, the Lordship and Barony of Cardross, the lands and Barony of Gargunnock, etc.

ERSKINE OF SYNTOUN IN SELKIRKSHIRE. On 10 March 1508, King James IV granted Robert Erskine, son and heir apparent of Lord Alexander Erskine, the lands of Syntoun, including Whitslaid, and Dalgleish with their mills, now incorporated in the Barony of Syntoun.

ERSKINE OF MORFY-FRYSSALE IN KINCARDINESHIRE. On 19 February 1532 King James V granted Sir Thomas Erskine of Haltoun, the lands and barony of Morfy-Fryssale, including the lands of Manis, Pitbleidy and Spittal, with fishing rights on the River North Esk.

ERSKINE OF KIRKBUDDO IN ANGUS. On 8 March 1532, King James V granted Sir Thomas Erskine of Haltoun, the lands and Barony of Kirkbuddo, with its mill. On 4 February 1534, King James V granted Sir Thomas Erskine of Kirkbuddo, the lands and Lordship of Brechin and Navar; on 22 April 1550, Queen Mary confirmed Lord John Erskin in the lands and Barony of Brechin and Navar, with castle, fort, mill, fishing rights on the River South Esk, etc.

ERSKINE OF KELLE IN ABERDEENSHIRE. On 20 May 1536, King James V granted Robert Erskine the lands and Barony of Kelle.

ERSKINE OF BALMAKELLE IN KINCARDINESHIRE. On 18 February 1538, King James V confirmed Lord John Erskine the lands and Barony of Balmakelly, including Bernis, Newtoun, Haltoun, Balmaschinnar and Smithhill, and salmon fishing rights on the River South Esk.

ERSKINE OF MORPHY IN ANGUS. On 8 August 1537, King James V granted Sir Thomas Erskine of Brechin, the lands and Barony of Morphy Wester etc, incorporated into the Barony of Easter Brechin; on 24 May 1541, King James V confirmed Sir John Erskine of Brechin, the Royal Secretary, in the lands of Cantirland and those of Kinnaird in Angus, incorporated into the Barony of Cantirland in Kincardineshire, and on 1 June 1541, King James V confirmed

Sir Thomas of Brechin in the lands of Hiltoun to be merged into the Barony of Easter Brechin, also the lands of Lumgair with its loch and fishing rights in Kincardineshire; on 29 August 1541, King James V confirmed Sir Thomas Erskine of Brechin in the lands of Nether Craigie, Snawtoun, Rachirhill, etc. in Kincardineshire.

ERSKINE OF BAQUHADRAK IN STIRLINGSHIRE. On 26 May 1557, Queen Mary granted Janet Erskin, wife of John Murray of Tuchadam, the lands and Barony of Baquhadrak.

ERSKINE OF FINTRY IN STIRLINGSHIRE. On 29 May 1593, King James VI granted John Erskine, the Earl of Mar, the lands and Barony of Fintry also the lands and Barony of Buchlyvie in Stirlingshire.

ERSKINE OF COLINTON IN MIDLOTHIAN. On 25 January 1597, King James VI granted John Erskine the Earl of Mar, the lands and Barony of Colinton.

ERSKINE OF DIRLETOUN IN EAST LOTHIAN. On 15 November 1600, King James VI granted Thomas Erskine of Gogar various lands incorporated into the Barony of Dirletoun, and the Barony of Corntoun.

ERSKINE, ..., on 28 December 1625, ... Erskine was created as a Baronet of Nova Scotia. [Henry Erskine, Lord Cardross, promoter of settlement by Scots in Carolina, around 1685] [Erskine-Halcro Genealogy, Edinburgh, 1895]

ERSKINE OF ALLOA IN CLACKMANNANSHIRE. On 5 March 1639, King Charles I confirmed Jean Erskine the Countess of Mar, the lands, lordship, Barony and Regality of Alloa, also the lands and Baronies of Strathdon, Braemar, Cromar and Strathdie, and the lands, Lordship and Regality of the Gareoch, the lands and Barony of Kelly.

ERSKINE OF ALVA IN STIRLINGSHIRE. On 20 March 1642, King Charles II granted Charles Erskine of Cambuskenneth, the lands and Barony of Alva.

ERSKINE OF CAMBO IN FIFE. On 20 August 1666, Charles Erskine of Cambo, Lord Lyon King of Arms in 1663, was created as a Baronet, he died in February 1677, his son Sir Alexander Erskine, a Jacobite in 1715, became the 2nd Baronet until his death in 1727, his son Sir Charles Erskine was the 3rd Baronet of Camo from 1727 until 1753.

ERSKINE OF ALVA IN CLACKMANNANSHIRE. King Charles II created Charles Erskine, the son of Sir Charles Erskine of Alva and Cambuskenneth and his wife Mary Hope, as the Baronet of Alva on 30 April 1666, he was a Member of Parliament, he died in 1690, his son Sir James Erskine became the second Baronet of Alva, but died at the Battle of Landen on 23 July 1693, his brother, Sir John Erskine, born 1672, succeeded him becoming the third Baronet of Alva, died on 12 March 1739, next came Sir Charles Erskine, another British Army officer, who was killed at the Battle of Laffeldt on 2 July 1747, his successor was his brother Colonel Sir Henry Erskine, who was an army officer and politician.

EVIOTH OF BALHOUSIE IN PERTHSHIRE. John Evioth, the son and heir of Richard Evioth of Balhousie, was granted the lands and Barony of Balhousie, with its mill, by King James IV on 1 February 1490. [A territorial surname derived from Eviot in Angus, examples date from the twelfth century]

FALCONER OF LETHIN IN NAIRNSHIRE. On 25 February 1507, King George IV, granted George Falconer of Halkertoun, the lands of Lethin, Lethinbar wil mills, Lichtnes, Auchmore, Auchinvalzyn, Ar, Dunnern, Little Dulceis, Meikle Dunceis, now incorporated into the Barony of Lethin; on 12 October 1593, King James VI granted Alexander Falconer the younger, the lands and Barony of Lethin. [An occupational surname, examples date from the thirteenth century][John Falconer settled in East New Jersey in 1682, while Robert Falconer was a merchant in New York before 1851]

FALCONER OF HALKERTOUN IN KINCARDINESHIRE. On 27 January 1595, King James VI confirmed Alexander Falconer, son and heir apparent of Alexander Falconer of Halkerton, the lands and Barony of Halkertoun.

FARNELL OF BRAID IN MIDLOTHIAN. On 27 February 1517, King James V granted Archibald Farnell, the lands and Barony of Braid. [A territorial surname from Angus, examples date from the thirteenth century][Robert Farnell was in Virginia by 1624]

FERGUSON OF DOWNIE IN PERTHSHIRE. On 6 May 1510, King James IV confirmed the sale by William Scott of Balwearie to John Ferguson in Dunfallandy, of the lands and Barony of Downie, including Downie, Bordland, Edyrnarnochty, Cultony, Stronymuk, Fanyeand, Invereddre with its mill, Bynnan, Randeweyoch, Keruach, Couthill, and Dalmonge, with parts of Pitbrane, Glengaisnot and Glenbeg. [a patronymic, possibly from MacFergus, examples date from the fourteenth century][Alexander Ferguson, a forger, was banished to Virginia in 1670, while Daniel Ferguson, was captured at the Battle of Dunbar in 1650 then transported to Boston]

FERGUSON OF BALEDMOND in MOULIN, PERTHSHIRE. Papers 1328-1948. [Perth & Kinross Archives.ms79][The Clans of Atholl, Blair Atholl, 1997]

FERGUSSON OF KILKERRAN IN AYRSHIRE. John Fergusson of Kilkerran was created as a Baronet on 30 November 1703, when he died in February 1729 he was succeeded by his son Sir James Fergusson as second Baronet of Kilkerran, he died on 20 January 1759.

FERNIE OF WESTER FERNIE IN FIFE. On 12 February 1528, King James V granted Andrew Fernie of that Ilk, the lands of Wester Fernie, the forest of Kilface, the office of Forester of Falkland and Constable of Cupar, the lands of Nuthill, now incorporated into the Barony of Wester Fernie, this was confirmed on 19 December 1540; on 22 March 1552, Queen Mary, granted William Fernie, son and heir apparent of Andrew Fernie of that Ilk, the lands and Barony of Wester Fernie; on 3 November 1590, King James VI confirmed William Fernie, son and heir apparent of Andrew Fernie of that Ilk, in the lands and Barony of Wester Fernie. [a territorial name from a location in Fife, examples date from the fourteenth century]

FLEMING OF KIRKINTILLOCH IN DUNBARTONSHIRE. King Robert Bruce granted Sir Malcolm Fleming, son of Robert Fleming of Biggar, the barony of Kirkintilloch formerly held by John Comyn, around 1315. His son, Sir Malcolm Fleming built Cumbernauld Castle. [a surname indicating Flanders as the place of origin, examples date from the twelfth century] [Patrick Fleming from Kirkintilloch settled in Virginia before 1663, while Thomas Fleming, a clergyman, died in Jamaica in 1741]

FLEMING OF BIGGAR IN LANARKSHIRE. King David II granted Sir Malcolm Fleming, son of Robert Fleming of Biggar, the barony of Kirkintilloch, also the Barony of Dalziel, by King David II, also, the lands and Barony of Lenzie around 1345; Robert, Duke of Albany, [the Regent], granted Malcolm Fleming the barony of Biggar in Lanarkshire on 28 June 1413; on 31 March 1451 Biggar was created a burgh of Barony. [Earlier Biggar was a centre of Flemish settlement, for example Waltheof son of Baldwin the lord of Biggar was captured at Alnwick in 1174 by the English], Baldwin was Sheriff of Lanark in 1162. [Biggar and the House of Fleming, Biggar, 1862]

FLEMING OF LENZIE IN DUNBARTONSHIE. In 1480, King James III granted Sir David Fleming, son of Malcolm Fleming, the land and Barony of Lenzie, the lands of Cumbernauld with its castle and forest, the lands and Barony of Biggar, the lands of Thankertoun in Lanarkshire, also lands of the Barony of Monycabo in Aberdeenshire, land in Lour, Angus, lands in Dunbullys in Forgandenny in Perthshire, and the lands of Auchtermune in Stirlingshire.

FLEMING OF THANKERTON IN LANARKSHIRE. King James IV granted Lord John Fleming the lands and Barony of Thankertoun in Lanarkshire on 5 May

1496. On 18 January 1589, King James VI granted Lord John Fleming, the lands and Barony of Auchtermonye in Stirlingshire, the lands and Barony of Lenzie in Dunbartonshire, the lands and Barony of Biggar in Lanarkshire, etc.; on 31 January 1596, King James VI confirmed Lord John Fleming in the lands and Barony of Auchtermonie in Stirlingshire, the lands and Barony of Biggar in Lanarkshire, also the Lordship and Barony of Cumbernauld.

FLEMING OF MONICABO IN ABERDEENSHIRE. On 8 May 1510, King James IV granted Lord John Fleming the lands and Barony of Monicabo with its mill.

FLEMING OF KILBUCHO IN PEEBES-SHIRE. On 26 September 1535, King James V confirmed the grant by the Earl of Morton of the lands and Barony of Kilbucho in the Regality of Dalkeith to Lord Malcolm Fleming.

FLEMING OF AUCHTERMONEY IN STIRLINGSHIRE. On 9 April 1538, King James V granted Lord Malcolm Fleming, the lands and Barony of Auchtermoney, and the lands and Barony of Lenzie, also Cumbernauld with its castle, fort and forest, in Dunbartonshire, the lands and Baronies of Thankerton and Biggar, in Lanarkshire, various lands in Peebles-shire, Lour in Angus, Dunbullis in Perthshire, Fresillsland in East Lothian, with mills, fishing rights, castle, towers, forts, etc.; on 17 January 1558, Queen Mary confirmed John Fleming, the brother and heir of Lord James Fleming, in the lands and Barony of Auchtermoney, also the lands and Barony of Lenzie, and the lands and Baronies of Thankerton and Biggar, etc

FLEMING OF FERME IN LANARKSHIRE. Archibald Fleming, an advocate, was created a baronet in September 1661, he died in January 1662 and was succeeded by his son Sir William Fleming as 2nd Baronet of Ferme, his wife Margaret Stewart was a prominent Covenanter, on his death on 6 February 1707 their son Sir Archibald Fleming became the 3rd Baronet, he married Elizabeth, daughter of Sir George Hamilton, Sir Archibald died at Ferme on 14 April 1714. The next baronet was his son Sir Archibald Fleming, husband of Janet Bogle, who died in August 1738. The title Baronet of Ferme then went to Sir Gilbert Fleming and after him to Sr William Fleming possibly his brother who died in Elgin, Moray, on 25 November 1746. Finally, the title went to Sir Collingwood Fleming who died in Virginia on 17 April 1764.

FLETCHER OF SALTOUN. Andrew Fletcher of Saltoun was born in 1655 son of Sir Robert Fletcher [1625-1664], he died in September 1716. In 1668, King Charles II united the barony of Saltoun with the burgh of Barony of Over Saltoun creating an enlarged barony for Andrew Fletcher. Andrew Fletcher was a politician opposed to the Stuart regime and to the Union of

Scotland and England in 1707, he lived in Europe for many years including a spell as an exile in Holland.[an occupational surname meaning an arrow-maker, examples date from the fourteenth century][Alexander Fletcher was a British officer during the American War, later in Prince Edward Island] [Fletchers of Glen Orchy, Dorset, 1973][Fletcher of Saltoun papers from 1592 until 1900 [NLS.GB2933, mss 17498-17605]; Letters of Andrew Fletcher of Saltoun, 1715-1716. [NLS.Acc.2933]

FORBES OF FORBES IN ABERDEENSHIRE. King James I granted the Barony of Forbes to William Forbes on 27 July 1429; the King granted the Barony of Forbes with the lands of Alford, Logie, and Banchory now in the united Barony of Forbes to Sir Alexander Forbes on 6 October 1429, this was confirmed by King James III on 9 July 1477; on 8 August 1547, Queen Mary, granted William Forbes, son and heir apparent of Lord John Forbes, the lands and Baronies of Forbes and Alford; on 28 December 1598, King James VI confirmed Arthur Forbes, son of Lord John Forbes, in the Lordship and Barony of Forbes. [a surname derived from the lands of Forbes in Aberdeenshire; examples of the surname date from the thirteenth century][John Forbes settled in Massachusetts in 1636, while CharlesForbes, a soldier on the Darien Expedition, died in Cuba in 1700] [House of Forbes, Aberdeen, 1937][The Forbes Barony Court Book, 1659 -1678, Scottish History Society, Volume XIX, Edinburgh, 1919]

FORBES OF PITSLIGO IN ABERDEENSHIRE. On 10 October 1476, King James III granted the lands and Barony of Pitsligo to Sir Alexander Forbes, also the lands and Barony of Kinaldie in Aberdeenshire; on 23 January 1580, King James VI granted Alexander Forbes of Pitsligo, the lands and Barony of Pitsligo now incorporating other lands in Aberdeenshire; on 1 July 1600, King James VI confirmed John Forbes of Pitsligo in the Baronies of Pitsligo and of Kinnaldie. [Genealogy of the family of Forbes, Inverness, 1819]

FORBES OF BURCHIS IN MAR, ABERDEENSHIRE. On 24 January 1505, King James IV, granted John Forbes, brother of William Forbes of Tolleis, the lands of Burchis, with its woods and muir, Wester Drummellochy, Newtoun, Macharishalch, Glenkervy, and the Ord with its woods and mill in the district of Mar in Aberdeenshire, now incorporated into the Barony of Burchis; on 21 December 1561, Queen Mary granted Alexander Forbes, son and heir of John Forbes of Tolleis, the lands and Barony of Tolleis.

FORBES OF FIDDES IN ABERDEENSHIRE. On 26 February 1510, King James IV granted Lord John Forbes the lands and Barony of Fiddes with its mill, this was confirmed on 29 July 1515 by King James V.; on 4 January 1539, King

James V granted William Forbes the lands and Barony of Fiddes. Including Fiddes mor, Fiddes beg, Cultercullan, Auchnacant with mill and alehouse, lands of Pettymuk and Blairchelle, Lair, Strogarnik and Kirktoun of Aboyne; on 22 February 1595, King James VI confirmed Lord John Forbes in the lands and Barony of Fiddes including several lands in Aberdeenshire.

FORBES OF BALLINBREICH AND CUSHNY IN ABERDEENSHIRE. On 15 August 1511, King James IV granted George Forbes of Auchintoill, the lands of Carnecoully, Tomquhatty, Tomnacoulek, and Pitberne, in the Barony of Cushny, now formed into the Barony of Ballinbreich and Cushny.

FORBES OF BRUX IN ABERDEENSHIRE. On 18 October 1546, Queen Mary granted John Forbes, son and heir apparent of Alexander Forbes of Brux, the lands and Barony of Brux.

FORBES OF BARNIS-FORBES IN ABERDEENSHIRE. On 15 December 1550, Queen Mary granted William Forbes various lands in Aberdeenshire incorporated into the Barony of Barnis-Forbes.

FORBES OF RERES IN FIFE. On 21 February 1551, Queen Mary, granted John Forbes, son and heir apparent of Arthur Forbes of Reres, the lands and Barony of Reres, also the lands and Barony of Leuchars-Forbes, in Fife; on 14 July 1594, King James VI confirmed Arthur Forbes of Reres, in the lands, Lordship and Barony of Reres.

FORBES OF PORTLETHAN IN KINCARDINESHIRE. On 4 July 1608, King James VI confirmed William Forbes, son of William Forbes of Monymusk, the lands and Barony of Portlethan.

FORBES OF MONYMUSK IN ABERDEENSHIRE. William Forbes of Monymusk was created a Baronet of Nova Scotia on 30 March 1626; a sasine dated 4 April 1626. [Court Book of Monymusk, 1710-1771, NRS.GD345.786]

FORBES OF CRAIGIEVAR IN ABERDEENSHIRE. William Forbes was created a Baronet of Nova Scotia on 20 April 1630.

FORBES OF CULLODEN IN INVERNESS-SHIRE. On 12 March 1642, King Charles I granted Duncan Forbes of Bucht, a merchant burgess of Inverness, the lands and Barony of Culloden.

FORBES OF STRECHIN IN ABERDEENSHIRE. On 6 April 1649, King Charles II granted John Forbes of Pitnacaddell the Barony of Strechin.

FORBES OF FOVERAN IN ABERDEENSHIRE. On 10 April 1700, Samuel Forbes, born 1663, an MP, was created as a Baronet, he died on 16 July 1717, to be followed by his son Sir Alexander Forbes as 2nd Baronet.

FORRET OF FORRET IN FIFE. On 5 March 1508, King James IV granted John Foret, son and heir apparent of Robert Foret of that Ilk, was granted the lands of Forret, and Cottoun with its mill, now the Barony of Forret; on 9 September 1545, Queen Mary granted David Forrett, son and heir apparent of John Forrett of that Ilk, the lands and Barony of Forrett. [a surname derived from the lands of Forret in Logie, examples of the surname date from the mid thirteenth century] [James Forret was on Long Island, New York, by 1639, while Mary Forret emigrated to East New Jersey in 1685]

FORMAN OF EDGARSTOUN IN BERWICKSHIRE. On 5 December 1506, King James IV confirmed the grant to John Forman of Davan of the Lordship of Edgarstoun with its mill, the lands and Barony of Broundean, Eddillshed and Elphinshope part of Hownam, Capehope with its mill, the lands of Fillogar and Crunzeartoun, also fishing rights on the River Tweed; on 9 August 1511 King James IV granted John Forman of Edgarstoun the lands of Rutherford and Wellis, with fishing rights on the River Tweed, in Roxburghshire, united into the Barony of Rutherford. [As a surname Foreman has been recorded in Scotland since 1296] [John Forman, a Covenanter, was transported to East New Jersey in 1685]

FORRESTER OF CORSTORPHIN IN MIDLOTHIAN. On 12 September 1533, King James V confirmed Alexander Forrester in the lands and Barony of Corstorphin, with its castle and fort, Clerkington, Nether Libertoun, Drylaw and Meadowfield.

FORRESTER OF MORFY-FRESALE IN KINCARDINESHIRE. On 12 September 1533 confirmed the sale of the lands and Barony of Morfy-Fresale, the lands of Manis, Pitbeidly and Spittal, with fishing rights on the River North Esk, to Alexander Forrester of Corstorphine.

FORRESTER OF CLERKINGTOUN IN MIDLOTHIAN. Adam Forrester was granted the Barony of Clerkingtoun, around 1397. [A surname of occupational origin dating from the twelfth century, examples date from 1184] [John Forrester, guilty of forgery, was transported to the colonies in 1751, while Thomas Foster, a shoemaker emigrated to New York in 1775]

FORRESTER OF CORSTORPHINE IN MIDLOTHIAN. On 10 July 1424 John Forrester of Corstorphine was granted the Barony of Lower Libertoun to be united with the barony of Corstorphine in into the Barony of Libertoun, this was confirmed by King James I on 4 February 1430; On 24 November 1533, King James V confirmed Sir John Forrester of Corstorphine, in Corstorphine, Drylaw, Nether Liberton, Meadowfield, and Clerkington, formed into the Barony of Corstorphine. On 17 December 1625, Sir George Forrester was created as Baronet of Corstorphine in Nova Scotia. On 22 July 1633 he was created Lord Forrester of Corstorphine, making the Barony dormant. [an occupational surname, examples date from the twelfth century][Andrew Forrester was Commander at Port Royal, Nova Scotia, before 1633, while John Forrester, guilty of forgery, was transported to the colonies in 1751.]

FORRESTER OF SKIPINCH IN ARGYLL. On 3 July 1495, King James IV granted Sir Duncan Forrester the lands of Skipinch, with its castle, the lands of Nethourlee and Killllelee, Colintre, Altgallereas, Altwowar, Glen Skipincn, Glen Restill, Clynneagir, Orgagir, Stonrestill, Garworle, Laganrowak, Allemor, in Knapdale, Argyll, united into the Barony of Skipiinch; on 15 January 1496, King James IV granted Duncan Forrester of Skipinch, the lands of Garden-Sinclair with its tower and fort in Menteith, Perthshire, also the lands of Mye and Finneich-tennand in Lennox, Stirlingshire; on 1 June 1496 he was also granted the lands and Barony of Gibletstoun, and the lands of Cowbaky and Langside in Fife; on 28 January 1497, King James IV confirmed Sir Duncan Forrester in the lands of Malaris in Perthshire; on 26 November 1497 King James IV granted Sir Walter Forrester, son and heir apparent of Sir Duncan Forrester, the lands of Garden with its tower, fort and mill in Perthshire, the lands of My, Torwood, Torwoodhead, the office of forester there in Stirlingshire, the lands of Qwoyg mill, the lands of Kirktoun Malare and Hiltoun Malare in Perthshire, also the Barony of Skipinch with its castle and fort in Knapdale, Argyll; on 16 May 1508, King James IV confirmed Sir Walter Forrester of Torwood in the lands of Gardene with its tower, fort, manor and mill, the lands of Dischore with mills, parts of Carbrock and Gartyncaber, the lands of Goosecroft, in Stirlingshire, the lands of Mye in Dunbartonshire, the lands of Montdoy and Over Glenny in Menteith, Perthshire, and the lands of Myl-coig in Strathearn, now incorporated into the Barony of Garden-Forrester; on 9 September 1528, King James V granted David Forester, son and heir apparent of Sir James Forester of Garden-Forester, the lands and Barony of Garden-Forester, with its tower, fort and mill, also the lands of Goosecroft, Claycroft, Mye, Montdowy, Over Glenny, Little Coggs with its mill, also part of Carbrok and Gartincabir, now merged into the Barony of Garden-Forester, plus part of Cambusbarron, the lands of Torwoodhead, Kingside Muir, and Torwood forest, in Stirlingshire, this was confirmed by King James V on 1 February 1542

FORRESTER OF MORPHY-FRISELL IN KINCARDINESHIRE. On 18 August 1537, King James V confirmed Alexander Forbes of Corstorphine with the lands and Barony of Morphy, with fishing rights on the River North Esk.

FOTHERINGHAM OF BRICHTY IN ANGUS. On 31 January 1532, King James V granted Thomas Fotheringham of Powrie the lands and Barony of Brichty, with its mill, in Angus; on 16 February 1541, King James V granted Thomas Fotheringham of Powrie the lands of Bawmuir, with its grain and fulling mills in Angus incorporated into the Barony of Bawmuir; on 8 August 1598, King James VI confirmed Thomas Fotheringham of Brichty in the Barony of Haltoun of Inverarity now incorporated into the Barony of Brichty. [a surname derived from Fotheringhay in Northamptonshire, England, via a site in Angus] [John Fotheringham, was a Jacobite transported to South Carolina in 1716, while Thomas Fotheringham, died in Jamaica in 1768]

FOULIS OF COLINTON IN MIDLOTHIAN. On 6 June 1540, King James V confirmed James Foulis the Barony of Colinton, including Colinton with its grain mill and fulling mill, lands of Swanstoun, Dreghorn, Oxgang, etc in Midlothian, the lands of Manuel Foulis in Stirlingshire; on 13 December 1581, King James VI confirmed James Foulis of Colintoun in the lands and Barony of Colintoun, also the Barony of Maxwell. On 7 June 1634, Alexander Foulles was created as a baronet of Nova Scotia. [Andrew Foulis was a tailor in Boston in 1684, while Reverend James Foulis settled in Virginia in 1750]

FRASER OF DURRIS, KINCARDINESHIRE. King David II granted Alexander Fraser the Thanedom of Durris and Dures around 1369; on 1 February 1578, King James VI confirmed Alexander Fraser in the Barony of Durris; on 24 June 1549, Queen Mary granted Thomas Fraser, nephew of Alexander Fraser of Duris, the lands and Barony of Duris, with tower, fort, mill, fishing, etc, also the lands of Mid Belty in Aberdeenshire, now incorporated into the Barony of Duris. [originally de Friselle or variant, examples of Fraser date from the twelfth century] [John Fraser of Pitcalzean, a Covenanter, was transported to East New Jersey in 1685, while Andrew Fraser, emigrated to Pennsylvania in 1695] [Memorial of the family of Frasers of Durris, Edinburgh, 1904]

FRASER OF KINNELL IN ANGUS. King James I granted Hugh Fraser of Lovat the Barony of Kinnell on 14 September 1430.

FRASER OF LOVAT IN INVERNESS-SHIRE. Hugh Fraser was Baron of Lovat since 1367; on 14 October 1501, King James IV granted Lord Thomas Fraser of Lovat the lands and Barony of Kinnell in Angus, on 14 October 1501; Hugh Fraser of Lovat was killed at the Battle of Flodden on 9 September 1513; on 2 March 1529, King James V granted Hugh Fraser of Lovat part of the lands of Inglistoun, the lands of Kingyle with its fishing rights, Drumbaloch, part of Belladrum, the lands of Ardblair, part of Fenclare, the lands of Kelauch and, with mills crofts, brewhouse, and fishing rights, Culmolenbeg, part of Culmolen, Kintallagie, the lands of Inchbarry in the Barony of Arde in Inverness-shire, and the lands of Arcles, and several lands in Strathglass in County Ross, now in the Barony of Arcles. On 26 March 1539, King James V confirmed Lord Hugh Fraser of Lovat in the lands and Baronies of Lovat, Stratheric, Ard, Abertarf, Strathglass, part of Glenelg, etc, with castles towers, forts, mills fishing rights, etc, in Inverness-shire, incorporated in the Barony of Lovat; on 14 February 1572, King James VI confirmed Lord Hugh Fraser of Lovat in the lands and Barony of Beauly. [The Clan Fraser of Lovat, Edinburgh, 1952]

FRASER OF STONEYWOOD IN ABERDEENSHIRE. On 22 May 1528, King James V granted Thomas Fraser of Stonywood, the lands and Barony of Alathy with its mill; on 30 June 1535, King James V confirmed the grant by Thomas Fraser of Stoneywood of the lands and Baronies of Stonywood and Muckwell to his nephew Andrew Fraser, the son and heir apparent of Andrew Fraser of Kilmundy; Andrew Fraser granted them to his father Andrew Fraser on 15 February 1536; on 18 January 1583, King James VI confirmed Adrew Fraser, son of Michael Fraser of Stoneywood, in the lands and Barony of Stoneywood. By 1588 Michael Fraser was Baron of Stoneywood etc in Aberdeenshire. [NRS.GD138.2]; on 21 March 1601, King James VI confirmed Andrew Fraser of Stoneywood, the lands and Barony of Stoneywood and Muckwell.

FRASER OF STRICHEN IN ABERDEENSHIRE. On 8 October 1573, King James VI, granted Thomas Fraser of Strichen, the lands and Barony of Strichen; on 25 January 1591, King James VI granted Thomas Fraser of Knokie, the lands and Barony of Strichen.

FRASER OF LUGTOUN IN MIDLOTHIAN. On 10 June 1581, King James VI granted James Fraser the lands and Barony of Lugtoun; on 29 July 1581, King James VI confirmed its transfer to Patrick Crichton.

FRASER OF PHILORTH IN ABERDEENSHIRE. On 9 April 1588, King James VI granted Alexander Fraser of Philorth, the lands and Barony of Philorth, this was confirmed on 1 July 1592; on 4 April 1601, King James VI confirmed Sir Alexander Fraser of Philorth and Fraserburgh in the lands and Barony of Philorth, etc [The Frasers of Philorth, Edinburgh,1879]

FRASER OF DORES IN KINCARDINESHIRE. On 2 August 1673, Alexander Fraser was created as a Baronet, when he died on 28 April 1681, his son Sir Peter Fraser succeeded as 2nd Baronet of Dores, but when he died, childless, on 10 May 1729 the barony became extinct.

FYFFE OF GLASCLUNE IN PERTHSHIRE. King David II granted Isabell, the Countess of Fife, the Barony of Glasclune in 1366 a territorial surname from the county of Fife, examples date from the thirteenth century.][Alexander Fyfe, from Angus, was transported to Jamaica in 1726, while William Fyfe, a clergyman, emigrated to Virginia in 1729.]

GARDYNE OF HARTSWOOD IN LANARKSHIRE. King David II granted William Gardyne the lands and barony of Hartiswood around 1345. [A surname from Gardyne in Angus, examples date from the thirteenth century]

GARDYNE OF LEYIS IN ANGUS. On 28 July 1532, King James V granted David Gardyne of Leyis, the lands of Leyis, Little Gardyne, with mills, part of the Lordship of Rossie, and Ballinschois in Angus, incorporated into the Barony of Leyis; Queen Mary, granted David Gardyne, son and heir apparent of David Gardyne of Leyis, the lands of Conansyth now incorporated into the Barony of Leyis.

GARDYNE OF GARDYNE IN ANGUS. On 14 November 1538, King James V confirmed Patrick Gardyne of that Ilk in the lands and Barony of Gardyne, including the lands of Middletoun, Eastertoun, Legistoun etc, incorporated in the Barony of Gardyne; on 15 March 1567, Queen Mary confirmed Patrick Gardyne of that Ilk, in the lands and Barony of Gardyne etc now incorporated into the Barony of Gardyne.

GASCOIGNE OF BARNBOW IN THE ORKNEY ISLANDS. Sir John Gascoigne was created as a baronet of Nova Scotia on 8 June 1635.

GIBB OF FALKLAND IN FIFE. Henry Gibb of Falkland, son of Sir John Gibb of Knock near Dunfermline in Fife, was created as a Baronet of Nova Scotia by King Charles I in 1634, he died childless in Falkland on 8 April 1650, the title was assumed by his cousin Sir John Gibb. The third Baronet was John Gibb of Dairsie who died near Dairsie in Fife in 1734. Next was his son Benaiah Gibb born 1756, settled in Montreal, Quebec, father of his son and heir Thomas Gibb who died in London around 1777. [a diminutive of Gilbert, examples date from the sixteenth century][Alexander Gibb, a cordiner, emigrated to Maryland in 1730][Pedigree of the family of Gibb, Guildford, 1874][The story of the Gibbs, Edinburgh, 1961]

GIBSON OF KEIRHILL IN MIDLOTHIAN. On 31 December 1702, Queen Anne created Thomas Gibson as Baronet of Keirhill, he died by 1713 his son Sir Edward Gibson became the 2nd Baronet of Keirhill. [a patronymic meaning son of Gilbert, examples date from the fourteenth century] [Agnes Gibson was transported to the colonies in 1695, while George Gibson, a surgeon's mate, was bound for Darien in 1699.]

GILMOUR, Sir JOHN, President of the College of Justice, became Baron of Craigmillar in 1660. On his death in 1671 he was succeeded by his son Sir Alexander Gilmour who was created a Baronet in 1678. His son Sir Charles Gilmour inherited the land and title. [a surname from Gaelic *Gille Moire* meaning 'servant of Mary', examples date from the twelfth century] [Alexander Gilmour, a weaver, emigrated to Philadelphia in 1774, while Robert Gilmour was a merchant in Virginia by 1779]

GLENDINNING OF PARTOUN IN KIRKCUDBRIGHTSHIRE. Adam Glendinning was granted the baronies of Clifton and Merbotel in Roxburghshire before 1286. King James II granted Simon Glendinning the lands and Barony of Partoun on 23 February 1459; on 6 September 1510, King James IV granted Ninian Glendinning, son and her apparent of John Glendinning of Partoun, the lands and Barony of Scraisburgh, including Maderspart and Gledstanes of Langtoun in Roxburghshire; on 26 July 1595, King James VI granted Robert Glendinning , son of Alexander Glendining of Partoun, the lands and Barony of Partoun. [A surname derived from a place in Dumfries-shire, examples date from the thirteenth century][Agnes Glendinning emigrated to Barbados in 1663, while William Glendinning was a merchant who died in North Carolina in 1816][House of Gendinning, Edinburgh, 1879]

GORDON OF STRATHBOGIE, ABERDEENSHIRE. On 16 June 1375 King Robert II granted Adam Gordon the Barony of Strathbogie. [probably a name of territorial origin in Berwickshire, examples date from the twelfth century] [Alexander Gordon, was a planter in Jamaica by 1780, while Annabel Gordon, was a Covenanter transported to East New Jersey in 1685] [The Earls of Aboyne, Huntly, 1908]

GORDON OF PANBRIDE IN ANGUS. King James II confirmed Alexander Gordon, Earl of Huntly as Baron of Panbride on 29 January 1450.

GORDON OF BADENOCH IN INVERNESS-SHIRE. On 28 April 1451 King James II granted to Alexander Gordon, Earl of Huntly, the Lordship of Badenoch with Ruthven Castle as a free Barony.

GORDON OF KINGUSSIE IN BADENOCH, INVERNESS-SHIRE. King James III created Kingussie a Burgh of Barony, held by Alexander Gordon the Earl of Huntly on 1 September 1464.

GORDON OF CHIVAS IN ABERDEENSHIRE. On 3 February 1480, King James III granted Adam Gordon, son of George Gordon the Earl of Huntly, the

Barony of Chivas; on 16 May 1498, King James IV granted William Gordon the lands and Barony of Chivas, formerly held by George Gordon the Earl of Huntly.

GORDON OF KENMURE IN KIRKCUDBRIGHTSHIRE. On 23 March 1488, King James III granted Alexandro Gordon, son and heir apparent of John Gordon of Lochinver, the lands of Kenmure with its mill, the lands of Lagan and Balmaclellan in Kirkcudbrightshire, united into the Barony of Kenmure.

GORDON OF MIDMAR IN ABERDEENSHIRE. On 26 May 1496, King James IV confirmed a grant by George Gordon the Earl of Huntly, to his brother Sir Alexander Gordon of the lands and Barony of Midmar on 26 May 1496; on 9 November 1501 King James IV granted Sir Alexander Gordon of Midmar the lands of Aberyeldy and Easton in Aberdeenshire now united into the Barony of Abiryeldy, which was confirmed by the king on 27 February 1507.

GORDON OF HUNTLY IN ABERDEENSHIRE. On 1 February 1503, King James IV granted Alexander Gordon, the Earl of Huntly, the lands of Rymiltounlaw in the Lordship of Gordoun in Berwickshire, now incorporated into the Barony of Huntly; on 12 January 1506 King James IV, confirmed the grant to Alexander Gordon, the Earl of Huntly of the Barony of Strathbogie, Touch, Cluny, Aboyne, Glen Tannar, and Glen Muick, in Aberdeenshire, now incorporated into the Barony of Huntly; on 25 March 1506, King James IV granted Alexander Gordon, the Earl of Huntly, the lands and Barony of Forthergill in Perthshire, with its castle and fort of Garth, also the lands of Pitdorny, Tullochcurren, and Dalnagarn; on 26 February 1507, King James IV granted Alexander Gordon, the Earl of Huntly, the lands of Cullarleis with its mill, now incorporated into the Barony of Huntly; on 20 February 1510, King James IV granted Alexander Gordon, the Earl of Huntly, the lands of Redpath, Nether Reidcleuch, Wolstruther, Quykiswood, and Spotswood in Berwickshire, now formed into the Barony of Gordoun; on 2 May 1545, Queen Mary confirmed George Gordon, Earl of Huntly, in the Barony of Huntly, alias Strathbogie; on 24 March 1559, King Francis and Queen Mary, granted Lord George Gordon, son and heir apparent of the Earl of Huntly, the lands and Lordship of Badenoch' also on 2 June 1566; on 10 December 1591, King James VI, granted George Gordon, the Earl of Huntly, the barony of Delny.

GORDON OF KNOCINBLEUIS IN ABERDEENSHIRE. On 30 August 1505, King James IV granted Patrick Gordon of Methlick the lands of Brekauch, Middletoun of Knockinbleuis, Drummeis, Glasschaw with its mill, also the forest of Drumcoutan in the Regality of Garioch in Aberdeenshire, now incorporated into the Barony of Knockinbleuis.

GORDON OF BADENOCH IN INVERNESS-SHIRE. On 26 April 1510, King James IV granted Lord John Gordon, son and heir apparent of the Earl of Huntly, the lands and Lordship of Badenoch, with Ruthven Castle, also, the lands of Fothergill with the fort at Garth in Perthshire.

GORDON OF KENMURE IN KIRKCUDBRIGHTSHIRE. On 11 May 1517, King James V granted Sir Robert Gordon of the Glen, son of John Gordon of Lochinvar, land at Kenmure and Lagan with its mill, the tower and fort of Kenmure, part of Balmaclellan with its mill, now united into the Barony of Kenmure, also land in the Barony of Stichill in Roxburghshire; on 2 January 1564, Queen Mary, confirmed William Gordon, brother and heir of John Gordon of Lochinver, in the lands and Barony of Stichell in Roxburghshire. [The Records of the Baron Court of Stichill, 1655-1807, Edinburgh, 1905]

GORDON OF METHLICK IN ABERDEENSHIRE. On 11 September 1533, King James V granted James Gordon, nephew and heir apparent of Patrick Gordon of Methlick, the Barony of Methlick including the lands of Archaidlie, Andatt and Brauchla, in Aberdeenshire, King James V confirmed James Gordon in the Barony of Meikle-Methlick on 31 May 1539.

GORDON OF KENNERTY IN ABERDEENSHIRE. On 24 July 1548, Queen Mary granted John Gordon, son and heir apparent of Thomas Gordon of Kennarty, the lands and Barony of Kennarty.

GORDON OF KINMOND IN ABERDEENSHIRE. On 23 September 1580, King James VI confirmed John Gordon of Pitlurg in the lands and Barony of Kinmond, similarly on 21 October 1588.

GORDON OF AUCHINDOUN IN BANFFSHIRE. On 28 August 1581, King James VI confirmed a charter by James Ogilvy of Findlator, transferring the lands and Barony of Auchendoun to Adam Gordon.

GORDON OF BARCLAY IN BANFFSHIRE. On 24 December 1582, King James VI confirmed Sir Patrick Gordon of Auchendoon, in the Barony of Barclay.

GORDON OF SCHEVAS IN ABERDEENSHIRE. On 5 April 1585, King James VI confirmed George Gordon, eldest son of William Gordon of Gight, the lands and Barony of Schevas.

GORDON OF FARR IN SUTHERLAND. On 21 May 1588, King James VI granted John Gordon, son and heir apparent of Alexander Gordon the Earl of Sutherland, the lands and Barony of Farr; on 29 April 1601, King James VI granted John, the Earl of Sutherland, the lands and Barony of Farr.

GORDON OF WRANGHAME IN ABERDEENSHIRE. On 2 October 1594, King James VI confirmed James Gordon, son and heir of John Gordon of Culsamond, the lands and Barony of Newtoun Wranghame.

GORDON OF MEIKLE METHLICK IN ABERDEENSHIRE. On 10 December 1600, King James VI granted James Gordon of Haddach, the Barony of Meikle Methlick.

GORDON OF CLUNIE, On 31 August 1625 Sir Alexander Gordon of Clunie was created a baronet of Nova Scotia.

GORDON OF LOCHINVAR IN DUMFRIES-SHIRE. Robert Gordon of Lochinvar was created a baronet of Nova Scotia on 1 May 1626.

GORDON OF GORDON IN NOVA SCOTIA, ALSO OF GORDONSTOUN IN MORAY. Sir Robert Gordon, son of the Earl of Sutherland, was born at Dunrobin, Sutherland, on 14 May 1580, was created a baronet of Nova Scotia with 16,000 acres there, on 28 May 1625, also the Regality of Gordon, and on 20 June 1642 became 1st baron of Gordonstoun in Moray. He married Louisa Gordon on 16 February 1613 and died in March 1656. Their son Sir Ludovic Gordon succeeded to the barony of Gordonstoun. He died in 1685 and was followed by his son Sir Robert Gordon [1647-1704] who was a politician, scientific mechanist and inventor. He married [1] Margaret Dow, Lady Duffus, and [2] Elizabeth Dunbar – their son Sir Robert Gordon succeeded to the barony of Gordonstoun in 1704. He too was a politician but was a Jacobite in 1715. He married Agnes Maxwell and died on 8 January 1772.

GORDON OF LESMOIR. On 2 September 1625 James Gordon of Lesmoir was created a baronet of Nova Scotia.

GORDON OF CAMBO. John Gordon was created a Baronet of Nova Scotia on 18 June 1631.

GORDON OF HADDO IN ABERDEENSHIRE. King Charles I created Sir John Gordon as the Baronet of Haddo on 13 August 1642. During the War of the Three Kingdoms, he fought as a Royalist but was captured and beheaded in Edinburgh on 19 July 1644. His son then became the second Baronet, he died childless in 1665 when the title went to his brother Sir George Gordon born 3 October 1637. Sir George was an advocate, MP, and High Chancellor, and on 30 November 1682 became Earl of Aberdeen when the Baronetcy merged into the Earldom.

GORDON OF ROTHIEMAY IN BANFFSHIRE. On 19 April 1649, King Charles II granted James Gordon of Rothiemay the lands and Barony of Rothiemay.

GORDON OF EARLSTOUN IN KIRKCUDBRIGHTSHIRE. On 31 July 1657, Oliver Cromwell, Lord Protector, granted the lands and barony of Earlston with its castles, woods, fishing rights, mills, mill-lands and others, to William Gordon; on 9 July 1706 Lieutenant Colonel William Gordon of Afton, was created Baronet of Earlstoun, he died in December 1718, when his son Sir Alexander Gordon became the second Baronet of Earlstoun and Afton, he died on 10 November 1720, then followed Sir Thomas Gordon as the third baronet until his death on 23 March 1769.

GORDON OF DALPHOLLY IN SUTHERLAND. On 3 February 1704, William Gordon of Dalpholly was created as a Baronet, he died on 9 June 1742.

GORTHY OF GORTHY IN STRATHEARN, PERTHSHIRE. On 15 October 1507, King James IV granted Tristram Gorthy of that Ilk the lands of Gorthy with its mill and lands in Dalpatrick now incorporated into the Barony of Gorthy. [a surname derived from the lands of Gorthy, examples of the surname date from around 1200][George Gortie, a Jacobite, was transported to Antigua in 1716][The Barony of Gorthy, Perth, 1878]

GRAEME OF INCHBRAKIE IN PERTHSHIRE. Patrick Graeme succeeded his father the Earl of Montrose, who was killed at the Battle of Flodden on 9 September 1513 in the lands of Inchbrakie and later Pyreny in Strathearn. [a surname of Anglo-Norman origin, examples date from the twelfth century] [William Graeme a Covenanter, was transported to East New Jersey in 1685, while Patrick Graham, an apothecary, settled in Georgia by 1736] [Or and Sable, a book of the Graemes and Grahams, Edinburgh, 1903][The Lairds of Dun, London, 1931][Family Letters 1745-1793, Edinburgh, 1857]

GRAHAM OF MUCKDOW IN STIRLINGSHIRE. King James II granted Sir Patrick Graham the Barony of Muckdow, comprising the lands of Balligrochane, Caristoun, Dougalstoun, Barloch, Killcrinan, Kilmoran, Mukdow, Clochbar, Gartferin, Erouquhybeg, Ardule, Rimochastel, Corry, Arclet and Achinroish, all in Stirlingshire, on 24 October 1458.

GRAHAM OF FINTRY IN STIRLINGSHIRE. King James III granted Robert Graham of Fintry the lands of Balmanoch in Stirlingshire, as a Barony on 31 August 1464. On 13 January 1549, Queen Mary confirmed Sir David Graham in the lands and Barony of Fintry; on 29 January 1586, King James VI granted

David Graham the lands and Barony of Fintry. [Pedigree of the Grahams of Fintry, Dundee, 1962]

GRAHAM OF ABERUTHVEN IN PERTHSHIRE. King James IV granted Lord William Graham the lands of Aberuthven wth its mill, also the lands of Pothill, Balhie, Auchenbanze, parts of Nether Pirny, parts of Strathboys, and parts of Strathfenton in Perthshire united into the Barony of Aberuthven, on 20 February 1500.

GRAHAM OF MORPHY IN KINCARDINESHIRE. On 30 March 1507, King James IV granted Henry Graham of Morphy, the lands of Morphy, Meikle Pilmure, Stone of Morphy, Smiddyland, Hill of Morphy, Sillecottis the mill of Morphy, fishing rights in the River North Esk in Kincardineshire, incorporated in the Barony of Morphy; on 24 December 1597, King James VI confirmed John Graham, son and heir of John Graham of Morphy in the lands and Barony of Morphy.

GRAHAM OF STRATHDICHTY IN ANGUS. On 8 January 1530, King James V granted William Graham of Fintry the lands of the Mains of Strathdichty, the outfield of Kirriemuir with its mill, the lands of Inchbrauchty, Inchmilne, Glenowick, Balnaboth, Daldavo, Pitcaridy, the forest of Glen Prossan, the lands of Dallinch, Balloch and the Kirktoun of Kirriemuir, in the Lordship, Regality and Barony of Kirriemuir, now incorporated in the Barony of Strathdichty, in Angus. [The Regality of Kirriemuir, Edinburgh, 1909]

GRAHAM OF COWGASK IN PERTHSHIRE. On 28 May 1584, King James VI granted John Graham the Earl of Montrose, the lands and Barony of Cowgask.

GRAHAM OF KINCARDIN IN PERTHSHIRE. On 23 May 1488, King James III granted Lord William Graham the lands and Barony of Kincardin with its castle and mills, also, the lands and Baronies of Muddock and Dundaffmure, the land of Aithry in Stirlingshire, and the lands and Barony of Old Montrose, Kinnaber and Charlestoun with manors, mills, orchards, and fishing rights on the North and South Esk in Angus; on 28 February 1509, King James IV granted William Graham, the Earl of Montrose, the lands of Callender-more, Callendar-beg, Dalrainich, Culterannych and Buchry in Perthshire, now merged into the Barony of Kincardine; on 3 August 1525, King James V granted William Graham, the Earl of Montrose, the lands and Barony of Old Montrose including its manor-house, mill, and fishing rights.

GRAHAM OF ABERRUTHVEN IN PERTHSHIRE. On 17 March 1505, King James IV granted William Graham the Earl of Montrose, the lands and

Barony of Aberruthven, with the exception of Inchbreckie and Pitinclerach; on 12 December 1511, King James IV confirmed William Graham, the Earl of Montrose, with the lands and Barony of Aberruthven.

GRAHAM OF STRATHICHTY IN STIRLINGSHIRE. On 13 July 1541, King James V granted David Graham son and heir apparent of William Graham of Fintry, the lands of Cragtoun, of Balmannoch, of Carscarrow, Weltoun, Crynnokkis, in Stirlingshire, also the lands of Strachichty, with mills etc, lands at Kirriemuir, lands of Inchbrachty, Inchmylne, Glennewik, Daldavo, Pitcaride the forest of Glen Prossin, etc in Angus, now incorporated into the Barony of Strathichty; also, the lands of Bochlivy-Graham with mill, in Perthshire, now incorporated as the Barony of Buchlivy-Graham.

GRAHAM OF BOQUHEN IN STIRLINGSHIRE. On 18 November 1565, King Henry and Queen Mary confirmed Andrew Graham of Gartavrtane the lands and Barony of Boquhen.

GRAHAME OF BRACO. Sir William Grahame of Braco, was created as a Baronet of Nova Scotia on 28 December 1625, a sasine dated 26 January 1630.

GRAHAM OF GORTHIE IN PERTHSHIRE. Oliver Cromwell, the Lord Protector, granted the Barony of Gorthie, with the Tower of Gorthie as its principal messuage, to Mungo Grahame, on 17 July 1657.

GRAHAM OF GARTMORE IN STIRLINGSHIRE. On 28 June 1665 William Graham was created 1st Baronet of Gartmore by King Charles II, he married Elizabeth Graham, sister of the Earl of Airth and Menteith in 1663, he died in 1684, when he was succeeded by his only son Sir John Graham as 2nd Baronet of Gartmore, however he became insane in 1696 and died unmarried on 12 July 1708 causing the barony to become extinct. [The Grahams of Gartmore, Glasgow, 1885]

GRAEME OF NEWTON IN STIRLINGSHIRE. John Graeme, son of James Graeme of Newton and his wife Elizabeth Moray, born 1688, a diplomat in the service of King James VIII, was created a knight and a baronet on 6 September 1726, on 20 January 1760 he was created Lord Newton, Viscount Falkirk, and Earl of Alford, he died in the Scots College in Paris on 3 January 1773. [a Jacobite baronetcy with castle and mills, the lands of Aithrey in Stirlingshire.]

GRAYME OF ...... On 9 June 1525, King James V confirmed the grant by George Leslie, the Earl of Rothes, to Elizabeth Grayme, Countess of Huntly, of the Barony of Ballinbrech with its castle and mills, the Barony of Leslie with its castle and mills, the Barony of Taudyis with its castle and mill, the lands of Nyde,with superiority over the lands of the Barony of Kennochy, its mansion-house, Drummard, Outermarny, Lalethin, and fishing rights on the River Tay, in Fife, the lands and Barony of Carny, in Perthshire, the lands and Barony of Dunlappie in Angus, the land and Barony of Quisny and Foulis-Mowat, and the lands of Rothienorman in Aberdeenshire, the land and Barony of Rothes, with its castle and mill, in Moray, also the lands of Kildeis in Inverness-shire.

GRANT OF URQUHART IN INVERNESS-SHIRE. On 8 December 1509, King James IV granted John Grant of Freuchy the lands, castle and fort of Bordland of Urquhart, St Ninian with its mill, lands at Carowgar, Drumboy, Bunlaod, Ballimakauchan, Gartal, Polmale, Dulchangy, Inchbrims, Meikle Devauch, with the office of forester of Cluny in the Lordship of Urquhart, now incorporated in the Barony of Urquhart.

GRANT OF GLENMORISTON IN INVERNESS-SHIRE. On 8 December 1509, King James IV granted John Grant, eldest son of John Grant of Freuchy, the lands of Glen Moriston, including Conechane, Auchlyn, Tullylechart, Duldragin, Innerwick, Blair, Inver, Coulnakirk, Meikle Cluny, now integrated into the Barony of Glen Moriston. [A surname of Norman origin introduced into Scotland in the thirteenth century] [Alexander Grant, a minister, settled in Antigua in 1748, while several Jacobite Grants were transported to Barbados in 1747][Reminiscences of the Grants of Glenmoriston, Edinburgh, 1887][A history of Clan Grant, Chichester, 1983]

GRANT OF TULLYCHCARROUN IN BANFFSHIRE. On 5 September 1595, King James VI confirmed Patrick Grant of Ballandalloch, in various lands in Banffshire also salmon fishing rights in the River Spey, incorporated into the Barony of Tullycharroun.

GRANT OF MONYMUSK IN ABERDEENSHIRE. On 7 December 1705, Francis Grant of Cullen, was created a Baronet, later of Monymusk, when he died in March 1726, his son Sir Archibald Grant became the second baronet, he died in Monymusk on 17 February 1778.

GRAY OF LONGFORGAN IN PERTHSHIRE. King Robert I granted the Barony of Longforgan, and land in Dundee to Andrew Gray around 1320; on 7 January 1509, King James IV granted Lord Andrew Gray the lands and Barony of Longforgan, including Huntly with its tower and fort, Bullion, Gedpick, Balbunnock, Kingaidy, Ebrukis, Thrisstleholme, Rashycrook, Dron,

Knap, Lairistoun,, Littletoun, land in Inchmartin, the lands of Montskeide, Montramyche alias Dysart, and Killebroiche, in Perthshire, incorporated into the Barony of Longforgan; on 22 February 1510, King James IV granted Lord Andrew Gray, Broughty in Angus with its castle, fort and fishing rights; on 16 April 1524 King James V granted Lord Patrick Gray the Barony of Forgan, with its mansion-house, and mills, the castle and fort of Huntly, the lands and Barony of Foulis with its manor-house and mill, in Perthshire, the lands of King's Law, with the church of Lundy, the lands and Barony of Dundee, with its mills, Pitarrow with its mill, Broughty with its castle, fort and fishing rights, the lands of Balgillo with its mills, Gutterstoun with its fishing, in Angus; the lands of Kinneff with its tower, Herbartshiels and Blacklaw with fishing in Kincardineshire. On 14 September 1542, King James V granted Lord Patrick Gray the lands and Barony of Forgan. [The surname probably comes from Gray in France, a name found in Scotland since the mid-thirteenth century][John Gray, emigrated to East New Jersey in 1685, while William Gray was transported to Virginia in 1696.] [Generations of Gray, Australia, 1996]

GRAY OF LUNDY IN ANGUS. King James III granted Lord Andrew Gray the lands and Barony of Lundy also the lands of Millhill with mill, also, the lands of Birflat in the Barony of Forgan in Perthshire, on 29 June 1489.

GRAY OF FOULIS IN PERTHSHIRE. On 28 April 1542, King James V granted Patrick Gray of Buttergask, the lands and Barony of Foulis, Blacklaw, the lands and Barony of Longforgan, with Huntly Castle, etc in Perthshire, land in Dundee, the lands of Crag of Broughty with castle, fort, and fishing rights, the lands of Balgillo, the lands of Gottarstone, part of Pitcarrow in Angus, now incorporated into the Barony of Foulis. On 5 March 1639, King Charles I granted William Gray of Pittendrum, a merchant burgess of Edinburgh, the lands and Barony of Forgan, the lands and Barony of Foulis, the lands and Barony of Buttergask and Leigertlaw.

GRAY OF KILMALAMOCK IN MORAY. On 16 December 1581, King James VI granted Patrick Gray, master of Gray, the lands and Barony of Kilmalamock.

GRAY OF DENMILN. On 5 March 1707 James Gray of Denmiln was created a Baronet, on his death in 1722 his son Sir James Gray became the second Baronet of Denmiln.

GRIERSON OF LAG IN DUMFRIES-SHIRE. On 21 November 1526, King James V granted John Grierson, the lands of Lag with its tower, fort, and mill, the lands of Makraithshill, Dalgarnock-holmis, Ardis and its mill, the superiority of Grennan, Blackmyre, and the land of Schaws, in Dumfries-shire, the land of Rockall, Collin with its mill, the lands of Kirkbride-rig in Annandale, and others in Kirkcudbrightshire, now incorporated into the Barony of Lag; on 20 August 1548, Queen Mary granted William Grierson, son and heir apparent of John Grierson of Lag, the lands and Barony of Lag; on 20 May 1593, King James VI confirmed William Grierson, son of Roger Grierson of Lag, in the Barony of Lag including several lands in Dumfries-shire and in Kirkcudbrightshire. [a surname associated with Dumfries, examples date from the fifteenth century][James Grierson settled in Augusta, Georgia, by 1773, while William Grierson emigrated to Philadelphia in 1775.][The Lag Charters, 1400-1720, Edinburgh, 1958]

GRIERSON OF ROCKHALL LAG IN DUMFRIES-SHIRE. On 25 March 1685 Robert Grierson was created as a Baronet he died on 15 April 1736 when his son Sir William Grierson succeeded to the Baronetcy.

GUTHRIE OF GUTHRIE IN ANGUS. King James III confirmed David Guthrie of Kingoldrum, as Baron of Lour, with the lands of Muirtoun, on 19 October1464; He also granted David Guthrie of Kingoldrum, the lands, tenants and tenantries of Guthrie on 25 March 1466; King James III confirmed David Guthrie of that Ilk in the lands and Barony of Guthrie on 2 February 1470. On 9 March 1539, King James V confirmed Andrew Guthrie in the lands and Barony of Guthrie; on 13 March 1544, Queen Mary granted Alexander Guthrie, son and heir apparent of Andrew Guthrie of that Ilk the lands and Barony of Guthrie; on 30 November 1583 King James VI granted Alexander Guthrie, the heir of Alexander Guthrie of that Ilk, the lands and Barony of Guthrie. [A surname derived from Guthrie in Angus, examples date from the thirteenth century][John Guthrie, a Jacobite, was transported to South Carolina in 1716, while Thomas Guthrie, from Orkney, settled in Georgia in 1774] [The Barony Court Book of Guthrie, ms. NRS.GD188.31.11] [The Guthrie family, 1178-1900, Northampton, 1906]

GUTHRIE OF GLENSAUCH IN KINCARDINESHIRE. King James III granted the Barony of Glensauch to Thomas Guthrie on 16 October 1473.

GUTHRIE OF KINGOLDRUM IN ANGUS. On 28 August 1508, King James IV confirmed Alexander Guthrie, son and heir of Sir Alexander Guthrie of that Ilk, of the lands and Barony of Kingoldrum, with its mill, also the lands of Lour and Muirtoun, etc, in Angus. Sir Alexander Guthrie was killed at the Battle of Flodden on 9 September 1513.

HAILES OF BOTHWELL IN LANARKSHIRE. King James IV granted Lord Patrick Hailes the lands and lordship of Crichtoun in Midlothian, the lands of Vogry, Sauchnale Furd with mills, Capristoun, Muirhouse, Castellaw all lands of the

Lordship of Crichtoun, the lands and Baronies of Dryfesdale, and Kirkmichael in Dumfries-shire, the lordships and baronies of Farannis, Blackhill, Mylnehill, Coilanehouse, Aikhorneholm, Greenside, Becktoun, Lammynby, Bettyshill the mill of Patrick, Earl of Bothwell, Dryfesdale, Bengale, Blackwood, Beckhouse, Drifeholme, the house of Dryfesdale, Torwood, Bellhill, Carruthers, Rispod, Townlands, Over Kirkmichael, Nether Kirkmichael, Rahill, Molynnis, Monygip and Crunzanetoun, also the lordship of Bothwell and its lands, castle, messuage, fisheries, mills etc., Uddingston with Cotelands and its mill, Scherehills, Ricardionstoun, Knockubill and others, fishing rights on the River Clyde, in Lanarkshire, also lands of Easter Barmukkis, Murschede Hirst, Foresterseat, Starryshaw, Gudockhills, Dunteling, Wester Brekhalch, Swynsty Parkhill etc in Lanarkshire, formed into the Lordship and Barony of Bothwell on 13 October 1488; on 26 February 1491, King James IV granted Patrick, Earl of Bothwell, the lands and Baronies of Yestir, Duncanslaw and Morham united into the Barony of Morham on 26 February 1491; Patrick, Earl of Bothwell, was granted the lands and Barony of Yetholm in Roxburghshire, also the lands and Barony of Weltoun also in Roxburghshire, on 18 May 1495; King James IV granted the lands and Dominion of Bothwell with its house, castle and manor with lands, fisheries etc. to Patrick Hailes, Earl of Bothwell on 12 September 1498; on 9 March 1499, King James IV granted Patrick the Earl of Bothwell the lands and Barony of Chawmirlane-Newtoun with its mill in Roxburghshire; on 24 January 1507, King James IV granted Patrick, the Earl of Bothwell, the lands and Barony of Fermingtoun in Roxburghshire; on 8 July 1511, King James IV granted Adam, the Earl of Bothwell, the lands of Dolphintoun to be united into the Barony of Hailes; on 8 November 1512, King James IV granted Adam the Earl of Bothwell, Moreham with its castle and fort, the lands of Plewfield and mill, in East Lothian, also the lands and Barony of Duncanlaw there, now united into the Barony of Hailes. The Earl of Bothwell was killed at the Battle of Flodden on 9 September 1513; on 29 July 1587, King James VI granted Francis Stewart, Earl of Bothwell, Lord Crichtoun, Haile an Liddesdale, Great Admiral of Scotland, the Barony of Hailes and the Barony of Bothwell.[The surname comes from Hailes in Midlothian, examples date from the twelfth century]

HALDANE OF GLENEAGLES IN PERTHSHIRE. On 28 January 1483, King James III granted John Haldane, the Barony of Gleneagles and Berdrale-Haldane, parts of Dysart in Fife, the lands of Knockhill, Ballarde, Balboure, Kepdoury, Carbeth, Camquhell, and Argess in Stirlingshire, now united into the Barony of Gleneagles; on 29 July 1498, King James IV granted Sir James Haldane of Gleneagles, the lands of Culzemore, Rosmukrath, Lurglorne, Killedin, and others in Stirlingshire and Dunbartonshire, also fishing rights of Loch Lomond; on 20 January 1509, King James IV granted Sir John Haldane of

Gleneagles, the lands of Calzemore, Ross, Lughorne, Killedean, part of Drummeikle, Lateris with its mill, Fenykintennand, Barquhois, Barnahill, Scheneglas, Ladrisbeg, with their mills, Bothurches, Trenbeg, Knockkoure with fishing rights, Croft, Ladrismore, Auchinkerachis, the islands of Ross, Durinch and Islanddarg on Loch Lomond in Dunbartonshire, also the lands of Ardonan, Finglen, Halch, Kerre, the mill of Ardonane, Tarquhone and Cawer, now incorporated into the Barony of Haldane; on 17 April 1546, Queen Mary granted James Haldane of Gleneagles, the lands of Kippanis and Craigbaky in Perthshire now united into the Barony of Gleneagles; on 8 December 1563, Queen Mary granted George Haldane, son and heir apparent of John Haldane of Gleneagles, the lands and Barony of Gleneagles, and the lands and Barony of Haldane. [An Old English name *Healfdene* meaning 'half-Dane', examples in Scotland date from the twelfth century][a prisoner of war named .....Hadden was banished to Virginia or Barbados in 1667, while George Haldane of Gleneagles, was Governor of Jamaica before 1759] [Haldane of Gleneagles, Edinburgh, 1929]

HALIBURTON OF DIRLETON IN EAST LOTHIAN. King James II granted the lands, Lordship, and Barony of Dirletoun to Patrick Haliburton, son and heir of John Hamilton on 24 March 1451; On 24 May 1505, King James IV, granted Lord Patrick Haliburton, the lands and Barony of Segy in Kinross-shire. [The surname is derived from a place in Berwickshire, examples date from the thirteenth century] [William Halliburton, a soldier, died at Darien, Panama, in 1699, while Margaret Halyburton emigrated to East New Jersey in 1684][Memorials of the Haliburtons, Edinburgh, 1820]

HALIBURTON OF BOLTON IN EAST LOTHIAN. King James IV granted Archibald Haliburton, son and heir apparent of Lord George Haliburton, the lands and Barony of Bolton on 30 June 1488.

HALIBURTON, OF ARCLES IN INVERNESS-SHIRE. On 13 May 1512, King James IV granted James Haliburton of Gask, part of Inglistoun, the lands of Kingily with its fishing rights, the lands of Drumballoch with it fishing rights, part of Balladrum, the lands of Ardblair, part of Fenblair, lands of Kelauch and Clonvaike, Crew, Fenelane with crofts and fishing rights, Cowlauch, Dounys with its mill, crofts, and fishing rights, Culmoninbeg, part of Colmolinmore, part of Kinlargy with fishing in the River Forne, and the lands of Inchbarry, in Inverness-shire, also the land of Arcles in Ross-shire, also the Kirktoun of Inglistoun, the lands of Struse, Cullguyry, Croychell, Wester Comyr, Kilbladdy and Daheny with fishing rights in Strathglass, now united into the Barony of Arcles; on 2 October 1529, King James V confirmed George Haliburton of Gask in the part of the lands of Ochtertyre, Balgrag and is mill, also the mill of Ochtertyre, now merged into the Barony of Gask in Angus.

HALIBURTON OF PITCUR IN PERTHSHIRE. James Haliburton was created as a baronet of Nova Scotia on 12 January 1628.

HALKETT OF PITFIRRANE IN FIFE. Charles Halkett or Hacket of Pitfirrane was created a baronet by King Charles II on 25 January 1662, he was a Member of Parliament, and husband of Janet Murray, and died in 1697. He was succeeded by Sir James Halkett as Baronett of Pitfirrane, who died unmarried in March 1705 when the barony became extinct. [A surname of territorial origin in Renfrewshire or Lanarkshire; examples of the surname date from the thirteenth century] [in 1698, John Halkett was a sailor bound for Darien, while Charles Halket, a Jacobite, was transported to the West Indies in 1747][Inventory of Pitfirrane writs, 1230-1794, Edinburgh, 1932]

HAMILTON OF KINNEILL IN WEST LOTHIAN. King Robert III granted the Barony of Kinneill to James Hamilton around 1397; King James II granted Lord James Hamilton, the lands and Barony of Drumsergart in Lanarkshire, and the lands and Barony of Kinneill in West Lothian, now incorporated int the Barony of Hamilton, on 23 October 1455; Sir James Hamilton, was granted lands in Lanarkshire by King James III all incorporated into the Barony of Hamilton on 26 February 1471; and on 12 July 1474, King James III, granted Lord James Hamilton the lands and Barony of Kinneill in West Lothian, the lands of Drumsergart, the Barony of Carmunnock, in Lanarkshire, to be integrated into the Barony of Hamilton; King James IV granted Lord James Hamilton, the lands and Barony of Kinneill with the castle of Craigtoun, the colliery and saltpans on 28 April 1490; On 11 August 1503, King James IV granted Lord James Hamilton, the lands and island of Arran in Bute-shire, with its castle, forts, mills and fishing rights, was created as a Barony; on 17 January 1513, King James IV confirmed James Hamilton, the Earl of Arran, the lands and Barony of Hamiltoun, with its castle, fort, grain mills, fulling mills, the lands and Barony of Mauchanshire with its mills, the lands and Baronies of Drumsargat and Carmunnock, with mills etc, the Barony of Stonehouse, the Barony of Crawford-John with its mills, the lands of Kirkle and Ricardsjohnstoun, in Lanarkshire, also Kinneill with its castle, forts, parks, grain mill and fulling mill, in West Lothian, Loch Finnart in Renfrewshire, the lands of Kirkinnan with its mills in Kirkcudbrightshire, and Birkinside with its mills in Berwickshire, now incorporated into the Barony of Hamilton; on 16 November 1528, King James V granted James Hamilton, the Earl of Arran, the lands and Lordship of Bothwell; on 1 July 1584, King James VI granted James Hamilton the Earl of Arran, the lands, Lordship and Barony of Cockburnspath in Berwickshire. [a surname possibly derived from a place in Northumberland, examples date from the thirteenth century] [Amos Hamilton was in Virginia by 1650, while Alexander Hamilton, settled in Annapolis in 1739]. [The House of Hamilton, Edinburgh, 1933]

HAMILTON OF CRAWFORDJOHN IN LANARKSHIRE. King James III granted the Barony of Crawfordjohn to Lord James Hamilton on 24 October 1464; on 20 April 1565, Queen Mary granted Sir James Hamilton of Crawfordjohn, the lands, Lordship and Barony of Avendaill

HAMILTON OF STONEHOUSE IN LANARKSHIRE. On 7 April 1498 King James IV granted Patrick Hamilton, brother and heir of Lord James Hamiltoun, the lands of Stonehouse, Wynelands, Tweedy.in the Barony of Stonehouse.

HAMILTOUN OF CAMBUSNETHAN IN LANARKSHIRE. On 25 September 1524, King James V granted Sir James Hamilton of Finnart the lands and Barony of Cambusnethan with its tower, fort, mills and church, in Lanarkshire, the lands of Whiterig in Stirlingshire, also the lands of Carswell in Lanarkshire.

HAMILTOUN OF MENSTRIE IN CLACKMANNANSHIRE. On 27 August 1529, King James V granted Helen Hamilton, daughter of the Earl of Arran, the lands and Barony of Menstrie with its mill and fishing rights.

HAMILTOUN OF SANQUHAR IN AYRSHIRE. On 11 January 1530, King James V granted William Hamilton of McNaristoun, and in Sanquhar-Lindsay, land on Sanquharmuir, land of Prestwickshaws, land in Auchindrane, in Ayrshire, now incorporated into the Barony of Sanquhar. On 10 May 1539, King James V, confirmed William Hamilton in the lands and Barony of Sanquhar, with tower, fort, mills, fishing rights, the lands of Over Auchinstewart, etc, in Ayrshire, the lands and Baronies of Bernewell and Symontoun, etc in Ayrshire, now incorporated in the Barony of Sanquhar-Hamilton, which was confirmed on 8 January 1540; on 9 December 1556, Queen Mary granted William Hamilton of Sanquhar, son and heir of William Hamilton of Glenmuir, the lands and Barony of Sanquhar-Hamilton.

HAMILTON OF OCHILTREE IN AYRSHIRE. On 19 December 1530, King James V granted Sir James Hamilton of Finnart, the lands and Barony of Ochiltree with its castle, fort, mills, etc, the lands of Barnwell and Symontoun with mills, fishing in Ayrshire, also the lands and Barony of Easter Wemyss and Lochore, with fort, mills, fishing, in Fife, and part of Balmakewan in Kincardineshire; on 12 January 1568, King James VI confirmed William Hamilton in the lands and Baronies of Barnewell and Symontoun in Ayrshire.

HAMILTON OF AUCHINLECK IN AYRSHIRE. On 12 February 1532, David Hamilton resigned the lands and Barony of Auchinleck, including the lands of Crakstoun, Over and Nether Kethstoun, and Rogertoun with tower, fort, mills, etc. which King James V then granted to Janet Hamilton, sister of the Earl of Arran.

HAMILTON OF OCHILTREE IN AYRSHIRE. On 3 July 1533, King James V, including granted Sir James Hamilton of Finnart, the lands and Barony of Ochiltree, with its castle, fort, mills, fishing rights, also the lands and Barony of Crawfordjohn, with its fort etc, in Lanarkshire, part of Crage in Avendale, Lanarkshire, the lands of Whiterig in Stirlingshire, the lands of Gorgie in Renfrewshire, also land in Stonehouse, Lanarkshire, now incorporated in the Barony of Ochiltree; on 18 November 1542, King James V granted Lord Ochiltree the Barony of Trabeauch in Ayrshire.

HAMILTON OF AVENDALE IN LANARKSHIRE. On 2 September 1534 King James V confirmed the grant by Andrew, Lord Avendale, of the lands and Barony of Avendale with its castle, fort, mill, fishing rights, also the Barony of Ochiltree, with its castle, fort, mill, fishing rights, etc, to James Hamilton of Finnart; on 22 September 1539 the king added the lands of Newtoun and Brakenbrig in the Barony of Avendale, the lands of Hazeldea and Melmuir in 1539, Barony of Stonehouse and the lands of Sandeholm and Broom, the lands and Barony of Crawford-John, in Lanarkshire, the lands of Whitrig in Stirlingshire, the lands of Gorgy in Midlothian, the lands of Kincavill in West Lothian, etc, now incorporated into the Barony of Avendale; on 20 April 1565, Queen Mary granted Sir James Hamilton of Crawfordjohn, the lands, Lordship and Barony of Avendaill; on 4 October 1589, King James VI granted James Hamilton of Libertousn, son and heir apparent of Sir James Hamilton of Crawfordjohn, the lands and Barony of Avendale, which together with lands in Bathgate, Stirlingshire, West Lothian, Ayrshire, united into the Barony of Avendale; on 27 November 1591, King James VI granted James Hamilton of Liberton, the lands and Barony of Avendaill

HAMILTON OF KILMARNOCK IN AYRSHIRE. On 8 February 1536, King James V granted Sir James Hamilton of Finnart the lands and Barony of Kilmarnock, with its orchards, castle and fort, mills, fishing rights, various tenantries, etc.

HAMILTON OF MAUCHANSHIRE IN LANARKSHIRE. On 15 September 1540, King James V granted James Hamilton, Earl of Arran, the lands and Barony of Mauchanshire, also the lands and Barony of Drumsargat, and land in the Barony of Stonehouse, all with towers, forts, mills, fishing rights, etc., plus the lands of Kirkinnan in Kirkcudbrightshire, now united into the Barony of Mauchanshire; on the same day the king confirmed James Hamilton, Earl of Annan, in the Barony of Hamilton.

HAMILTON OF STONEHOUSE IN LANARKSHIRE. On 27 September 1543, Queen Mary granted James Hamilton, son and heir apparent of James Hamilton of Stonehouse, the land and Barony of Stonehouse and mill in Lanarkshire, land in Brochtoun in Peebles-shire, etc, now formed into the Barony of Stonehouse.

HAMILTON OF LIVINGSTOUN IN WEST LOTHIAN. On 15 October 1546, Queen Mary granted James Hamilton of Kincavill, the Barony of Livingstoun.

HAMILTON OF INNERWEIK IN RENFREWSHIRE. On 4 September 1550, Queen Mary granted Alexander Hamilton, son and heir apparent of Alexander Hamilton of Innerweik, the lands and Barony of Innerweik etc.

HAMILTON OF CARSTAIRS IN LANARKSHIRE. On 29 July 1588, King James VI granted James Hamilton, son and heir apparent of James Hamilton of Libertoun, the lands and Barony of Carstairs.

HAMILTON OF BOTHWELLMUIR IN LANARKSHIRE. On 1 December 1590, King James VI confirmed Lord John Hamilton, in the lands and Lordship of Bothwellmuir.

HAMILTON OF PAISLEY IN RENFREWSHIRE. On 20-22 March 1592, King James VI confirmed Claude Hamilton in the lands, Lordship and Barony of Paisley. On 8 February 1642, King Charles I confirmed James Hamilton, Earl of Abercorn and Lord Paisley, in the Lordship and Barony of Abercorn, also in the Lordship and Barony of Paisley etc.

HAMILTON OF BATHGATE IN WEST LOTHIAN. On 11 November 1608, King James VI confirmed Robert Hamilton, son and heir of Robert Hamilton of Bathgate, the lands and Barony of Bathgate.

HAMILTON OF BROOMHILL. James Hamilton was created as a Baronet of Nova Scotia on 6 January 1635. His son Sir John Hamilton succeeded to the Baronetcy around 1647 but as he died childless on 20 June 1679 the baronetcy became extinct. On 26 March 1639, King Charles I confirmed John Hamilton of Broomhill the younger in the lands and Barony of Skirling in Peebles-shire.

HAMILTON OF JEDBURGH FOREST IN ROXBURGHSHIRE. On 12 February 1639, King Charles I granted Sir John Hamilton of Orbiston, Senator of the College of Justice, the lands, Lordship and Barony of Jedburgh Forest.

HAMILTON OF ERSKINE IN RENFREWSHIRE. On 24 December 1638, King Charles I granted Sir John Hamilton of Orbiestoun, the lands, Lordship and Barony of Erskine, the lands and Barony of Dunottar.

HAMILTON OF BEILL IN EAST LOTHIAN. On 15 September 1641, King Charles I granted John Hamilton of Skirling, the lands and Barony of Beill.

HAMILTON OF PRIESTFIELD IN MIDLOTHIAN. On 29 January 1642, King Charles I granted James Hamilton the Barony of Priestfield.

HAMILTON OF SILVERSTONHILL IN LANARKSHIRE. King Charles I granted Robert Hamilton the Barony of Silvertonhill around 1646, he was an Member of Parliament, he died by 1670 and was succeeded by his son Sir William Hamilton, a soldier, as the second Baronet, and died in 1708. The third Baronet was his son Sir John Hamilton who died in Jersey in 1748. The fourth Baronet of Silvertonhill was Sir Robert Hamilton, an army officer, who died on 10 August 1786.

HAMILTON OF PRESTON IN EAST LOTHIAN. On 5 November 1673 William Hamilton of Preston was created as a Baronet, later settled in the Netherlands where he died around 1690, his brother, Sir Robert Hamilton became the 2nd Baronet of Preston until his death in 1701.

HANNAY OF MOCHRUM. Sir Robert Hannay was created a baronet of Nova Scotia on 31 March 1630. [A surname possibly of Gaelic origin; examples, mainly in Dumfries and Galloway, date from the late thirteenth century] [William Hanna, a clergyman, emigrated to Virginia in 1772, while James Hannah, emigrated to New York in 1774][The Hannays of Sorbie, London, 1961]

HAY OF OLIVER CASTLE IN PEEBLES-SHIRE. John Hay, son and heir of David Hay the lands of Over Kingildurris, Frude, Polmude, Cockland, Glen Quotho, in Peebles-shire, by King James III on 12 July 1470; on 2 February 1512, King James IV granted John Hay, son and heir of John Hay, Lord of Yester, the lands of Oliver Castle, also the lands of Todrik in Selkirkshire, and part of Glen Rusco, now the Barony of Oliver Castle; Lord Hay of Yester was killed at the Battle of Flodden on 9 September 1513. [originally de la Haye, from France, examples date from the twelfth century][Henry Hay, a shipmaster trading between Virginia and Aberdeen in 1665, while Thomas Hay was in Boston in 1694][The Story of the Hays, Edinburgh, 1977]

HAY OF URY IN ABERDEENSHIRE. On 7 October 1487, King James III granted William Hay of Ury the lands and Barony of Crimond, in Aberdeenshire; on 12 January 1588, King James VI, confirmed William Hay, nephew of William Hay of Ury in Kincardineshire, in the lands of Ury; on 3 April 1588, King James VI confirmed John Hay of Ury in the lands and Barony of Crimond; John Hay, of Ury in November 1604; William Hay of Ury from May 1607 to 1630. Colonel David Barclay had a charter from James VII creating the free barony of Urie in 1679. [The Court Book of the Barony of Urie, 1604-1747. Edinburgh, 1892]

HAY OF SLAINS IN ABERDEENSHIRE. On 19 May 1565, Queen Mary granted Andrew Hay, son and heir apparent of George Hay the Earl of Errol, the lands and Barony of Slains and Inverpeffer, now incorporated in the Barony of Slains; on 29 March 1584, King James VI granted Francis Hay, son of Andrew Hay the Earl of Errol the lands and Barony of Slains and Inverpeffrey, incorporated into the Barony of Slains, the lands and Lordship of Errol, the lands and Barony of Caputh, the lands and Barony of Cowie, incorporated in the Barony of Errol, the lands and Barony of Logie, etc.

HAY OF LOGIEALMOND IN PERTHSHIRE. King James IV granted Thomas Hay, son of William Hay the Earl of Errol the lands and Barony of Logiealmond on 4 October 1493; On 29 June 1503 King James IV granted William Hay, the Earl of Errol, the lands and Barony of Glendoick, with its mill, in Perthshire.

HAY OF KILMALAMAK IN BANFFSHIRE. King James IV granted Gilbert Hay the lands and Barony of Kilmalamak, including the lands of Pitgony, St Andrews Kirkton, Bareflathills, and Dunkempty, also the lands of Cottis within the Barony of Innes in Morayshire, on 4 October 1501.

HAY OF SNAYD IN DUMFRIES-SHIRE. On 24 May 1505, King James IV granted Sir John Hay of Beltoun the lands and Barony of Snayd.

HAY OF YESTER IN EAST LOTHIAN. On 10 November 1512, King James IV granted Lord John Hay the lands and Barony of Yester, and the lands and Barony of Duncanslaw, now united into the Barony of Yester; on 27 February 1591, King James VI confirmed Lord William Hay in the lands and Barony of Yester, the lands and Barony of Loch Wharret, the Barony of Oliver Castle, the lands and Barony of Lyne and West Hoprew, the lands and Barony of Snaid, now incorporated into the Lordship and Barony of Yester; on 29 May 1591, King James VI granted James Hay, brother of the deceased Lord William Hay of Yester, the lands and Barony of Yester.

HAY OF BRODIE IN MORAY. On 15 February 1577, King James VI confirmed Alexander Hay, the Royal Chancellor, the lands and Barony of Brodie; on 4 March 1577, the king confirmed George Brodie, son of Alexander Hay of that Ilk, in the lands and Barony of Brodie.

HAY OF SMITHFIELD. James Hay of Smithfield was created a Baronet of Nova Scotia by Sir William Alexander the Earl of Stirling on 10 December 1635. [Regist.Precept. Cart. Pro Baronettis Nova. Scotiae.] [The surname Hay is derived from a William de Haga who was granted the lands of Errol in the Carse of Gowrie around 1180 by King William the Lion.] [William Hay, a gardener, emigrated to Maryland in 1754, while Edward Hay, from Perth, was the Governor of Barbados, died there in 1779]

HAY OF AUCHENHUIFF IN ABERDEENSHIRE. On 15 January 1658, Oliver Cromwell, the Lord Protector, granted the lands and barony of Auchenhuiff, with its mains, and heughs, mills and mill-lands, the towns and lands of Pitkean with its tower, fortalice, manor place, etc, formerly held by Patrick Murray of Auchinhuiff to John Hay, the Keeper of the Register of Sasines at Aberdeen.

HAY OF CAPUTH [?], Perthshire. King Robert III granted Thomas Hay, the Constable of Scotland, the Barony of Capet [Caputh?] around 1403.

HAY OF COWIE IN KINCARDINESHIRE. On 14 May 1415, Robert, Duke of Albany, the Regent, granted the Barony of Cowie to William Hay of Errol, the Constable of Scotland, this was confirmed by King James I on 16 June 1430, Colly was formerly held by Fraser of Kilorth.

HAY OF LOCHLOY IN NAIRNSHIRE. On 23 February 1510, King James IV confirmed William Hay in the lands of Lochloy with its mill, Park, Incheoch, Knocknakilze and Urchy, now incorporated into the Barony of Lochly.

HAY OF NAUGHTOUN IN FIFE. On 8 April 1513, King James IV granted Janet Hay of Naughtoun part of Seggy, now united with the Barony of Naughtoun.

HAY OF ERROL IN PERTHSHIRE. On 21 March 1522, King James V granted William Hay, the Earl of Errol, the lands and Barony of Downie, including Downie, Murclye, Inverquhorsky, Dalrilzeance, Leonacht, Dulmaen, Glen Ganot, Pitbrayne and its mill, in Perthshire; on 10 April 1546, Queen Mary granted Andrew Hay, son and heir apparent of the Earl of Errol the lands and Barony of Errol; on 10 February 1549, Queen Mary granted Andrew Hay, son and heir apparent of George Hay, the Earl of Errol, Lord Hay, the Constable of Scotland, the lands, Barony and Lordship of Errol; on 13 January 1574, King James VI granted Andrew Hay, the Master of Errol, the lands and Barony of Logie in Perthshire; on 7 June 1608, King James VI granted Francis Hay the Earl of Errol, the land and Barony of Crimond in Aberdeenshire; on 10 August 1600, King James VI granted Francis Hay the Earl of Errol, the lands and Lordship of Errol, the lands and Barony of Caputh, the lands and Barony of Cowie, also the lands and Barony of Logie, etc.

HAY OF DALGATHY IN ABERDEENSHIRE. On 24 May 1549, Queen Mary granted William Hay, son and heir apparent of Alexander Hay brother german of William Hay of Dalgathy, in the lands and Barony of Dalgathy; on 4 April 1580, King James VI confirmed William Hay of Dalgathy in the lands and Barony of Ardgrane, Caldwalls and Pittachie; on 29 April 1698, King James VI confirmed Alexander Hay, son of Alexander Hay of Dalgetty, the lands and Barony of Dalgatty etc. [The Hay of Park family, London, 2005]

HAY OF TUYNAME IN KIRKCUDBRIGHTSHIRE. On 19 November 1608, King James VI confirmed John Hay, the deputy town-clerk of Edinburgh, the lands and Barony of Tuyname.

HAY OF SMYTHFIELD. The lands and Barony of Smythfield together with certain lands in Peebles-shire, formerly pertaining to Lord Hay of Yester, to be erected into the free barony of Smythfield on 14 July 1654 were granted to William Hay. [Edward Hay was Governor of Barbados before 1779].

HAY OF LINPLUM IN ……. On 26 March 1667, James Hay of Linplum was created as a Baronet, he died on 3 April 1702, and was succeeded by his son Sir Robert Hay, an officer in the British Army, who died on 20 December 1751.

HAY OF PARK IN WIGTOWNSHIRE. On 25 August 1663 King Charles II created Sir Thomas Hay as a Baronet, on his death around 1680 the lands and title went to his son Sir Charles Hay who died in 1737, the 3rd Baronet was Sir Thomas Hay who died in 1777.

HAY OF ALDERSTOUN IN EAST LOTHIAN. On 22 February 1703, John Hay, was created by Queen Anne as the Baronet of Alderston, he died in 1706 when his son Sir Thomas Hay became the 2nd Baronet.

HENDERSON OR HENRYSON OF FORDELL IN FIFE. On 11 January 1512, King James IV granted James Henryson, clerk of the Court of Justiciary, part of the lands and Barony of Fordell with its mill, now the Barony of Fordell; on 9 September 1513 Henderson of Fordell was killed at the Battle of Flodden. On 12 April King James VI son and heir apparent of James Henryson of Fordell, was granted the lands and Barony of Fordell. On 16 July 1664, King Charles II created John Henderson a Baronet of Fordell, on his death in 1683 his son Sir William Henderson became the 2nd Baronet, on his death in 1709, the lands and title went to his son Sir John Henderson, and when he died in 1730 his son Sir Robert Henderson became the 4th Baronet. [a patronymic meaning 'son of Henry', examples date from the fourteenth century] [Alexander Henderson, born 1737, a merchant, died in Virginia in 1815, while James Henderson, a wright, emigrated to New Hampshire, in 1773.] [The Hendersons of Caskieben, Aberdeen, 1963]

HEPBURN OF HAILES IN MIDLOTHIAN. On 20 December 1451 King James II granted Patrick Hepburn the Lordship of Hailes, together with lands of Whittingham, Gamilshiels, etc in Midlothian, the lands of Hershope and Oldhamstocks, Mersington, Lambden and others in Berwickshire, united as the Barony of Hailes; on 27 August 1511, King James IV granted Adam Hepburn, the Earl of Bothwell, son of Patrick Hepburn the Earl of Bothwell, the Lordship and Barony of Hailes, the lands and Barony of Oldhamstocks, the lands and Lordship of Crichtoun, the lands and Barony of Whitsom, the lands and Barony of Tounyetame, the lands and Barony of Wiltoun, the lands and Barony of Chalmerlae-Newtoun, the lands and Barony of Dryfesdale and Carruthers, the lands and Barony of Kirkmichael, the lands and Barony of Earlstoun, the lands and Barony of Bothwell, the lands and Barony of Dolphinstoun, the lands and Barony of Dunsire, and many other properties, castles, mills, etc, now incorporated into the Earldom and Barony of Bothwell. Sir Adam Hepburn was killed at the Battle of Flodden on 9 September 1513. [a territorial surname based on Hebburn in Northumberland, examples in Scotland date from the thirteenth century] [Mary Hepburn, from Edinburgh, was transported to Maryland in 1704, while Charles Hepburn settled on Cape Fear, North Carolina, by 1741.]

HEPBURN OF WALCHTOUN. On 9 July 1462, King James II granted Sir Patrick Hepburn the lands of Walchtoun with Whitfield in Midlothian, land in Cockburnspath, Berwickshire, also Athelstaneford in Midlothian, united into the Barony of Walchtoun; on 21 September 1498, King James IV granted Kentigern Hepburn, son and heir apparent of David Hepburn of Wauchtoun, the lands and Barony of Wauchtoun in Midlothian, the territory of Coldingham in Berwickshire, and the lands of Athelstaneford in Midlothian, also the land of Tolly in Fife.

HEPBURN OF DUNSIRE IN LANARKSHIRE. King James III granted the lands and Barony of Dunsire to Adam Hepburn, son and heir of Lord Patrick Hepburn of Hailes, on 13 October 1475; on 1 February 1480, King James III granted Patrick Hepburn, son of Patrick Hepburn, the lands and Barony of Dunsire, also the lands of Sheriffbigging in Berwickshire.this was confirmed on 6 February 1483.

HEPBURN OF POLGONY IN ABERDEENSHIRE. King James IV granted Adam Hepburn part of the lands and Barony of Dunloppy with its mill in Angus on 30 March 1498; On 18 November 1503, King James IV granted the Barony of Polgony to Sir Adam Hepburn of Craigs and his wife Elizabeth Ogston., and on 24 March 1504, the king granted them the lands and Barony of Craggis with Meigle in Perthshire and Connante with fishing rights on the North Water of Esk, Belllochquhy, Killaree, Wester Darre, Easter Darre with its mill,

Over Crag of Glenisla, Easter Crag of Glenisla, Nether Crag of Glenisla, Auchwary, Cookstoun with its mill, Blackstoun, Bauchlownas, Kinbraid and Auchnansis in Angus, also Wester and Easter Eglismaldis with their mills in Kincardineshire now all incorporated in the Barony of Craggis; this was confirmed by King James IV on 20 August 1505; on 22 February 1510, King James IV granted Adam Hepburn of Craggis, the lands and Baronie of Dunloppie in Angus with its mill and tenantries; Sir Adam died in battle in Northumberland later that year; King James IV King James V granted the lands and barony of Polgony to Patrick Hepburn, son and heir of Sir Adam Hepburn on 22 February 1528. [Charles Hepburn died in 1741 in North Carolina][Genealogical notes of the Hepburn family, London, 1925]

HEPBURN OF BANNOCKBURN IN STIRLINGSHIRE. On 19 September 1601, King James VI granted Elizabeth Hepburn, daughter of Sir Patrick Hepburn of Lufnes, and wife to be of Alexander Drummond of Carnok, the lands and Barony of Bannockburn

HEPBURN OF ESSILMONT IN ABERDEENSHIRE. On 25 February 1608, King James VI confirmed Patrick Hepburn of Smetoun in the lands and Barony of Essilmont in Aberdeenshire.

HERING OF GLASCLUNE IN PERTHSHIRE. On 23 February 1510, King James IV granted Andrew Hering of Glasclune, the lands and Barony of Glasclune with its manor Calbridistoun, Fornochthouse and fort, Glasclune, Over Balcarne, Balburdo, part of Over Fernocht, Ballany and Cothill with grain mills and fulling mills, the lands of Balkelly, Nether Balkarne, the lands of Lethendy, also the lands of Kirktoun, Pittendreich and Blackloch with mills in Perthshire, now incorporated into the Barony of Glasclune; on 10 March 1593, King James VI confirmed David Hering, son and heir of Andrew Hering of Glasclune the lands and Barony of Glasclune; on 23 July 1599, King James IV granted the lands and Barony of Glasclune to Andrew Hering of Glasclun. [Hering is an Old English surname, recorded in Scotland since the thirteenth century] [Patrick Herron, a prisoner of war, was transported to Boston in 1652, while Janet Herring, a Jacobite, was transported to Maryland in 1747]

HERIOT OF BURNTURK IN FIFE. On 14 June 1512, King James IV granted Walter Heriot, son and heir apparent of Walter Heriot of Burnturk, the lands of Burnturk, and parts of Ballingall and of Glaslie, now incorporated into the Barony of Burnturk; on 28 January 1557, Queen Mary confirmed Andrew Heriot, son and heir of Walter Heriot of Burnturk, in the lands and Barony of Burnturk. [A territorial surname derived from a place in Midlothian, examples date from the twelfth century][Captain Richard Heriot was bound for Nova Scotia in 1627, while David Heriot emigrated to East New Jersey in 1685][The Heriots of Ramornie, Dumfries, 1931]

HERKERS OF PRESTOUN IN DUMFRIES-SHIRE. King David II granted the Barony of Prestoun to Thomas Herkers around 1350. [A surname probably derived from Harcarse in Berwickshire] [Thomas Harkness, a Covenanter from Dumfries, was transported to the colonies in 1684, while Peter Harkness was a merchant in Montreal before 1822]

HERRIES OF TERREGLES IN KIRKCUDBRIGHTSHIRE. John Herries was granted the Barony of Terregles by King David II on 27 October 1365; on 1 June 1486, King James III, granted Andrew Herries, son and heir apparent of Herbert Harries, the lands and Baronies of Terreglis and of Kirkgunzeane, also part of the Barony of Ur in Dumfries-shire, plus the lands of Moffatdale, Avondale, Tornyngarth, Lockarby and Hoddam in Annandale, and the lands of Barnwell and Symondstoun in Ayrshire; on 25 February 1500, King James IV granted Andrew Herries, son and heir apparent of Herbert Herries, Lord Herries of Terregles, the lands and Baronies of Terregles and of Kirkgunzeane, with land in the Barony of Urr in Kirkcudbrightshire, the lands of Hoddam, Tolligarth, Lockerbie, Huttoun, Avondale, Moffatdale and Kirkandrews in Annandale, Fewrule in Roxburghshire, the lands of H. Bernwell and Symingtoun in Ayrshire; on 23 December 1506, King James IV granted Lord Andrew Herries, the lands of Myretoun-Makke in Wigtonshire also land in Douchire, Barskeuch, Ochiltree, Clouchlach, etc formed into the Barony of Myretoun-Herries; on 18 April 1510 King James IV granted Lord Andrew Herries the lands and Barony of Terregles, with its mills, the lands and Barony of Kirkgunzean, with tower, fort, mill tenantries, part of the Barony of Ur in Kirkcudbrightshire, the lands of Moffatdale and Avondale, part of Lockerbie, Huttoun, Tolnagarth, Hoddam, Ecclesfechan, Nether Ormandsby, Skelis, the lands and Barony of Morton Woods, with its mill, fishing rights in the Solway, the lands and Barony of Myretoun-Herries in Wigtonshire, the lands and Barony of Bernwell and Symontoun in Ayrshire, the lands of Fewrule in Roxburghshire, all incorporated into the Barony of Herries. Lord Herries was killed at the Battle of Flodden on 9 September 1513. [A surname recorded in Dumfries and Galloway since the thirteenth century.][Robert Herries, a Covenanter, was transported to the West Indies in 1678, while Walter Herries, a surgeon participated in the Darien Expedition of 1698.]

HERRIES OF COUSLAND IN MIDLOTHIAN. On 15 November 1600, King James VI granted Hugh Herries the lands and Barony of Cousland.

HILL OF WAUGHTON IN EAST LOTHIAN. On 4 February 1707 Colonel Scipio Hill, a Colonel of Cavalry, was created Baronet of Waughton, on his death on

21 November 1729, the baronetcy became dormant. [a locational surname, examples date from the thirteenth century][Thomas Hill, a joiner, was bound for South Carolina in 1775, while Janet Hill, from Edinburgh, was transported to Virginia in 1696]

HOLBURN OF MENSTRIE IN CLACKMANNANSHIRE. On 21 June 1706 James Holburn of Menstrie was created Baronet of Menstrie, on his death in January 1737 the title went to his son Sir James Holburn who died on 26 July 1758.

HOPE OF CRAIGHALL IN FIFE. On 19 February 1642, King Charles I granted Sir Thomas Hope of Craighall, an advocate, the Baronies of Hilltarvit and Craighall. Thomas Hope of Craighall, was created as a baronet of Nova Scotia on 19 February 1628; a sasine dated 9 May 1628, he died on 1 October 1646, and was succeeded by his son Sir John Hope as second Baronet of Craighall, he became a Lord of Session and an MP, he died in Edinburgh on 28 April 1654. His eldest son Sir Thomas Hope, born 1633, succeeded as third Baronet of Craighall, he died by 1663, then his son Sir Thomas Hope became the fourth baronet, the next baronet was Sir William Hope who died 14 November 1706, his brother Sir Thomas Hope then became the Sixth Baronet however when he inherited Kinross he became Bruce-Hope, and sold Craighall in 1729. [a territorial surname, examples date from the thirteenth century][Thomas Hope, a soldier, died in Jamaica around 1700, while John Hope, a merchant from Glasgow, settled in Virginia by 1776.]

HOPE OF KERSE IN STIRLINGSHIRE. On 30 May 1672, Alexander Hope, son of Sir Thomas Hope, was created as a Baronet, on his death in December 1673, his son Sir Alexander Hope became the 2nd Baronet, he died on 10 February 1719, when his son became the 3rd Baronet until his death on 24 February 1749.

HOPE OF KIRKLISTON IN WEST LOTHIAN. On 1 March 1698 Sir William Hope, born 1660, son of Sir James Hope of Hopetoun, was created Baronet of Kirkliston he was a career soldier and latterly Deputy Governor of Edinburgh Castle, he died on 1 February 1724 and was succeeded by his son Sir George Hope as 2nd Baronet, also a soldier who died in Ireland on 20 November 1729, the last Baronet was his son Sir William Hope, he was a Lieutenant of the Royal Navy, afterwards was a Lieutenant of the 31st Regiment of Foot, finally a Captain in the Service of the East India Company until killed in Bengal in 1763.

HOPPRINGLE OF MENNAR IN PEEBLES-SHIRE. David Pringle of Smailholm was killed at the Battle of Flodden on 9 September 1513. On 2 January 1535, King James V confirmed the grant of the Barony of Menner by David Hoppringle of Smailholme to his son James Hoppringle. [from a place in Roxburghshire, examples of Hoppringle or Pringle, date from the thirteenth century] [John Pringle settled on Prince Edward Island by 1769, while Walter Pringle was Governor of Dominica before 1768][Records of the Pringles or Hoppringles, Edinburgh, 1933]

HUME OF LANGSHAWS IN AYRSHIRE. King James II granted the lands of Langshaws, Castleton, Gallowbraes, Whitlees, Robertoun, Crennachblair, Kirkwood, and Mcbehill, all in the Lordship of Stewarton in Ayrshire, now incorporated into the Barony of Langshaws to Alexander Hume of that Ilk on 20 July 1451. A surname from a place in Berwickshire, examples date from the thirteenth century][George Home of Wedderburn, a Jacobite, was transported to Virginia in 1721, while Jean Home, an arsonist, was transported to the colonies in 1769.][Family History of the Homes, 1927]

HUME OF HUME IN BERWICKSHIRE. On 28 February 1452, King James II granted Alexander Hume, son and heir of Sir Alexander Hume of that Ilk, the lands of Dunglas, Hume, Susterpath and Kello in Berwickshire now incorporated and united as the barony of Hume; King James II granted the lands of Chirnside in Berwickshire to Alexander Hume which were included into the Barony of Hume; also, on 28 February 1452 the King granted some land in Berwickshire to be incorporated in the Barony of Hume, confirmed on 4 January 1490; King James IV granted Alexander Hume of that Ilk, the lands and Barony of Tulchadam in Stirlingshire on 1 April 1489; King James IV granted Alexander Hume the lands and Barony of Broxfield in Roxburghshire now united into the Barony of Hume on 26 June 1490; King James IV granted Alexander Home of Home the Barony of Dunbar on 28 April 1491; on 4 July 1491 King James IV granted Lord Alexander Hume the lands of Easter Upsidlintoun with fishing rights at Haliwell on the Tweed and Todrick in Berwickshire; on 4 February 1510, King James IV granted Lord Alexander Hume, the lands and Barony of Hume and Dunglas, with castles, forts, etc., the lands of Susterpeth, Kello, Chirnside, with mills, lands in Letham, Leyhouse, Hulawis, Manderstoun, Hassingtoun, the lands and Barony of Easter Upsettlingtoun with fishing rights at Holywell on the River Tweed, lands of Todrick, Betseschiell, land in Duns, Panlaurig, lands of Foulshotlaws, in Berwickshire, the lands and Barony of Hassingdean, the lands of Appletreehall, the lands and Barony of Broxfield with its mills in

Roxburghshire, part of the lands of Inverallon with mill in Stirlingshire, plus the lands and Barony of Hownam Mains, Over Chatto, Over Crailing with manor house and mill, and the lands of Lyn in Roxburghshire, now incorporated into the Barony of Hume; on 9 June 1516, King James V confirmed the grant of the lands and Lordship of Dunglas to Lord Alexander Hume, now part of the Lordship and Barony of Hume; on 22 June 1535, King James V granted Lord George Hume part of the Barony of Dirltoun, part of the lands of the Barony of West Fentoun in East Lothian, part of the Lordship of Haliburton, the Barony of Lambdean in Berwickshire, part of the lands and Barony of Segie in Kinross-shire, part of the Baronies of Balgarno, Abernyte, Forgandenny in Perthshire, the lands and Barony of Broxfield in Roxburghshire, the lands and Baronies of Hume and Dungl in Roxburghshire with castles, forts, mills etc, the lands and Barony of Upper Settlington, the lands of Greenlaw, in Berwickshire, the lands and Barony of Hassindene, the lands and Barony of Hownam in Roxburghshire, the lands of Inverallan in Stirlingshire, the lands and Barony of Ewisdale in Dumfriesshire, etc, incorporated into the Barony of Hume; on 1 April 1538, King James V granted Lord George Hume many lands and Baronies now incorporated into the Barony of Hume; on 4 February 1558, Queen Mary confirmed Lord Alexander Hume in the lands and Barony of Broxfield; on 14 July 1638, King Charles I granted James Hume, Earl of Home, the lands and Barony of Dunglas, the lands and Barony of Home, the lands and Barony of Hassinden, the lands and Barony of Broxfield, etc. [a surname derived from Home in Berwickshire, examples date from the late thirteenth century] [Benjamin Hume died in Jamaica in 1733]

HOME OF EARLSTOUN IN BERWICKSHIRE. On 26 November 1489 King James IV granted John Hume of Whiterig the lands and town of Earlston with its mill, the lands of Brotherstone and Whiterig with mill-land in Merton, now united into the Barony of Earlstoun; on 4 March 1506 King James IV granted Kentigern Hume the lands and Barony of Earlstoun; on 24 March 1564, Queen Mary granted John Hume of Coldinknowis, the lands and Barony of Earlstoun; on 31 August 1592, King James VI confirmed John Home, son and heir of James Home of Coldinknowis, the lands and Barony of Earlstoun.

HUME OF GLENESK IN ANGUS. King James IV granted Mariota Hume, daughter of Lord Alexander Hume, the lands and Barony of Glenesk with the manor of Dalbeg, in Angus, also the lands and Barony of Meigle with its mill in Perthshire, on 4 August 1493.

HUME OF WEDDERBURN IN BERWICKSHIRE. Sir David Home of Wedderburn was killed at the Battle of Flodden on 9 September 1513. On 12 September 1597, King James VI, confirmed David Hume, son and heir apparent of George Home of Wedderburn, in the Barony of Hornden. In 1638 King Charles I created Sir David Hume, the Baronet of Wedderburn by King Charles I n 1638, he was an M.P. and was killed at the Battle of Dunbar on 3 September 1650. On 23 March 1649, King Charles I granted George Home, eldest son of George Home of Wedderburn, the Barony of Horndean; he was succeeded by his grandson, George Hume, as second Baronet, however, as he supported the Jacobites in 1715 his title was forfeited to the Crown in 1716.

HOME OF BEDRULE IN ROXBURGHSHIRE. On 14 June 1589, King James VI granted James Home of Coldinknows, the lands and Barony of Bedrule.

HOME OF NORTH BERWICK IN EAST LOTHIAN. On 16 October 1591, King James VI confirmed Alexander Home in the lands and Barony of North Berwick.

HOME OF LADYKIRK IN BERWICKSHIRE. On 18 November 1591, King James VI confirmed George Home, son of Alexander Home of Huttounhall, in the lands and Barony of Upsettlingtoun alias Ladykirk.

HOME OF SPOTT IN BERWICKSHIRE. On 10 June 1592, King James VI granted Sir George Home of Primroknow, the lands and Barony of Spott; on 14 June 1594, King James VI granted Sir George Home of Spott, the lands and Barony of Gairtlie; on 2 July 1595, King James VI granted Sor George Home of Spott, the lands and Barony of Greenlaw-Redpath.

HUME OF POLWARTH IN BERWICKSHIRE. Patrick Hume was created as a baronet of Nova Scotia on 28 December 1625. [Sir George Home emigrated to Port Royal, Nova Scotia, in 1630].

HUME OF BLACKADDER IN BERWICKSHIRE. On 25 January 1671, John Hume or Home was created as a Baronet, he died in France on 23 January 1675, and was succeeded by his son Sir John Hume as 2nd Baronet of Blackadder, he died 4 April 1706 to be succeeded by his son Sir John Hume the 3rd Baronet.

HOME OF RENTON IN BERWICKSHIRE. Around 1675 Sir Alexander Home was created as a Baronet, on his death on 28 May 1698, his son Sir Robert Home became the 2nd Baroner of Renton.

ILES OF LUNDY IN ANGUS. King David II granted the Barony of Lundy to John Iles around 1322.

INGLIS OF MANER IN PEEBLES-SHIRE. King Robert III granted William Inglis the Barony of Maner on 2 October 1395. [The surname means 'English', examples date from the mid twelfth century] [Mungo Inglis, a tutor at the College of William and Mary from 1694 until 1705, while Peter Inglis, from Edinburgh, was transported to Maryland in 1772.][Inglis of Auchendinny and Redhall, Edinburgh, 1914]

INGLIS OF TARVIT IN FIFE. On 6 March 1488 King James III granted Andrew Inglis the lands of Tarwald and Caploquhy with their mills, and the lands of Balbirnie in Fife now formed into the Barony of Tarwald, [Tarvet], on 7 February 1541, King James V confirmed Alexander Inglis of Tarvit in the lands, tower and mill of Tarvit, Caple with mills, Bawbirne, and fishing rights, in Fife, incorporated into the Barony of Tarvit; on 1 December 1579, King James VI granted John Inglis, son and heir apparent of Alexander Inglis of Tarvit, the lands and Barony of Tarvit.

INGLIS OF STRICHEN IN ABERDEENSHIRE. On 23 March 1649, King Charles II granted Marjorie Inglis, widow of George Peacock an apothecary burgess of Aberdeen, and wife of Paul Collison, the lands and Barony of Strichen.

INNES OF TOUGH IN ABERDEENSHIRE. On 13 December 1507, King James IV granted Walter Innes the lands of Tough, and part of Pitfour, now incorporated into the Barony of Tough. [The surname is derived from a location in Moray called 'innis' which is Gaelic for an island, a site of Flemish settlement in the thirteenth century, examples of the surname date from the thirteenth century] [Reverend Alexander Innes, emigrated to New England in 1693 and died in New Jersey in 1713, while Katherine Innes emigrated to Philadelphia in 1775][The Family of Innes, Aberdeen, 1864]

INNES OF MONYCABO IN ABERDEENSHIRE. On 2 September 1531, King James V confirmed Robert Innes of Invermarky, in the lands and Barony of Monycabo with its mill.

INNES OF ARDGRANE IN ABERDEENSHIRE. On 19 January 1535, King James V confirmed the grant by Robert Innes of Invermerky to his son Alexander Innes of the lands and Barony of Ardgrane, Cauldwells and Peltauchty in Aberdeenshire

INNES OF UGSTOUN IN MORAY. The lands of Ugstoun and Pleulands, which had been inherited by Elizabeth Hepburn, daughter of the deceased Sir Adam Hepburn, were granted by King James V to Robert Innes of Invermarky who then incorporated them into the barony of Ugstoun on

1 September 1539; on 12 June 1553, Queen Mary, confirmed Margaret Innes, daughter of Alexander Innes of that Ilk, in the lands and Barony of Ugstoun.

INNES OF INNES IN MORAY. On 25 March 1539, King James V, confirmed Alexander Innes of that Ilk, including various lands in Moray and Banffshire, incorporated in the Barony of Innes; Sir Robert Innes in Urquhart, Moray, was created a baronet of Innes, Nova Scotia, on 28 May 1625, by King Charles I, a sasine dated 20 May 1628; and was also baronet of Delny in 1631. Sir Robert was a politician and a Royalist. His wife was Grizel Stewart, daughter of the Earl of Moray. Their son Robert inherited the barony around 1655. Sir Robert Innes of Innes was a Member of Parliament and husband of Margaret Scott, daughter of Walter Scott of Buccleuch. Their son Sir James Innes succeeded to the barony around 1690. He married Margaret Hay, daughter of the Earl of Erroll. Their son Sir Harry Innes [1670 -1721] became the 4TH Baronet around 1700. His wife was Anne Grant, daughter of Sir James Grant, their son inherited the barony of Innes. He married Jean Forbes in 1694. He died on 12 November 1721. The next baronet was Sir Harry Innes who married Anne Colquhoun in 1727, and he died on 31 October 1762.

INNES OF PLAIDIS IN ROSS-SHIRE. On 20 February 1552, Queen Mary confirmed Alexander Innes of Catboll in the Barony and Lordship of Plaidis.

INNES OF TOUGH IN ABERDEENSHIRE. On 5 September 1595, King James VI granted Walter Innes of Auchintoule the lands of Tough and Pitfour incorporated into the Barony of Tough.

INNES OF CARNOUSIE IN BANFFSHIRE. On 5 September 1595, King James VI granted George Ogilvy, son of George Ogilvy of Dunlugas, the land and Barony of Carnousie.

INNES OF BALVENY IN BANNFSHIRE. On 12 January 1628, Robert Innes of Balveny was created as a Baronet by King Charles I, when he died around 1650 he was succeeded by his son Sir Walter Innes who was a Royalist during the Wars of the Three Kingdoms and had to sell Balveny in the aftermath.

INNES OF COXTOUN IN BANFFSHIRE. On 11 June 1658, Oliver Cromwell, the Lord Protector, granted Sir Alexander Innes of Coxtoun the lands, Lordship and Barony of Balveney with its manor-place, castles, towers, fortalices, teinds and others, formerly held by Sir Robert Innes.

IRVINE OF DRUM IN ABERDEENSHIRE. On 26 February 1507, King James IV granted Sir Alexander Irvine of Drum the lands of the Park of Drum with its forest and mills in Kincardineshire, also the lands of Lonmay, Largneis, Auchindore, Fulzemont, and Tarland with mills in Aberdeenshire, now created as the Barony of Drum. [a territorial surname from Irving in Dumfries-shire, and Irvine in Ayrshire, examples date from the thirteen century][Andrew Irvine from Shetland emigrated to Barbados in 1684, while David Irvine, emigrated from Dumfries to Prince Edward Island in 1775.] [The Irvines of Drum, Peterhead, 1920]

IRVINE OF LENTURKS IN ABERDEENSHIRE. On 15 July 1597, King James VI confirmed Alexander Irvine of Easter Beltie, in the Barony of Lenturks.

JARDINE OF APPLEGIRTH IN DUMFRIES-SHIRE. On 16 September 1559, King Francis and Queen Mary confirmed Alexander Jardine, son and heir apparent of John Jardine of Applegirth, in the lands and Barony of Hartside; Alexander Jardine of Applegirth was created as a Baronet on 25 May 1672, he died in August 1683 when his son Sir Alexander Jardine became the 2nd Baronet, on his death in 1699 the Baronetcy went to his brother Sir John Jardine who died in 1737. [possibly a surname of Norman French origin, examples date from the twelfth century][Andrew Jardine, a Covenanter, was transported to the colonies in 1685, while William Jarden died in Antigua in 1705.]

JOHNSTOUN OF KIRKMICHAEL IN DUMFRIES-SHIRE. On 5 March 1464 King James III granted Herbert Johnstoun of Dalebank, the Barony of Kirkmichael, comprising the lands of Nese and Gleneybank, Dalcrom, Cragshiels, in Dumfries-shire. [a surname dating from the twelfth century, which may originate in Perth, once known as St John's town] [John Johnston, settled in Boston by 1665, while Gabriel Johnston was Governor of North Carolina, died there in 1752] [A History of the Johnstones, 1191-1909, Edinburgh 1909]

JOHNSTOUN OF NEWBY IN DUMFRIES-SHIRE. On 8 January 1542, King James V, granted the lands of Newby, with its tower, fort, manor, mill, etc also fishing rights, plus other lands in Annandale, now incorporated into the Barony of Newby.

JOHNSTOUN OF JOHNSTOUN IN DUMFRIES-SHIRE. On 2 March 1543, Queen Mary granted John Johnstoun of that Ilk the Barony of Johnstoun; on 7 October 1548, Queen Mary granted George Johnstoun, nephew of James Johnstoun of Johnstoun, the lands of Johnstoun now incorporated into the Barony of Johnstoun; on 23 August 1587, King James VI confirmed John

Johnstoun, son and heir apparent of George Johnstoun of that Ilk, in the lands and Barony of Johnstoun.

JOHNSTOUN OF WAMPHRAY IN DUMFRIES-SHIRE. On 24 January 1550, Queen Mary confirmed James Johnstoun in the lands and Lordship of Wamphray.

JOHNSTOUN OF CASKIBEN IN ABERDEENSHIRE. George Johnston of Caskieben was created as Baronet of Johnston in Nova Scotia on 31 March 1626; a sasine dated 25 May 1626.

JOHNSTON OF ELPHINSTONE IN NOVA SCOTIA. On 18 October 1628, King Charles I granted Samuel Johnston, of Elphinstone in East Lothian, son of Patrick Johnston, a Baronet of Nova Scotia. He died around 1644 and was succeeded by his son Sir John Johnston as the second Baronet, when he died around 1666 his son Sir James Johnston became the third Baronet.

JOHNSTONES OF LIBERTON IN MIDLOTHIAN. On 1 January 1658, Oliver Cromwell, the Lord Protector granted Samuel Johnston of Chiennes, the lands and Barony of Nether Liberton, which with the lands and Barony of Over Liberton now united into one Barony of Liberton. [Most Johnston families trace their origins back to a John Johnstoun who settled in Annandale during the twelfth century. By the Early Modern Period the Johnstones were one of the most powerful reiving families on the Wester Borders.

JOHNSTONE OF WESTERHALL IN DUMFRIES-SHIRE. On 25 April 1700, John Johnstone, son of Sir James Johnstone MP, was created as a Baronet, he died at Tournai, Flanders, on 30 September 1711.

KEITH OF STRACHAN IN KINCARDINESHIRE. King Robert II granted Robert Keith, son of William Keith and his wife Margaret Frazer, the Barony of Strachan around 1380. [An account of the Ancient and Noble family of Keith, Peterhead, 1820]

KEITH OF TROUP IN BANFFSHIRE. Robert Keith, son of Robert Keith the Marischal of Scotland, was granted the Barony of Troup before 1424.

KEITH, WILLIAM, was granted the castle and Barony of Dunnottar by King Robert III before 1424; William Keith, the Earl Marischal, was granted the lands of Aldene in Aberdeenshire, also Pitinblae in the Barony of Kinedward on 10 November 1505; on 5 August 1587, King James VI confirmed George Keith, the Earl Marischal, the lands, Lordship and Barony of Keith Marischal, also the lands and Barony of Owres in Kincardine, the lands and Barony of Kintore in Aberdeenshire, the lands and Barony of Troup in Banffshire, the lands and Barony of Inverugy in Banffshire, the lands and Barony of Strabrok in West Lothian, the lands and Barony of Dunnottar, the lands and Barony of Fetteresso, the lands and Barony of Garvok, the lands and Barony of Bordland of Rattray, etc; on 22 April 1525, William Keith, nephew and heir apparent of William Keith, the Earl Marshall, was granted the lands and Barony of Dunnottar, with its castle, mills, etc, the lands and manor-house of Fetteresso, the lands and Barony of Garvock with fishing rights at Bervie, Cowie and Durris with crofts in Kincardineshire, the lands and Barony of Keith with its tower and fort, the office of Earl Marshall of Scotland and Constable of Haddington, etc; was created as a Baronet of Nova Scotia on , the 28 May 1625. This baronetcy was forfeited in 1716 due to the baron's Jacobitism, he joined the Jacobite Rising in 1745, and was killed at the Battle of Culloden on 12 April 1746. [the surname is derived from the lands of Keith in East Lothian; examples date from the twelfth century] [Dr James Keith settled in Barbados by 1678, while Sir Basil Keith was Governor of Jamaica before 1777]

KEITH OF INVERUGY IN ABERDEENSHIRE. On 6 October 1508, King James IV granted William Keith of Inverugy the lands of Straloch in Banffshire, now united into the Barony of Inverugy; on 30 June 1538 King James V had various properties in Caithness merged into the Barony of Inverugy; on 26 September 1592, King James VI granted George Keith, the Earl Marischal, the Lordship and Barony of Inverugy, also the Baronies of Strachan, Kintore, Easter Skryne, Auden, etc.

KEITH OF BENHOLME IN KINCARDINESHIRE. On 30 July 1587, King James VI confirmed Robert Keith of Benholme in the lands and Barony of Benholme; on 15 July 1594, King James VI granted Robert Keith, brother german of George Keith the Keith Marischal, the lands and Barony of Benholme etc.

KEITH OF DINGWALL IN EASTER ROSS. On 3 August 1587, King James VI granted Sir Andrew Keith of Dingwall, the castle and burgh of Dingwall with several local lands now incorporated into the Lordship and Barony of Dingwall; on 24 November 1591, king James VI confirmed Lord Andrew Keith in the lands, Lordship and Barony of Dingwall; on 22 January 1593, King James VI granted William Keith of Delny, the lands, Lordship and Barony of Dingwall.

KEITH OF LESLIE IN ABERDEENSHIRE. On 15 January 1589, King James VI granted Sir William Keith of Delnie, the lands and Barony of Leslie.

KEITH OF LUDQUHARME. Sir William Keith was created as a Baronet of Nova Scotia on 28 July 1629.

KEITH OF POWBURN IN KINCARDINESHIRE. On 4 June 1663, King Charles II created James Keith as a Baronet. On his death around 1690 the Baronetcy became extinct.

KEMPT OF BELHELVIE IN ABERDEENSHIRE. On 3 July 1538, King James V granted the lands and Baronies of Belhelvie and of Curtastoun to Henry Kempt of Thomastoun. [a surname recorded in Aberdeenshire since the fourteenth century][John Kemo was a militiaman in Virginia in 1757, while Archibald Kemp was a farmer in South Carolina by 1850][A general history of the Kemp families, London, 1902]

KENNEDY OF DALRYMPLE IN AYRSHIRE. In 1377 King Robert II granted the Barony of Dalrymple to a John Kennedy; on 27 January 1406 King Robert III granted the Barony of Dalrymple to James Kennedy; King James II granted James Kennedy, son of Sir Gilbert Kennedy, the Barony of Dalrymple on 21 November 1450; [the surname comes from the Gaelic name *Ceannaideach*, examples in Scotland date from the twelfth century] [Adam Kennedy settled in Antigua before 1698; while John Kennedy was transported to Virginia in 1666].

KENNEDY OF GLENSTINQUHARE IN AYRSHIRE. On 17 May 1473, King James III granted James Kennedy, son of Lord James Kennedy, the lands and Barony of Glenstinquhare and other lands in Ayrshire united into a barony on 17 May 1473.

KENNEDY OF ARDSTINCHELL IN AYRSHIRE. On 20 August 1429 King James I granted certain lands in Ayrshire, now united into the Barony of Ardstinchell. [Alexander Kennedy a cooper from Edinburgh, settled in Fredericksburg, Virginia, in 1774]

KENNEDY OF KIRKMICHAEL IN AYRSHIRE. King James I granted lands in Carrick, Ayrshire, now united into the Barony of Kirkmichael to David Kennedy on 24 August 1429.

KENNEDY OF DALCHQUHARNE IN AYRSHIRE. On 3 August 1450 King James II granted the Barony of Dalchquharne to Gilbert Kennedy.

KENNEDY OF MYRETOUN IN WIGTONSHIRE. On 10 December 1477, King James III granted John Kennedy of Blairwhan, the lands of Frethride, the lands of Skeche and Myretoun united into the Barony of Myretoun, which was made a burgh of barony.

KENNEDY OF LESWALT IN WIGTONSHIRE. King James III granted Lord James Kennedy the lands and Barony of Leswalt and the land of Slewdonale, the lands of Turnberry, Tawboyag, and Garvanhead in Ayrshire, on 24 January

1483, this was confirmed by King James IV on 24 January 1489; King James IV granted Alexander Kennedy, son of John Kennedy, the lands and Barony of Leswalt, Menybrig, and Barquhonny in Wgtonshire, also the lands of Mule, Gartrowan, Drummokloch, Balker, Meikle Larg, Auchmattill and Pollaneregane, on 21 February 1500, this was confirmed by King James IV on 30 March 1506.

KENNEDY OF BRAIDWOOD IN LANARKSHIRE. On 24 July 1498, King James IV granted Janet Kennedy, daughter of Lord John Kennedy, the lands and Barony of Braidwood with its fort and tenantries at Hewes, on 21 July 1498; the king also granted her the lands and Barony of Crawford-Lindesay, with its castle, fort and chapel on 25 September 1498; on 7 February 1510, King James IV confirmed Janet Kennedy, daughter of Lord John Kennedy, with the lands and Barony and Lordship of Bothwell with its castle and fort in Lanarkshire.

KENNEDY OF CASSILLIS AND DUNURE IN AYRSHIRE. King James IV granted David Kennedy, son and heir apparent of Lord John Kennedy, the lands and Baronies of Cassillis and Dunure on 17 February 1502; on 5 February 1512, King James IV granted David Kennedy, the Earl of Cassillis, the castle and manor house of Cassillis, including its mill, the Park of Cassillis, Blairboye, Crawfordstoun, Pinmureis, Giltremakgrane, Arinscheyn, Carsantoun, Hillhouse, Dounscheistoun, Bernfurd, Troquhan, Makilweynstoun, Montgomerystoun, Giltre, Ferdinwilliame, Kilmoris, Dalmortoun, Dalreoch, the lands of Glenschinschare, Row, Balloch, Knockiness, and many others now incorporated into the Barony of Cassillis. The Earl of Cassillis was killed at the Battle of Flodden on 9 September 1513. On 13 February 1542, King James V granted Gilbert Kennedy, Earl of Cassillis, the Barony of Culzeanand on 31 August 1542, the king also granted him the lands and Barony of Dunure, which included Dunure Castle, fort and mill, and the lands of Glennop in Ayrshire; on 8 March 1575, King James VI granted Gilbert Kennedy, Earl of Cassillis, the lands and Barony of Turnberry in Ayrshire; on 13 August 1597, King James VI granted John Kennedy the Earl of Cassillis, the lands and Barony of Culzean; on 26 January 1599, King James VI granted John Kennedy the Earl of Cassillis, several lands in Wigtonshire incorporated into the lands and Barony of Glen Luce. [The noble family of Kennedy, Marquess of Ailsa and Earl of Cassillis, Edinburgh,1849]

KENNEDY OF TWYNHOLM IN KIRKCUDBRIGHTSHIRE. On1 March 1505, King James IV granted Sir Gavin Kennedy, son of Sir John Kennedy of Blairwhan, the lands and Barony of Twynholm, with its castle, fort, mills, tenantries, etc, also the lands and Barony of Myretoun, with its tower, fort, mill, multures tenantries, etc in Wigtonshire, plus various lands in Ayrshire; On

27 February 1506, King James IV granted Sir Gavin Kennedy of Blairwhant, the lands and Barony of Frethird in Galloway; on 13 February 1551, Queen Mary, granted John Kennedy, nephew and heir apparent of James Kennedy of Blairwhan, the lands and Barony of Twynholm.

KENNEDY OF BARGALTOUN IN KIRKCUDBRIGHTSHIRE. On 21 April 1513, King James IV granted Sir John Kennedy of Culzean, the lands and Barony of Bargaltoun, including Bargaltoun, Largeschean, Deremole, Culevane, Donane, and Greensoderm.

KENNEDY OF MAKGUMRISTOUN IN AYRSHIRE. On 12 June 1542, King James V granted Hugh Kennedy, son of Hugh Kennedy of Girvan Mains, various lands in Ayrshire, now incorporated int the Barony of Makgumristoun, the king also granted him the Barony of Girvan.

KENNEDY OF DALQUHARRAN IN AYRSHIRE. On 24 June 1542, King James V granted David Kennedy, brother german of Gilbert Kennedy the Earl of Cassillis, various lands in Ayrshire incorporated into the Barony of Dalquharran.

KENNEDY OF CARDNES IN KIRKCUDBRIGHTSHIRE. On 23 January 1572, King James VI granted Thomas Kennedy of Bargany, the lands and Barony of Cardnes; on 7 January 1592, King James VI granted Thomas Kennedy of Bargany, the lands and Barony of Corswell in Wigtonshire.

KENNEDY OF BLAIRQUHAN IN KIRKCUDBRIGHTSHIRE. On 27 March 1575, King James VI confirmed John Kennedy of Blairquhan in the lands and Barony of Tuynan in Kirkcudbrightshire, the lands and Barony of Myrtoun in Wigtonshire, and lands in Ayrshire, now incorporated into the Barony of Blairquhan.

KENNEDY OF THORNTOUN IN KINCARDINESHIRE. On 17 December 1638, King Charles I granted John Kennedy of Ardgeight, the lands and Barony of Thorntoun.

KENNEDY OF GIRVANMAINS IN AYRSHIRE. On 4 August 1673, John Kennedy was created as a Baronet, on his death by 1700 his kinsman Sir Gilbert Kennedy became the 2nd Baronet of Girvan Mains.

KENNEDY OF CULZEAN IN AYRSHIRE. On 8 December 1682 Archibald Kennedy was created as a Baronet, he died in 1710 and was succeeded by his son Sir John Kennedy as the 2nd Baronet.

KENNEDY OF CLOWBURN IN LANARKSHIRE. On 8 June 1698, Andrew Kennedy, the Conservator of the Scots Privileges in the Low Countries, was created a Baronet, he died in February 1717.

KENNOWAY OF SAUCHIE IN CLACKMANNANSHIRE. On 12 February 1639, King Charles I granted Alexander Kennoway, son of Peter Kennoway of Kittilstoun, the lands and Barony of Sauchie etc. [a locational surname from Fife, examples date from the seventeenth century]

KERR OF ROXBURGH IN ROXBURGHSHIRE. King James II granted Andrew Kerr of Altounbourne the land and Barony of Old Roxburgh on 6 February 1452. [the surname may be derived from a location in the Borders, examples date from the twelfth century][Anna Kerr, from Edinburgh, was transported to Virginia in 1696, while Thomas Kerr, an engineer at Darien died in the West Indies around 1700]

KER OF CESFORD IN ROXBURGHSHIRE. King James III granted Walter Ker, son and heir apparent of Andrew Ker of Cesford, the lands and Barony of Cesford with its castle, with the lands of Huntersland in the Lordship of Caverton, also the lands and Barony of Auld Roxburgh, the lands of Altonburn, the lands of Primyside and land at Smailholm, merged into the Barony of Cesford on 5 April 1474, this was confirmed on 8 May 1481; King James IV granted Walter Ker the lands and Barony of Cesford on 13 March 1494; on 21 September 1542, King James V granted Walter Ker of Cesford, the lands of Cesford, parts of Cavertoun and Rutherfordsland, also the lands of Fotheringham with mills, towers, forts, fishing rights, etc, now incorporated in the Barony of Primside, also lands in Roxburghshire incorporated into the Barony of Cesford; on 12 March 1554, Queen Mary granted Andrew Ker, son and heir apparent of Sir Walter Ker of Cesford, the lands and Barony of Cesford; on 22 March 1574, King James VI granted Robert Ker, son and heir apparent of William Ker of Cesford, the younger, the lands and Barony of Cesford, and the lands and Barony of Auld Roxburgh, etc.; on 16 August 1587, King James VI granted William Ker of Cesford, the lands and Barony of Ormistoun; on 8 April 1588, King James VI granted William Ker of Cesford, the Barony of Roxburgh; on 20 July 1595. King James VI confirmed William Ker of Cesford, son of Walter Ker of Cesford, in the Barony of Erneheuch; on 29 January 1642, King Charles I granted Robert Ker of Cesford the lands and Barony of Broxfield. [Pedigree of Ker of Cesford, Newcastle, 1914]

KER OF LOWISLAW IN ROXBURGHSHIRE. King James IV granted Robert Ker, son of Walter Ker of Cesford, Lowislaw in Yetholm, with land in Kirk Yetholm, now united into the Barony of Lowislaw, on 18 February 1491.

KER OF BROXFIELD IN ROXBURGHSHIRE. On 22 November 1516, King James V granted Mark Ker of Dolphintoun, the lands and Barony of Broxfield with its mill, tenantries, etc, also Faircross, Fluris, Gallowlaw, and Easter Meirdean.

KER OF OXNAM IN ROXBURGHSHIRE. On 17 January 1524, King James V granted Andrew Ker of Fernyhurst the lands and Barony of Oxnam.

KER OF FERNIEHURST IN ROXBURGHSHIRE. On 21 May 1540, King James V confirmed Andrew Ker of Ferniehurst in the lands of Ferniehurst, Corrosheuch, Limekilwood, Quarterwood, Langlee and Gillistoinges in Jedburgh Forest, land in Langtoun, Rekiltoun, Wemyss-land, also the lands and Lordship of Oxnam, with tower, mansion, mills, fishing rights, etc, in Roxburghshire, now incorporated into the Barony of Ferniehurst.

KER OF PRESTONGRANGE IN MIDLOTHIAN. On 15 October 1591, King James VI granted Mark Ker, Lord Newbattle, the Barony of Prestongrange and the Barony of Newbattle; on 5 March 1642, King Charles I granted William Ker of Newbattle the Lordship and Barony of Jedburgh.

KER OF GREENHEAD IN ROXBURGHSHIRE. Andrew Ker was created as Baronet of Greenhead of Nova Scotia on 31 July 1637. [John Kerr, a surgeon at Hudson Bay in 1681]

KERR OF ORMESTOUN IN ROXBURGHSHIRE. On 24 January 1592, King James VI granted Mark Ker, son and heir of William Ker of Cesford – the Warden of the Marches, the lands and Barony of Ormestoun; on 8 December 1665, William Kerr of Chatto, son of Andrew Kerr of Chatto, deceased, was granted the lands and Barony of Ormestoun.

KER OF LANGNEWTOUN IN ROXBURGHSHIRE. On 19 February 1642, King Charles I granted Anne Ker, the Barony of Newbattle.

KER OF OXNAM IN ROXBURGHSHIRE. On 4 April 1649, King Charles II granted William Ker of Naetoun, the lands and Lordship of Oxnam.

KILPATRICK OF CLOSEBURN IN DUMFRIES-SHIRE. King James III granted Thomas Kirkpatrick, the lands and Barony of Closeburn, and the Barony of Birdburgh, also the lands of Auchenleck and Sundrum in Dumfries-shire on 15 October 1470. [a surname meaning 'church of [St] Patrick'; examples date from the late thirteenth century] [Reverend Robert Kilpatrick, settled in Newfoundland in 1730, died at Trinity Bay in 1741]

KINNAIRD OF KINNAIRD IN PERTHSHIRE. On 7 May 1440, King James II granted the Barony of Kinnaird to Alan Kinnaird, son of Thomas Kinnaird; on 2 March 1484, King James III granted Alan Kinnaird, the lands and Barony of Kinnaird and the Barony of Nauchton, also the ferry and Sea-mills, and fishing rights there. [A surname derived from the lands in Perthshire granted to Randolph Rufus in 1180, examples date from the twelfth century][Sir Alexander Kinloch died at Darien in 1699, while Robert Kinnaird settled in Barbados by 1679] [The Kinnairds of Culbin, Inverness, 1938]

KINNAIRD OF INCHTURE IN PERTHSHIRE. King Robert III granted the Barony of Inchture to Ronald Kinnaird around 1403.

KINNEAR OF KINNEAR IN FIFE. King Robert II granted the barony of Kinnear in Fife to a John Kinnear, son of Reginald Kinnear, in 1378; on 21 December 1483 King James III granted John Kinnear, son of David Kinnear, the lands and Barony of Kinnear; on 11 March 1512, King James IV granted John Kinnear of that Ilk, the lands and Barony of Kinnear, with its manor-house, tower and fort also its mill, Caithlock with its mill, the lands of Thanisland, part of Strobirne, Fordale, Fothers, plus part of the land of Kittidy and Craigsumqhar, in Fife, now incorporated into the Barony of Kinnear.; on 7 February 1548, Queen Mary granted David Kinnear, son and heir apparent of John Kinnear of that Ilk, the lands and Barony of Kinnear. [A surname of territorial origin based on a location in Fife; examples date from the thirteenth century] [Alexander Kinnear was a sailor bound for Darien in 1698, while John Kinnear emigrated to New York in 1774].

KINNINMOND OF CRAIGHALL IN FIFE. On 26 March 1474 King James III granted Sir John Kinninmond of Craighall part of the lands the Barony of Ceres, part of the lands of Craighall and Callench, of Baltuly, Kingarroch, and Pitscottie, incorporated into the Barony of Craighall; on 28 November 1510, King James IV granted Andrew Kinninmonth part of the Barony of Ceres, part of Craighall, and of Callench, Baltuly, Kingarroch, and Pitscottie, the lands of Urquhart also part of Pitferran, now incorporated into the Barony of Craighall; on 21 February 1527, King James V confirmed Andrew Kinninmonth in the lands and Barony of Craighall, Ceres, and Callangis, with mills, fishing, etc; on 9 July 1589, King James VI confirmed David Kinninmont, son of Andrew Kinninmonth of Craighall, the lands and Barony of Craighall. [A placename in Fife, as a surname examples date from the twelfth century] [Ambrose Kinamont was a juryman in Annapolis, Maryland, in 1699]

KINROSS OF KIPPANROS IN PERTHSHIRE. On 6 December 1584, King James VI granted James Kinross, son and heir apparent of James Kinross of

Kippanros, the lands and Barony of Kinross. [a surname derived from the lands of Kinross, examples date from the twelfth century]

KIRKCALDY OF GRANGE. On 4 February 1541, King James V, confirmed James Kirkcaldy of Grange, the Royal Treasurer, with the Barony of Auchtertool in Fife, including Auchtertool, Welltou, Hallyards, Easter Clyntray, and the loch of Orisburne; and on 7 February 1541, King James V confirmed James Kirkcaldy of Grange in the lands of Grangewith its tower, fort, manor, orchards, the collieries at Tiry, the lands of Banchrie, Pitedy, Pitkyne, Turlvany, Balberdy and the castle of Kinhorn, in Fife, all incorporated into the Barony of Grange; on 22 May 1564, Queen Mary granted William Kirkcaldy the lands and Barony of Grange in Fife; on 13 January 1599, King James VI confirmed William Kirkcaldy of Grange, in the lands and Barony of Grange including lands in Fife now incorporated in the said Barony; on 14 May 1664, King Charles II created John Kirkcaldy as a Baronet. [a surname derived a burgh in Fife, examples date from the late thirteenth century][Margaret Kirkcaldy was in Virginia by 1651] [A short history of the family of Kirkcaldy of Grange, London, 1903]

KIRKPATRICK OF TORTHORWALD, DUMFRIES-SHIRE. Duncan Kirkpatrick was granted the Barony of Torthorwald by King Robert III on 10 August 1398. [The surname is possibly derived from a chapel in Closeburn, examples of the surname date from the mid twelfth century][Hugh Kirkpatrick settled in Jamaica in 1691, while Henry Erskine Kirkpatrick emigrated to the Leeward Islands in 1768]

KIRKPATRICK OF CLOSEBURN IN DUMFRIES-SHIRE. On 16 September 1594, King James VI confirmed Thomas Kirkpatrick, the land and Barony of Closeburn and Brigburgh; on 26 March 1685, Thomas Kirkpatrick was created as a Baronet, he died in 1709 when his son became the 2nd Baronet of Closeburn, he was dead by 1720 when his son Sir Thomas became the 3rd Baronet. [Kirkpatrick of Closeburn, London, 1858]

LAMB OF BRACO IN PERTHSHIRE. On 10 March 1658, Oliver Cromwell, the Lord Protector, granted John Lamb, a merchant in Dunblane, Perthshire, the Barony of Athray in Stirlingshire with its corn and waulkmills, also the lands of Braco with its manor place. [A surname of Norse origin, examples date from the late thirteenth century][James Lamb, a watchmaker from Edinburgh and a Jacobite, was transported to the West Indies in 1747] [Some Annals of the Lambs, London, 1926]

LAMOND OF INVERAN IN ARGYLL. John Lamond was granted the lands of Ard Lamont, Cororowray, Kilbride, Ancletymory, Askak, Stewlag, Dragouch,

Glenne, Auchoqhorlmore, Auch;quhorobeg, Auchnyschellouch, Cragnaveach, Invyryn, Trlstor, Colstane, Strongerrick, Inverkellane, Kilmernak, Kilmichil, and Tollart, in Cowal, now united into the Barony of Inveran, by King James III on 16 April 1472. On 3 January 1539, King James V confirmed John Lamond in the Barony of Inveran including various lands in the Bailie of Cowal now incorporated in Inveran; on 5 January 1548, Queen Mary granted Duncan Lamond, son and heir apparent of Sir John Lamond of Inveran, the lands and Barony of Inveran; on 18 July 1600, King James VI confirmed Coll Lamond, son of James Lamont of Inveran, the lands and Barony of Inveran [A surname of Norse origin, examples date from the thirteenth century][Lauchlan Lamont, from Argyll, died in Norfolk, Virginia in 1773] [The Lamont Clan, 1235-1935, Edinburgh, 1938]

LANGLANDS OF WILTOUN IN ROXBURGHSHIRE. King James II granted the Barony of Wiltoun, formerly held by his father James Langlands, to John Langlands, on 10 April 1451. The Langlands of Wilton family ended with the death of a Miss Langlands there in 1814. [A surname derived from a place in Peebles-shire; examples date from the fourteenth century]

LAUDER OF BLYTH IN BERWICKSHIRE. On 31 May 1509, King James IV granted Alexander Lauder, the Provost of Edinburgh, the lands of Thirlstoun and Tullosfew, including Manys, Ernisheuch, Egrop, Windypark, Heuch, Blyth, Heatherwick, Garmuir, Tullos, Dodhouse and Simprin in Berwickshire, now incorporated into the Barony of Blyth. Sir Alexander Lauder was killed at the Battle of Flodden on 9 September 1513. [a surname derived from the village of Lauder in Berwickshire; examples of the surname date from the thirteenth century][Francis Lauder, a schoolmaster and minister, emigrated to Maryland in 1761; David Lauder, a Jacobite, was transported to Virginia in 1716]

LAUDER OF POPPILL IN EAST LOTHIAN. On 7 February 1589, King James VI confirmed George Lauder of the Bass in the lands and Barony of Poppill; on 21 March 1598, King James VI granted George Lauder of the Bass, the lands and Barony of Beill in East Lothian.

LAURIE OF MAXWELTON IN DUMFRIES-SHIRE. On 27 March 1685, Robert Laurie, son and heir of John Laurie of Maxwelton, was created a Baronet, he died in April 1698, was succeeded as 2nd Baronet by his son Sir Robert Laurie who died in 28 February 1702, the next Baronet was his brother Sir Walter Laurie died on 23 November 1731, his son and heir was Sir Robert Laurie who died on 28 April 1779. [a diminutive of Laurence, examples date from the seventeenth century][Gavin Laurie, emigrated to East New Jersey in

1684, he was Deputy Governor there, while James Laurie, a tailor from Selkirk, emigrated to Maryland in 1736] [The Lauries of Maxwelton, London, 1972]

LEIGHTOUN OF ULLISSHAVEN IN ANGUS. On 23 December 1511, King James IV granted Walter Lichtoun the lands of Ullisshaven, with its tower, fort, mill, and port, also the lands of Wester Campsie and the lands of Kinnaird in Angus, together with the lands of Dullauthy with its fishing, in Kincardineshire, now incorporated into the Barony of Ullisshaven; on 1 July 1548, Queen Mary granted John Lichtoun son and heir apparent of John Lichtoun of Ullisshaven, the lands and Barony of Ullisshaven etc in Angus, and lands in Kincardineshire; on 17 March 1567, Queen Mary confirmed John Lichtoun of Ullisshaven, in the lands and Barony of Ullisshaven etc now incorporated into the Barony of Ullisshaven; on 19 June 1592, King James VI granted Robert Lichtoun, a burgess of Montrose, the lands and Barony of Ullisshaven etc now incorporated in the barony. [an English territorial surname, examples date from the twelfth century][S. Leighton, a clerk from Edinburgh emigrated to Georgia in 1775, while Patrick Lighton, a sailor, was bound for Darien in 1699.][Memorials of the Leightouns of Ullishaven, London, 1931]

LESLIE OF PHILORTH IN ABERDEENSHIRE. [A territorial surname derived from the lands of Lesslyn in the Garioch, granted to a Flemish immigrant around 1185] [Captain John Leslie settled in Barbados by 1679, while Andrew Leslie was a clergyman in South Carolina from 1729 until 1740] [The Barony Court of Philorth, 1653-1676, Aberdeen University library.ms.2867]

LESLIE OF CARNY IN PERTHSHIRE. King Robert III granted George Leslie the Barony of Carny around 1397.

LESLIE OF LESLIE IN ABERDEENSHIRE. King James II granted the Barony of Leslie, comprising the lands of Bracath, Quiltis, the Millton of Knockinblewis, and Drummes, to Alexander Leslie, on 4 April 1460, formerly held by Sir William Leslie of Balquhan; on 27 November 1526, King James V confirmed Alexander Leslie in the lands and Barony of Leslie with its fort, mills, etc, also the lands of Edingarro, in Aberdeenshire; on 21 October 1542, King James V confirmed Norman Leslie son of George Leslie of Rothes, the lands and Barony of Leslie, also the lands ad Barony of Ballinbreich in Fife, the lands and Barony of Carny in Perthshire, the lands and Barony of Fethyis in Angus, the lands and Barony of Balmane in Kincardineshire, the lands and Baronies of Quysny and Foulis Mowat in Aberdeenshire, the lands and Barony of Rothes, etc in Moray; on 28 July 1543, Queen Mary granted John

Leslie, son and heir apparent of Alexander Leslie of that Ilk, the Barony of Leslie; on 7 June 1548, Queen Mary confirmed Andrew Leslie, son and heir of the Earl of Rothes, in the lands and Barony of Ballinbreich, and the lands and Barony of Tacis in Fife, the lands and Barony of Carny in Perthshire, the lands and Barony of Fethyis in Angus, the lands and Barony of Balmain and Woodfield in Kincardineshire, the lands and Baronies of Quisny and Foulis-Wester in Aberdeenshire, the lands and Barony of Rothes in Moray, the lands and Barony of Rothynorman in Aberdeenshire, the lands and Barony of Leslie in Fife, etc . [A surname derived from Leslie in Aberdeenshire, examples date from the twelfth century][Reverend William Leslie in Barbados in 1653, while Margaret Leslie, a Covenanter, was transported to East New Jersey in 1685][Historical Records of the family of Leslie, 1067-1869]

LESLIE OF BALMANE IN KINCARDINESHIRE. On 8 February 1475, King James III granted George Leslie, Earl of Rothes, the lands of Welfield, Fresky, and Pitnamone, also the mills of Kincardine and Fettercairn, the lands of Esly, Balmane and Strethis in Kincardineshire, now integrated into the Barony of Balmane; on 21 January 1478, King James III granted the lands and Barony of Balmane to John Leslie, the nephew and heir apparent of George Leslie the Earl of Rothes; on 1 April 1517, King James V granted George Leslie, the Earl of Rothes, the lands of Halltacis, the mill of Tacis, the lands of Ballinderane, Hecham, Logy, the Mains of Ballinbreich with its mill, part of Ballingall, the lands, castle and Barony of Ballinbreich with its mills, fishing, woods, in Fife, the lands and Barony of Carny with its mill in Perthshire, the lands and Barony of Fethis in Angus, the lands and Barony of Quisny and Fowlis-Mowar with its mill etc. in Aberdeenshire, the lands and Barony of Rothes with its castle, mills, fishing rights on the River Spey, woods forests. Etc, in Moray, the lands and Barony of Rothiemay with mills, in Aberdeenshire, the lands of Kildethis in Inverness-shire, part of the lands and Barony of Dunlopy in Angus, etc. The Earl of Rothes was killed at the Battle of Flodden on 9 September 1513.

LESLIE OF WARDES IN ABERDEENSHIRE. King James III granted Alexander Leslie the lands and Barony of Kinedward, the lands and Barony of Kinedward, the lands of Easter Tiry, Kinarquhy and Faithly in Aberdeenshire on 4 February 1479; on 27 March 1511, King James IV granted John Leslie of Wardes the lands of Garioch, including Duncanstoun, Gillanderstoun with its mill, Donidare with its mill, Rochmuriell, the Davoch of Ardene with its mill, Warthill, Dornoch with its mill, Milnetoun, Hairlaw, Inverowry with Daw and its mill, Tullifour, Torreis, Knockinbarde with its mill, and Knocmorgan, now a Barony.

LESLIE OF BALQUHANE IN ABERDEENSHIRE. On 29 July 1511, King James IV granted William Leslie, the lands of Balquhane, Knocinblew, land in Harlaw, lands of Selve, Lochtillach, Whitecors, Knocalloquhy with its mill, lands of Seggieden and Earlsfield in the Regality of the Garioch, now incorporated into the Barony of Balquhane. [Pedigree of the family of Balquhan, 1067-1861, Bakewell, 1861]

LESLIE OF PITCAPLE IN ABERDEENSHIRE. On 14 August 1511, King James IV granted the lands and mill of Pitcaple, also that of Crimond, part of Ardune, Hairlaw, in the Garioch, to David Leslie of Pitcaple, now incorporated into the Barony of Pitcaple; on 30 August 1588, King James VI granted Duncan Leslie of Pitcaple, the lands and Barony of Pitcaple.

LESLIE OF ROTHES IN MORAY. On 21 July 1536, King James V confirmed George Leslie with the lands and Lordship of Rothes, with its tower, fort, etc, in Moray, also Belhelvy in the Barony of Ballinbreich, in Fife; on 8 July 1539, King James V granted George Leslie, the Earl of Rothes, the lands and Barony of Ballinbreich, with castle, mill, fishing, ferries, etc., the lands and Barony of Cairnie, with castle, fort, mills, fishing etc, in Perthshire; the lands and Barony of Fethis in Angus, the lands and Barony of Balmain and Vodfield in Kincardineshire, the lands and Barony of Rothienorman in Aberdeenshire, now incorporated into the Barony of Ballinbreich; on 6 September 1547, Queen Mary, granted the Earl of Rothes, the lands and Barony of Ballinbreich, the lands and Barony of Tacis, the lands and Barony of Carnie in Perthshire, the lands and Barony of Fethyis in Angus, the lands and Barony of Balmany and Woodfield in Kincardineshire, the lands and Barony of Quysny and Foulis Wester in Aberdeenshire, the lands and Barony of Rothes in Moray, also the lands and Barony of Rothienorman in Aberdeenshire, and the lands and Barony of Leslie and Kennoway in Fife; on 22 July 1564, Queen Mary granted Andrew Leslie, the Earl of Rothes, the lands and Barony of Ballinbreich, the lands and Barny of Cairny, the lands and Barony of Fethys, the lands and Barony of Balmany and Woodfeild, the lands and Barony of Foulis-Mowat, the lands and Barony of Rothes, the lands and Barony of Rothienorman, also the lands and Barony of Leslie; on 22 September 1573, King James VI granted Andrew Leslie, Earl of Rothes, the lands and Barony of Newtoun in Fife; on 28 March 1575, King James VI granted James Leslie the master of Rothes, son and heir apparent of Earl Andrew, the lands and Barony of Ballinbreich, etc. also the Barony of Leslie; on 25 August 1584, King James VI granted Andrew Leslie the Earl of Rothes, the lands, Lordship, Regality and Barony of Abernethy in Fife.

LESLIE OF CLEISCH IN FIFE. On 11 December 1540, King James V granted John Leslie of Parkhill, the lands and Barony of Cleisch, including Middle

Cleisch, Haltoun of Cleisch, with its tower, fort, and parkland, Bordland of Cleisch, Nevinstoun, the lands of Blair and Cromby, etc; on 10 July 1542 the king granted John Leslie of Cleisch, the Barony of Cleisch as above now incorporated into the Barony of Cleisch.

LESLIE OF LESLIE IN FIFE. On 13 December 1540, King James V granted Norman Leslie, son of George Leslie the Earl of Rothes, the lands and Barony of Leslie, with its castle, fort, mill, fishing rights, etc, the lands of Kennoway, Drummard, Lalethin, Audy, Droswman, also the burgh of Leslie as a burgh of Barony; on 4 November 1592, King James VI confirmed Andrew Leslie the Earl of Rothes, in the lands and Barony of Newtoun in Fife.

LESLIE OF NEWTOUN IN FIFE. On 30 June 1541, King James V granted Andrew Leslie of Kilmany, son of George Leslie the Earl of Rothes, the lands of Newtoun, salmon fishing on the River Tay at Woodhaven, the lands of Woodhaven with mills, fishing rights, etc, in Fife, now the Barony of Newtoun. The land and Barony of Buchan.

LESLIE OF BUCHAN IN ABERDEENSHIRE. On 19 June 1545, Queen Mary granted John Leslie, son and apparent heir to William Leslie of Buchan, the lands and Barony of Buchan.

LESLIE OF TULLIGLENNIS IN MORAY. On 9 March 1554, Queen Mary granted Walter Leslie of Kilmany, the lands and Barony of Tulliglennis.

LESLIE OF FARINDONALD AND ARDMANOCH IN INVERNESS-SHIRE. On 8 December 1557 Queen Mary, confirmed Robert Leslie in the lands and Baronies of Farindonald and Ardmanoch.

LESLIE OF ATHIE IN EASTER ROSS. On 31 July 1593, King James VI granted Robert Leslie of Finrassie, the lands and Barony of Athie, on 24 June 1608, Robert Leslie, son and heir of Robert Leslie of Finrassie.

LESLIE OF FETTERNEAR IN ABERDEENSHIRE. On 4 March 1598, King James VI granted William Leslie of Civildie, the lands and Barony of Fetternear, including salmon fishing rights on the River Don, lands of Bonnington, lands of Lusk, lands of Auchlivie, lands of Tuilyeauche, etc

LESLIE OF BALLINBREICH IN FIFE. On 25 July 1598, King James VI granted James Leslie, eldest son and heir apparent of James Leslie of Rothes, the lands and Barony of Ballinbreich, the lands and Barony of Tasis, Haltasis,

Bandirran, Cocklaws and Kilmuck, the lands and Barony of Cairnie, the lands and Barony of Fetheis, the lands and Barony of Balmaine, the lands and Barony of Quisny and Foulis-Mowat, the lands and Barony of Rothes, the lands and Barony of Rothienorman, now incorporated in the Barony of Ballinbreich.

LESLIE OF ARDROSIER IN INVERNESS-SHIRE. On 14 February 1600, King James VI confirmed Robert Leslie of Duglie in the lands and Barony of Ardrosier.

LESLIE OF LINDORES IN FIFE. On 31 March 1600, King James VI granted Patrick Leslie, son of Patrick Leslie the Commandator of Lindores, the lands and Barony of Grange of Lindores.

LESLIE OF NOVA SCOTIA. On 1 September 1625, John Leslie was created as a Baronet of Nova Scotia, a sasine dated 14 June 1626.

LINDSAY OF SINDEGAITS. King Robert I granted William Lindsay the Chamberlain of Scotland, the Barony of Sindegaits around 1320.

LINDSAY OF BYRES IN MIDLOTHIAN. Alexander Lindsay was granted the Barony of Byres by King David II around 1345; on 7 August 1413, Robert, Duke of Albany, the Regent, granted John Lindsay of the Byres, the baronies of the Byres, Chalmer Newtoun in Roxburghshire, Airth in Stirlingshire, and Abercorne in Midlothian; King James IV confirmed the grant of the lands and Barony of the Byres with its tower, fort and manor-house to Lord John Lindsay on 8 November 1495; on 28 October 1497, King James IV granted Patrick Lindsay, brother of Lord John Lindsay of the Byres, the Lordship and Barony of the Byres, the Lordship of Drem, St Mungo's Wells and the Cots with its grain mills and fullery in Haddington, the lands and Barony of Abercorn, Phillipstoun, Duddingstoun, Dean and Newton with their grain mills and fulleries in East Lothian, the lands and Barony of Chamberlain-Newton with their grain mills and fulleries in Roxburghshire, the lands of Cragorth, the lands and Barony of Airth with fishing rights, and mills in Stirlingshire, the lands of Glendevon in Perthshire, the lands and Barony of Pitlessie with its mill, the lands of Pitcreavie and Montshiel with its castle and tower in Fife; on 8 August 1511, King James IV granted Lord Patrick Lindsay, the lands and Barony of Chamaurlane-Newton in Roxburghshire; also the lands of Sanquar-Lindsay with mills, in Ayrshire; on 30 May 1524, King James V confirmed the charter of Lord Patrick Lindsay of the Byres granting his son and heir Sir John Lindsay of Pitcreavie the Lordship, and Barony of the Byres, including Coitts, Mungo's Wells, Harviestoun, Sanyngs,

Drem, Cawdro, and Muirtoun in East Lothian, the Barony of Abercorn with Dean Tower in West Lothian, the lands and Barony of Pitlessie, Cashindolie, Mark Inch, and Piotstoun, in Fife, the lands of Glen Devon in Perthshire, and the lands of Sanquhar-Lindsay in Ayrshire, on 11 November 1546, Queen Mary granted Patrick Lindsay, son and heir apparent of John Lindsay of the Byres, the lands and Barony of the Byres, also the lands and Barony of Pitcruive in Fife, the lands and Barony of Pitlessie in Fife, the lands and Barony of p in West Lothian, etc; on 10 January 1588, King James VI granted James Lindsay, son and heir apparent of Lord Patrick Lindsay of the Byres, the lands and Barony of Byres, etc; on 8 February 1642, King Charles I confirmed [the surname is possibly of Norman origin but probably from Lindsay in Lincolnshire, England, examples date from the twelfth century][Alexander Lindsay settled in the New Netherlands in 1639, while Major George Lindsay, a shipmaster, was killed in Darien in 1700] [Lives of the Lindsays, Wigan, 1840]

LINDSAY OF BALWYNDOLOCH AND RUTHVEN IN ANGUS. In 1363, King David II granted Alexander Lindsay the lands and Barony of Balwyndoloch and Ruthven; also, on 10 May 1366, King David II granted Sir Alexander Lindsay, the lands of Newdusk in Kincardineshire as a Barony.

LINDSAY OF DOWNIE IN ANGUS. On 8 June 1372 King Robert II granted Sir Alexander Lindsay the Barony of Downie in Angus.

LINDSAY OF CRAWFORD IN LANARKSHIRE. In 1381 King Robert II granted the Barony of Crawford to James Lindsay.; on 8 April 1403 King Robert III granted the Barony of Meginch in Perthshire, and the Barony of Clova in Angus; on 10 December 1404 King Robert III granted the Barony of Crawford to David Lindsay the Earl of Crawford; on 3 July 1559, King Francis and Queen Mary granted David Lindsay, son and heir apparent of the Earl of Crawford, the lands and Barony of Finavon, the lands and Barony of the forest of Platane, the lands and Barony of Inveratitie, the lands and Barony of Downie, the lands and Barony of Alicht, the lands and Barony of Ballindoch, the lands and Barony of Melginch, the lands and Barony of Baltrody, the lands and Barony of Pitfour; on 22 March 1565, Queen Mary granted David Lindsay, son and heir apparent of David Linds, the lands and Barony of Inverarity, the Earl of Crawford, the lands and Barony of Finavon, the lands and Barony of the Forest of Platane, the lands and Barony of Inveraritie, the lands and Barony of Downie, the lands and Barony of Alyth, the lands and Barony of Ballindoch, the lands and Barony of Meigle, the lands and Barony of Melginch, the lands and Barony of Baltrody, and the lands and Barony of Pitfour, etc.

LINDSAY OF INVERARITY IN ANGUS. King David II granted the Barony of Inverarity to Alexander Lindsay, formerly held by Margaret Abernethy the

Countess of Angus, around 1370; on 11 January 1527, King James V granted David Lindsay, Earl of Crawford, the lands and Barony of Inverarity in Angus.

LINDSAY OF KIRKMICHAEL IN DUMFRIES-SHIRE. In 1377, King Robert II granted James Lindsay the Barony of Kirkmichael.

LINDSAY OF MEIGLE IN PERTHSHIRE. King Robert III granted the Barony of Meigle to David Lindsay on 28 July 1397.

LINDSAY OF SINDEGAT. William Lindsay, the Chamberlain of Scotland, was granted the Barony of Sindegat by King Robert I around 1315.

LINDSAY OF KINBLETHMONT IN ANGUS. On 7 November 1458, King James II granted Walter Lindsay the lands and Barony of the Aird and Beaufort in Inverness-shire.

LINDSAY OF PANBRIDE IN ANGUS. In 1453, King James III granted William Lindsay of Beaufort the Barony of Panbride, formerly held by the Earl of Huntly.

LINDSAY IN ABERDEENSHIRE. On 6 December 1474, King James III, granted Alexander Lindsay, son and heir apparent of David Lindsay the Earl of Crawford and Lord Lindsay, the lands and Barony of Tulenahilt, Tulebrok, and New Park in Aberdeenshire, also the lands and Barony of Newdosk in Kincardineshire, and the lands and Baronies of Glenesk, Kinblethmont, Doun, Finavon, the forest of Plattane and the lands and Barony of Kirkbuddo, in Angus, with the lands and Baronies of Alyth, Ballindoch, Ruthven, Meigle, Baltrody, Melginch, in Perthshire, also the land and Barony of Cambo in Fife, together with the lands and Barony of Kirkmichael in Dumfries-shire, on 6 December 1474; on 30 July 1507, King James IV granted John Lindsay, the Earl of Crawford, the lands and Barony of Auchteralloun, New Park of Kello, Tullibralloch, and Tualloun.Ilynahilt, in Aberdeenshire, incorporated into the Barony of Auchterallan; on 2 September 1527, King James V granted Alexander Lindsay, the Master of Crawford, the son and heir apparent of the Earl of Crawford, the lands and Barony of Finavon, the forest of Platane, the Barony of Glen Esk, the Barony of Kilbutho, the Barony of Downie, superiority of the lands of Lethnott in Clova, the lands and Barony of Fearn, the lands and Barony of Inverarity, in Angus, also the lands and Barony of Ballindalloch, the lands and Barony of Meigle, the lands, forest, and Barony of Alyth, the lands and Barony of Baltrody with the lands of Pitfour, the lands and Barony of Melginch, the lands and Barony of Carnebaddy, also property in Watergait of Perth; the lands and Barony of Newdosk in Kincardineshire, the lands and Barony of Strathnairn in Inverness-shire, the lands and Barony of Newhall in Fife, the lands and Barony of Tullynathill, Tullybrok, and Newpark, in Aberdeenshire; on 16 October 1541, King James V granted David Lindesay of Edzell, the lands of Auchterallen, Tulenahilt, Tulliebrollockan, and Newpark in Aberdeenshire, the lands and Barony of Newdosk in Kincardineshire, the lands and Barony of Glen Esk, the lands and Barony of Fearn, the lands of Cloway, and the lands and Barony of Finavon, the lands and Barony of the forest of Platane, the lands and Barony of Inverarity, the lands and Barony of Downie, all in Angus, the lands and Barony of Alyth, the lands and Barony of Ballindoch, the lands and Barony of Meigle, the lands and Barony of Baltroddy, the lands and Barony of Pitfour in Perthshire.

LINDSAY OF COLVANTOUN. King James III granted James Lindsay, the Provost of Lincluden, the lands of Clochburn, Millhill, and Paddockkeruke, also the lands of Wolfclyde, Isburnhil, and Stanegil, in Lanarkshire, the lands of Redhewis in Midlothian, the lands of Polbuthy in Dumfries-shire, the lands of Boyle in Peebles-shire, all now annexed and incorporated into the Barony of Colvantoun on 15 February 1477.

LINDSAY OF THANKERTOUN IN LANARKSHIRE. On 29 September 1480, King James III granted Margaret Lindsay, daughter of John Lindsay of Colvantoun, and wife of Lord Robert Fleming, the lands and Barony of Thankertoun, the lands of Westraw in the Barony of Biggar, also parts of the lands of Cormestoun and Quodqueen, Wolfclyde, Baitlaw, Bissyberry and Hevilside, united into the Barony of Biggar.

LINDSAY OF GLEN ESK IN ANGUS. On 15 August 1511, King James IV granted John Lindsay, the Earl of Crawford, the lands and Barony of Glenesk, including the Mains of Dalbog with its manor house, mill, alehouse, and fishing rights, the lands of Brabmarehill, Glen Mark, Glen Lee, Kirktoun, the alehouse of Glen Mark, Auchrenny, Migvie, Dalbrek, Auchlochry, Bailye, Glen Effy, the mill of Ratnovy, Cornvrane, Inverkenny, Carcarncors, Glen More, Auchory, Tullibernis, Drumcairn, Finnoch, Ardgeich, the mill at Lethno, Dunhasny, Shannach, and others, incorporated into the Barony of Glenesk; on 1 April 1554, Queen Mary, granted David Crawford, son and heir apparent of David Crawford, the Earl of Crawford, the lands, Lordship and Barony of Glen Esk; on 16 August 1587, King James VI confirmed David Lindsay, the Earl of Crawford, the lands and Barony of Finavon, the lands and Barony of Alyth, the lands and Barony of Meigle, the lands and Barony of Melginch, the lands and Barony of Baltrodie, the lands and Barony of Pitfour, etc now incorporated into the Lordship and Barony of Finavon; on

17 August 1588, King James VI confirmed Sir David Lindsay of Edzell and his son David Lindsay, in the lands, Lordship and Barony of Glen Esk, also the lands and Barony of Newdosk, the lands and Barony of Fearn, the lands and Barony of Morphy-Fraser, etc. [History of the House of Angus, 2 vols., Edinburgh, 2005][The Lindsay family of Glen Esk and Edzell, Arbroath, 1922]

LINDSAY OF DOWHILL IN FIFE. On 14 July 1541, King James V confirmed Adam Lindsay in the Barony of Dowhill, with tower, fort, and mills, etc; also the lands and Barony of Kinloch in Perthshire, now incorporated in the Barony of Dowhill.

LINDSAY OF CANGNOR IN STIRLINGSHIRE. On 19 February 1547, Queen Mary granted Alexander Lindsay, a burgess of Perth, the lands and Barony of Cangnor.

LINDSAY OF BALGAVY IN ANGUS. On 22 August 1587, King James VI granted Walter Lindsay of Balgavy, the lands and Barony of Balgavy.

LINDSAY OF SPYNIE IN MORAY. On 6 May 1590, King James VI granted Alexander Lindsay the lands, Lordships and Barony of Spynie, also the lands, Lordships and Baronies of Kineddar, Birneth, Raffort, Ardclayth, Kilmills, Strathspey and Moy, Keith, now incorporated in Spynie; on 17 April 1593, King James VI confirmed Alexander Lindsay, Lord Spynie, in the lands, Lordship and Barony of Spynie.

LINDSAY OF MORPHIE-FRASER IN KINCARDIN. On 19 February 1608, King James VI confirmed David Lindsay, son of Sir David Lindsay of Edzell, in the lands and Barony of Morphie-Fraser.

LINDSAY OF KINFAUNS IN PERTHSHIRE. On 25 February 1608, King James VI granted John Lindsay, son and heir apparent of Sir Henry Lindsay of Careston, the lands, Barony and Lordship of Kinfauns and Pitsindie.

LINDSAY OF KINLOCH IN PERTHSHIRE. On 29 September 1608, King James VI granted John Lindsay, brother german of James Lindsay of Dowhill, the lands and Barony of Kinloch. [Kinloch of that Ilk, 1922]

LINDSAY OF WEST NISBET IN BERWICKSHIRE. On 27 December 1639, King Charles I granted Lady Jean Lindsay, daughter of David the Earl of Crawford, the lands and Barony of West Nisbet.

LINDSAY OF EVELICK IN PERTHSHIRE. On 15 April 1666 Alexander Lindsay, son of Alexander Lindsay the Bishop of Dunkeld, was created Baronet of

Evelick by William and Mary, and died around 1690, his son Sir Alexander Lindsay succeeded as the Second Baronet of Evelick and died by 1720, his son Sir Alexander Lindsay succeeded to the Baronetcy becoming the Third Baronet of Evelick, he died there on 6 May 1762.

LINDSAY OF KINNEFF IN KINCARDINESHIRE. David Lindsay was granted the Barony of Kinneff on 15 April 1666.

LITTLE OF OVER LIBERTOUN IN MIDLOTHIAN. On 26 February 1642, King Charles I granted William Little of Over Libertoun the lands and Barony of Over Libertoun including the Barony of Dalmahoy. [a descriptive surname, examples dae fom the thirteenth century][Margaret Little, from Edinburgh was transported to Virginia in 1696, while Andrew Little emigrated to Antigua in 1724]

LIVINGSTOUN OF WISTON, IN LANARKSHIRE. King David II granted William Livingstoun the Barony of Wistoun in 1342.

LIVINGSTONE OF CALLANDER IN PERTHSHIRE. On 30 April 1457 King James II granted baronies and lands in Stirlingshire, Lanarkshire, and Perthshire, specifically the Barony of Callander with its castle, the lands of Airth, Slamannan Muir, Kilsyth, Polmais, Levilands, Croftfidlerdale, the Barony of Culter in Lanarkshire, also the lands of Calyn, Calindrade, Douglas and in Perthshire, united into the Barony of Callandar to Sir James Livingstone; on 3 February 1510, King James IV granted Alexander Livingstoun, son and heir apparent of Lord William Livingstone, the lands and Barony of Callander, with its castle and tenantries, the lands of Airth, Kilsyth, Polmais, Levilands and Croft-federal, with tenantries, in Stirlingshire, also part of the lands and Barony of Culter in Lanarkshire, plus the lands of Calen, Calentreth and Douglas in Perthshire, now incorporated into the Barony of Callender; on 20 May 1546, Queen Mary granted John Livingstone, son and heir apparent of Lord Alexander Livingstone, the lands and Barony of Culter in Lanarkshire, also lands in Stirlingshire, now annexed to the Barony of Callandar; on 14 June 1594, King James VI confirmed Lord Alexander Livingstone in the lands and Barony of Logie in Perthshire, on 8 July 1594, King James VI granted Lord Alexander Livingstone the lands and Barony of Callendar, also the lands and Barony of Feldys and Clochrist, also the Barony of Livingstone; on 13 March 1600, King James VI confirmed Alexander, Lord Livingstone in the lands and Barony of Callendar. [The name is of territorial origin and comes from an Anglian settlement in East Lothian; examples of the surname date from the twelfth century] [a William Livingstone was transported to East New Jersey in 1685, while Katherine Livingstone was transported to Maryland in 1704.][The Livingstones of Callendar, Edinburgh, 1920]

LIVINGSTON OF SALINE IN FIFE. On 28 March 1482, King James III granted John Livingstone a burgess of Edinburgh, the lands and Barony of Saline.

LIVINGSTONE OF EAST WEMYSS IN FIFE. On 19 May 1508, King James IV granted the lands of East Wemyss to Sir Robert Livingstone of East Wemyss, with its coal mines, salt, woods, etc, now incorporated into the Barony of East Wemyss. Sir Robet Livingstone was killed at the Battle of Flodden on 9 September 1513.

LIVINGSTONE OF GERVISWOOD IN LANARKSHIRE. On 8 February 1513, King James IV confirmed James Livingstone, in the lands of Gerviswood and Musbridge with its mill, the lands of Brownlee, the crofts of Inflathill and Selyholme, with the croft of Whitehill, Castlelands, Berrybank, Shoolbrades part of Kingson's Knoll, in Lanarkshire, now incorporated in the Barony of Gerviswood; on 6 March 1549, Queen Mary granted William Lison Sir Thomas Livingstone vingstone, nephew and heir apparent of James Livingstone of Gerviswood, the lands and Barony of Gerviswood.

LIVINGSTONE OF WESTER KILSYTH IN STIRLINGSHIRE. William Livingstone was killed at the Battle of Flodden on 9 September 1513. On 17 February 1540, King James V confirmed William Livingston of Kilsyth in the lands of Wester Kilsyth, Garvald with tower, fort, mills, etc., and Glasswells in Stirlingshire, also, part of Graden, fishing rights on the River Tweed, lands of Darnchester in Berwickshire, now incorporated into the Barony of Wester Kilsyth. [Kilsyth, a parish history, Glasgow, 1893]

LIVINGSTONE OF HERBERTSHIRE. On 22 December 1608, King James VI granted Alexander Livingstone, the Earl of Linlithgow, the lands and Barony of Herbertshire etc.

LIVINGSTONE, OF DUNIPACE IN NOVA SCOTIA. Sir David Livingstone was created a baronet of Nova Scotia, the Barony of Livingstone-Dunipace, with 16000 acres there, by King Charles I on 30 May 1625. He married Barbara Forrester. As he had disposed his assets before he died, his son made no claim to the barony which became dormant.

LIVINGSTONE OF NEWBIGGING IN LANARKSHIRE. On 29 June 1627, King Charles I created Thomas Livingstone of Newbigging, a soldier in Dutch Service, a Baronet of Nova Scotia with 16000 acres there, he died by 1660 when his son Sir Thomas became the Second Baronet, he too was a soldier, in Dutch service and later in British service, on 4 December 1696 he became Viscount Teviot when the baronetcy merged with the peerage.

LIVINGSTON OF KINNAIRD IN PERTHSHIRE. John Livingston of Kinnaird was created Baronet of Anti Costi in Nova Scotia on 25 June 1627, a sasine dated 23 July 1627.

LIVINGSTOUN OF SKIRLING IN PEEBLES-SHIRE. On 7 October 1641, King Charles I granted James Livingstoun, the lands and Barony of Skirling.

LIVINGSTONE OF WESTQUARTER IN STIRLINGSHIRE. On 30 May 1699, James Livingston was created a Baronet on 30 May 1699, he died in Edinburgh on 27 November 1701 with no child to succeed him.

LOCKHART OF CARSTAIRS IN LANARKSHIRE. On 28 February 1672, William Lockhart of Carstairs was created as a Baronet, when he died in 1710 his son Sir James Lockhart succeeded to the title of 2nd Baronet of Carstairs. He died on 31 July 1755. [from an Old French name 'Locard', examples date from the twelfth century][George Lockhart, a merchant trading in the West Indies around 1683, while Gavin Lockhart, a Covenanter, was transported to East New Jersey in 1685][Seven Centuries, a history of the Lockharts of Lee and Carnwath, Carnwath, 1976]

LOGAN OF GROGAR IN AYRSHIRE. On 19 January 1479, King James III granted Sir Robert Logan the lands and barony of Grogar in Ayrshire; on 14 September 1557, Queen Mary confirmed Robert Logan of Restalrig, in the lands and Barony of Grogar. [a surname probably from a place in Ayrshire, examples date from around 1200] [Alexander Logan was a fisherman in Boston in 1684, while Andrew Logan was a sergeant at Darien, Panama, in 1699] [The Logans, London, 1979]

LOGAN OF RESTALRIG IN MIDLOTHIAN. On 2 January 1540, King James V granted Robert Logan, son and heir apparent of Sir Robert Logan of Restalrig, the lands and Barony of Restalrig, including manor, mill etc, also, the lands and Barony of Grogar, in Ayrshire, now incorporated in the Barony of Restalrig, and on 2 January 1540 Robert Logan, son and heir apparent of Sir Robert Logan of Restalrig, was granted by King James V the lands and Barony of Restalrig, including Gogar and Mountlothian in Midlothian, the lands and Barony of Grogar in Ayrshire, now incorporated into the Barony of Restalrig, confirmed on 17 March 1543; on 30 November 1580, King James VI confirmed John Logan of Coitfield in the lands and Barony of Restalrig, also lands in Berwickshire united into the Barony of Hutton; on 2 April 1585, King James VI granted James Logan, son and heir apparent of John Logan of Coitfield, the lands and Barony of Restalrig, and other lands formed into the Barony of Hutton.

LOGAN OF COUSTON IN FIFE. Robert Logan was granted the lands, barony and Regality of Aberdour, also the lands and Barony. of Loch Leven, the burgh of Barony of Kinross, the lands and Barony of Seggie, the lands and Barony of Killour, also the Earldom of Orkney and the Lordship of Shetland, on 18 December 1657 by Oliver Cromwell, the Lord Protector. [The name is of territorial origin, possibly originated in Ayrshire, as a surname it is recorded from around 1200] [Alexander Logan was in Boston by 1684, while George Logan was a merchant in Virginia by 1750]

LOGIE OF TANNADICE AND GLAMIS IN ANGUS. In April 1364, King David II granted John Logie the Thanage of Tannadice also that of Glamis in Angus. [a surname of territorial origin, examples date from the thirteenth century]

LOVELL OF MONIFIETH IN ANGUS. On 11 May 1529, King James V granted Henry Lovell the lands and Lordship of Eglismonitho [Monifieth] including its manor-house, Brauchan, part of the Kirktoun of Monifieth, Justin-leys, also fishing rights in the North Sea and River Tay; on 30 May 1551, Queen Mary, granted John Lovell, son of Henry Lovell, nephew of Andrew Lovell of Ballumbie, the lands of Ballumbie. [a surname from the Norman French *lovel* meaning 'little wolf'][Richard Lovell, a soldier of the Virginia Regiment in 1760s].

LOWES OF WEST NISBET IN BERWICKSHIRE. On 27 December 1639, King Charles I, granted Alexander Lowes, a merchant burgess of Edinburgh, the lands and Barony of West Nisbet. A surname from a place in Selkirkshire, examples date from the fourteenth century]

LUMSDEN OF ARDRE IN FIFE. King James II granted John Lumsden of Ardre the lands of Pourane, Castlefields, part of Ramsay-Forthir in Fife, and the lands of Glegerno in East Lothian now united and formed into the Barony of Ardre, on 10 November 1450, On 18 July 1511, King James IV confirmed John Lumsden in the lands of Ardre, Letham, Redwalls, Schipseis, Powrane, the Castle-field of Cupar, part of Ramsay-Forthar, in Fife, also the lands of Glegarno in East Lothian, incorporated into the Barony of Ardre; on 8 August 1598, King James VI granted Robert Lumsden, brother german of James Lumsden of Ardre, the lands and Barony of Ardre etc incorporated into the Barony of Firtyhfield. [A surname from a place in Berwickshire, examples of the surname date from the twelfth century] [William Lumsden settled in South Carolina in 1671, while John Lumsden, died in Jamaica in 1770] [Memorials of the families of Lumsden, Edinburgh 1889]

LUMSDEN OF CONDOLANE IN FIFE. On 25 October 1507, King James IV granted James Lumsden, son and heir apparent of Thomas Lumsden of

Condolane the lands of Condolane with its manor-house and mill, and the lands of Drum in Fife, also the lands of Midlar in Aberdeenshire, now incorporated into the Barony of Condolane, this was confirmed by the king on 8 May 1512. Thomas Lumsden was killed at the Battle of Flodden on 9 September 1513.

LUMSDEN OF CUSHNIE IN ABERDEENSHIRE. On 15 November 1600, King James VI confirmed John Lumsden of Cushnie in the Barony of Cusnie-Lumsden.

LUMISDEN. John Lumisden, son of Andrew Lumisden, Episcopal Bishop of Edinburgh, was created a knight and baronet by King James VIII on 5 [January 1740, he died in France in 1751. [a Jacobite Baronage]

LUNDY OF LUNDIN IN FIFE. On 22 May 1540, King James V granted Walter Lundy the lands of Lundyn, with tower, fort, manor, etc, lands of Prateris, lands of Tuquhittis, Kame, Gelstoun, Bowsey, Stratharlie, the lands of Haltoun and Balcolmo, in Fife, incorporated into the Barony of Lundin; on 5 January 1555, Queen Mary, granted Walter Lundy of that Ilk, son and heir apparent of William Lundy, the lands and Barony of Lundin.[a surname possibly from a place in Angus, examples date from the fifteenth century] [Charles Lundy, a Jacobite, was transported to Antigua in 1716, while Archibald Lundy emigrated to New York in 1775.][History of the Clan Lundy, Lundie, Lundin, Glasgow, 2005]

LUNDY OF KINCRAIG IN FIFE. King James III granted William Lundy of that Ilk, son and heir apparent of Sir John Lundy of Lundy, the lands of Kincraig now incorporated and unified into the Barony of Lundy, on 1 December apparent of William Lundy of Lundy, the lands of Overpatris and part of Netherpatris in the Barony of Lundy on 29 April 1489.

LUNDY OF BALGONY IN FIFE. On 30 April 1511, King James IV granted Sir Andrew Lundy the lands of Balgony, Mylnetoun, the Byris, Innerlochty, the tower, for and manor-house of Balgony, lands of Dowene, Scheitham, the manor and lands of Blackfaulds, Cowdean with its fulling mill and grain mill, in Fife, also Nether Carnbo, Brachty and Gowlam with its mill, in Strathearn, Perthshire, now incorporated into the Barony of Balgony. Sir Robert Lundy of Balgonie was killed at the Battle of Flodden on 9 September 1513; on 21 October 1549, Queen Mary confirmed Andrew Lundy of Balgony in the lands and Barony of Mondynis.

LUNDY OF CONDLANE IN FIFE. On 15 April 1564, Queen Mary confirmed James Lundy, son of Robert Lundy of Balgony, in the lands and Barony of

Condlane etc. incorporated into the Barony of Condlane; on 22 December 1591, King James VI granted Andrew Lundie of Condland, the lands and Barony of Condland.

LUNDIN OF GORTHY IN PERTHSHIRE. On 25 May 1576, King James VI granted George Lundin the lands and Barony of Gorthie in Strathearn Perthshire. [a surname from a place in Fife, examples date from the twelfth century]

LYLE OF LUNDY, IN ANGUS. King Robert III granted the Barony of Lundy to Robert Lyle around 1397. [The surname is derived from the French 'L'Isle', examples date from the twelfth century.] [John Lyle, a farmer from Caithness, emigrated to New York in 1775, while James Lyle was a carpenter in Williamsburg, Virginia, by 1756]

LYLE OF LYLE IN RENFREWSHIRE. On 29 August 1541, King James V granted James Lyle, son and heir apparent of Lord John Lyle, the lands of Lyle, Mylton with mill, the lands of Auldtounrig and Colruth, with castles, manors, mills, fishing rights, etc, incorporated into the Barony of Lyle. [The Lyles of Renfrewshire, Glasgow, 1936]

LYON OF GLAMIS IN ANGUS. King Robert II granted John Lyon the Thane of Glamis, the barony of Glamis in 1371; on 12 December 1527, King James V confirmed John Lyon, Lord Glamis, the land and Barony of Baky, with its manor-house, fort, mill, etc, in Angus; on 6 February 1544, Queen Mary granted Lord John Lyon of Glamis the lands and Baronies of Balhelvy and Curtestoun, in Aberdeenshire; on 12 September 1548, Queen Mary granted John Lyon, Lord Glamis, the lands and Barony of Kinghorn in Fife; on 12 July 1569, Queen Mary confirmed John Lyon, Lord Glamis, the lands and Barony of Baikie, etc. [The surname may have come from France via England in the fourteenth century, examples date from that period] [Mary Lyon was bound from Leith aboard the Phoenix of Leith for Virginia in 1666, while James Lyon, a wright, settled in Barbados before 1676][The Lyons of Cossins and Wester Ogil, Edinburgh, 1901]

LYON OF KINBLETHMONT IN ANGUS. On 30 January 1507, King James IV granted David Lyon of Kinnell in Angus, the Barony of Kinblethmont including the lands of Gilchorn with its mill, Lawtoun with tenantries, Hunterstoun, Balmulistoun, etc.

LYON OF MELGUND IN ANGUS. On 6 May 1580, King James VI confirmed Thomas Lyon of Baldovie, in the lands and Barony of Melgund; and on 7 November 1587 he was granted lands in Angus incorporated into the

Barony of Dod; on 6 April 1594, King James VI confirmed Thomas Lyon of Auldbar, in the lands and Barony of Dod.

LYON OF TANNADICE IN ANGUS. On 17 May 1598, King James VI confirmed Sir Thomas Lyon of Auldbar, in the lands and Barony of Tannadice.

MACARLICH OF ARDGOUR IN ARGYLL. On 18 October 1542, King James V confirmed John MacArdlich in the lands and Barony of Ardgour, including various properties now incorporated into the Barony of Ardgour. [examples in Scotland date from the seventeenth century]

MCCLELLAN OF BOMBIE IN KIRKCUDBRIGHTSHIRE. On 26 February 1589, King James VI granted William McClellan of Gelstoun, the lands and Barony of Twynholm; on 5 June 1597, King James VI granted Robert McLellan, eldest son of Thomas McLellan of Bombie, the lands of Bombie and others in Kirkcudbrightshire now united into the Barony of Bombie; on 5 February 1642, King Charles I granted Thomas McLellan, Lord Kirkcudbright, the lands and Barony of Twynholm. [A surname derived from the Gaelic *macgill fhaolain* – son of the servant of St Fillan, examples date from the fourteenth century][Mathew MacLellan, from Galloway, emigrated to Barbados in 1655, while Andrew McClelland, a Covenanter, was transported to East New Jersey in 1685[Records of the McClellands of Bombie and Kirkcudbright, Castle Douglas, 1874]

MCCONNELL OF DUNNIVAIG IN ISLAY. On 21 April 1545 Queen Mary granted James McConnell of Dunnivaig and the Glens, many properties in Argyll and Inverness-shire, incorporated into the Barony of Bar in North Kintyre; on 11 March 1599, King James VI confirmed Archibald McConnell, son of Angus McConnell of Dunnevaig in the lands and Barony of Geya [Gigha?] [a variant of *macDhomhnuill*][James McConnell, a thief from Ayrshire, was transported to the colonies in 1717]

MACCORKILL OF FANTELEN IN ARGYLL. On 21 April 1542, King James V granted Malcolm MacCorkill, son and heir apparent of Ewen MacCorkill of Fantelen, various lands in Lochawe, Argyll, now incorporated into the Barony of Fantelen; on 3 February 1595 King James VI granted Duncan Maccorquadale, eldest son of Duncan MacCorquadale of Fantelen, Fantelen and other lands in Argyll, incorporated into the Barony of Fantelen. [an abbreviation of McCorquadale, examples date from the sixteenth century] [Archibald McCorkadale, a Covenanter, was transported to Jamaica, in 1685, while several McConnells were captured at the Siege of Worcester and banished to Boston in 1651]

MACCULLOCH OF MERTOUN IN WIGTONSHIRE. On 8 July 1504, Alexander MacCulloch's lands of Mertoun and Auchquhonwane with towers, forts, mills and tenantries in the Lordship of Galvidie [Galloway] in Wigtonshire, were incorporated into the Barony of Mertoun by King James IV; on 6 August 1532, King James V confirmed the grant by Simon McCulloch of Myrtoun to Henry MacCulloch off Kilasser of the lands and Barony of Myrtoun; on 3 July 1546, Queen Mary granted Simon MacCulloch, son and heir apparent of Margaret McCulloch of Myretoun, the lands and Barony of Myrtoun; on 3 February 1582, King James VI granted William Macculloch, son and heir apparent, the lands and Barony of Myretoun; on 8 March 1585, King James VI confirmed William McCulloch of Myretoun in the lands and Barony of Cardnes, etc; on 10 August 1664, Sir Alexander MacCulloch of Mertoun was created a Baronet, he was followed by his grandson Sir Godfrey MacCulloch as 2nd Baronet of Mertoun, but as he was executed for murder in 1697, the barony became extinct. [an old surname from Galloway, examples date from the thirteenth century] [Thomas McCulloch, a minister in Nova Scotia from 1802 to 1804, President of Dalhousie College there by 1838, died in 1843]

MACDONALD OF SLEAT ON THE ISLE OF SKYE IN INVERNESS-SHIRE. Donald MacDonald was created the First Baron of Sleat by King Charles I on 14 July He 1625 with a grant of 16,000 acres in Nova Scotia. During the Wars of the Three Kingdoms, he was a Royalist. his wife was Janet MacKenzie, sister of the Earl of Seaforth. He died in October 1643 and was succeeded by his son Sir James McDonald as Second Baronet of Slate. He also was a committed Jacobite in 1745. He married twice, firstly to Margaret Mackenzie, daughter of Sir Roderick Mackenzie of Lorgeach, and Margaret MacLeod; and secondly to Mary daughter, of John MacLeod of MacLeod. He died on 8 December 1678. The next Baronet of Slate was his son, Sir Donald MacDonald who married twice, his second wife was Mary Douglas, daughter of the Earl of Morton and his wife Elizabeth Villiers. The Third Baronet of Sleat died on 5 February 1695. Then followed their Sir Donald MacDonald as the Fourth Baronet of Sleat who was an active Jacobite in 1715, fought at Sherifffmuir, but avoided being attainted which would have made the Barony forfeit to the Crown. He died in 1718. His son was born about 1697 and matriculated at Oxford University in 1712. On his death in 1720 the Barony went to his uncle Sir James MacDonald as Baronet of Sleat and of Oransay. The Sixth Baronet married twice, firstly to Janet, widow of John MacLeod of Talisker, who was raised to the Peerage on 17 July 1776 and secondly to Margaret, daughter of John MacDonald of Castleton. He died in Forres, Moray, in 1723. Alexander, born 1711, son of Sir James MacDonald and his wife Janet McLeod, became the Seventh Baronet of Sleat on 24 April 1733. He supported the Hanoverians during the 1745

Jacobite Rising. He also married twice, firstly on 5 April 1733 to Anne, widow of Lord Ogilvy, and secondly to Margaret Alexander, daughter of the Earl of Eglinton. He James MacDonald, the son of Sir Alexander and Margaret Montgomerie, who was an officer of the Coldstream Guards, on 17 July 1776 was created Baron MacDonald of Sleat in Skye when the Baronetcy merged. [an Anglicised version of *MacDhomhnuill*, examples date from the thirteenth century][Donald McDonald emigrated to East New Jersey in 1684; while, another Donald McDonald was indentured in Pennsylvania in 1693] [Clan Donald, Loanhead, 1978][The Troublesome MacDonalds, Washington, 1974] [The Jacobite Peerage, Edinburgh, 1904]

MACDONELL OF KEPPOCH. Alexander MacDonell of Keppoch, son of the 15th Chief of the Clan, was born around 1695, served in the French Army for ten years, was created a knight and baronet by King James VIII in 1743. [a Jacobite Baronetage][an Anglicisation of the Gaelic *MacDhomnuill* – son of Donald, examples date from the fourteenth century][John McDonnell, was captured at the Siege of Worcester in 1651 and transported to Boston]

MACDOUGALL OF BRAXFIELD IN ROXBURGHSHIRE. On 28 December 1591, King James VI confirmed Thomas MacDougall, brother german of William MacDougall of Makerstoune, the lands and Barony of Braxfield. [An Anglicised version of the Gaelic name *MacDughaill* 'son of the dark stranger', examples date from the fourteenth century] [Duncan McDougall, a Covenanter, was transported to Jamaica in 1685, while William MacDougald, a merchant from Edinburgh, died in East Florida in 1774.]

MACDOWEL OF MAKARSTOUNE. King James III granted the lands and Baronies of Yester, Duncanlaw and Morham, and the lands of Giffordgait and Moscolly, to Dougal MacDowel, formerly held by William Maxwell of Tealing in Angus and Polgavy in Perthshire, on 23 August 1463; on 3 February 1478, King James III granted Andrew MacDowell, son and heir apparent of Dougal MacDowell, the lands and Baronies of Makarstone and Yetholm in Roxburghshire, also the lands and Baronies of Yester, Duncanlaw, and Moreham in East Lothian. [an Anglicisation of *MacDhughaill* – son of Dougall, examples date from the thirteenth century][Alister MacDoell, was captured at the Siege of Worcester in 1651 and transported to Boston, while Fergus McDowell was in Boston by 1684].

MCDOWALL OF GARTHLAND IN WIGTONSHIRE. On 13 November 1591, King James VI confirmed Uthred McDowell of Garthland in the lands and Barony of Garthland including various lands throughout Wigtonshire.

MCDOWELL OF LOGAN IN WIGTONSHIRE. On 18 March 1595, King James VI confirmed John McDowell in the Barony of Logan.

MCGHIE OF LIVINGSTONE IN WEST LOTHIAN. Alexander McGhie of Balmachie, Kirkcudbrightshire, was confirmed by King James VI in the lands and Barony of Livingstone, on 7 May 1591. [a surname from the Gaelic *Mac Aoidh* meaning 'son of Hugh', examples date from the late thirteenth century][Hugh McGhie, a highwayman, was transported to the colonies in 1750, while John McGee settled in Lanark, Upper Canada, in 1821]

MCGILL OF BALGAVY IN ANGUS. On 12 August 1550, Queen Mary confirmed James McGill, a burgess of Edinburgh, in the lands and Barony of Balgavy.

MACGILL OF CRANSTOUN-RIDDELL IN MIDLOTHIAN. On 6 December 1585, King James VI, granted David McGill the younger the lands and Barony of Cranstoun-Riddell; on 29 March 1592, King James VI confirmed David McGill, son and heir apparent of David Riddell of Cranstoun-Riddell, an advocate, the lands and Barony of Cranstoun-Riddell; on 3 February 1601, King James VI confirmed David McGill in the lands and Barony of Cranston-Riddell; on19 July 1627 James Makgill of Cranstoun-Riddell was created as a Baronet of Nova Scotia; on 12 February 1639, King Charles I granted Sir James McGill of Cranstoun-Riddell, the lands and Barony of Cousland He was a Lord of Session and an MP, he died on 8 December 1706 with no heir when the Baronetcy became extinct. On 8 September 1641, King Charles I confirmed Sir James cGill of Cranston-Riddell in the lands and Barony of Cousland. [An Anglicisation of *Mac an ghoill* -son of the stranger][James MacGill, a prisoner of war, was transported to Boston in 1652, while, another James McGill was a fur trader in Canada by 1776]

MCGILL OF WEST NISBET IN BERWICKSHIRE. On 27 December 1639, King Charles I, granted Robert McGill, an advocate, the lands and Barony of West Nisbet.

MACGILLEAN or MCLEAN OF DUART IN ISLAY. On 8 October 1496, King James IV granted Lachlan McLean son of Hector McLean of Duart the Barony of Duart including the lands of Toresay, castle Duart with mill, lands of Browlos, land in Ardmanach, Burg, Glen Kennir, Tressines, Calgary, Enynvoy, Calzoch, Lag, Soneboll, Gilzacrest, Peymore, Ardenis, Mandelon, Crosobol, Herne, the stewartry of Tiereig, Carnabog, Achnaha, Achkalen, Dougree, Kinloch, Achranich, and many others all united into the Barony of Duart. [an Anglicised version of the Gaelic -*Mac Gille Eoin* -son of the servant of John, examples date from the thirteenth century][Alexander McLean settled in Delaware by 1696, while Daniel McLean, from Inverness via Panama died in Carolina in 1699]

MACGREGOR. Alexander MacGregor or Drummond was born around 1660 was elected as last chief of Clan Gregor, was a prominent Jacobite who was created a knight and baronet by King James VIII on 14 March 1740, he married Margaret Cameron, and died in Dunblane on 1 March 1749. [a Jacobite Baronetage] [from the Gaelic *MacGriogair* – son of Gregory] [Colonel Patrick McGregor, Militia Muster Master of New York, died there in 1691, while Donald Glass McGregor was transported to East New Jersey in 1684][Clan Gregor, Edinburgh, 1825]

MACKANE OF ISLAY IN ARGYLL. King James IV granted John MacKane [MacEan?] of Ardnamurchan, various lands united into a Barony on Islay – Skanlastill, Kinbeloquhane, Capolse, Robolse, Little Capolse, Kilbraan, Dulloch, Auchtownwruch, Balluchter, Achvern, Ballechtach, Arrevore, Correre, Curloch, Alane-Mackindow, Alastill, Laald, Dawundak, Nynneemor, also the office of Baillie of Islay formerly held by the Lord of the Isles. [a Gaelic name *MacAin* meaning 'son of John'; examples date from the fourteenth century][several MacKeans, prisoners of war captured at the Siege of Worcester, were transported to New England in 1651]

MCKAY OF FARR IN STRATHNAVAR IN SUTHERLAND. On 16 December 1539, King James V granted Donald McKay in Strathnaver, the lands of Farr, Armidale, Straye, Rynewe, Kinnald, Golspie, Dilrid, Cattach, Bronych, Kilchalumkill in Strathbrora, Davach Lochnaver, Davach Erebull, etc, now incorporated into the Barony of Farr.

MCKAY OF STRATHNAVER. Sir Donald McKay of Strathnaver was created as a Baronet of Nova Scotia on 18 March 1627. [from *Mac Aoidh* – meaning Son of Hugh, examples date from the fourteenth century][Aeneas MacKay, settled in Boston by 1745, while Patrick Mackay settled in Georgia in 1737] [The Book of Mackay, Edinburgh, 1906]

MCKENZIE OF EILEAN DONAN IN WESTER ROSS. On 25 February 1509, King James IV confirmed John McKenzie of Kintail in lands of Kintail, Comissaig, Letterfearn, Glenselle, Glenlik, Lettirhall, Croo, the waters of Keppach and of Luing, with the castle and fort of Eilean Donan, etc., now incorporated into the Barony of Eilean Donnan; MacKenzie of Kintail was killed at the Battle of Flodden on 9 September 1513. On 30 August 1538, King James V granted John McKenzie of Eilean Donan several properties in Inverness-shire to be merged into the Barony of Eilean Donan.

MCKENZIE OF ASSYNT IN SUTHERLAND. On 20 January 1592, King James VI granted Colin McKenzie of Kintail, in the lands and Barony of Assynt.

MCKENZIE OF TARBET IN EASTER ROSS. Sir John McKenzie was created as a Baronet of Nova Scotia on 21 May 1628. [Some MacKenzie Pedigrees, Inverness, 1965]

MCKENZIE OF ALFORD IN ABERDEENSHIRE. On 22 January 1642, King Charles I granted Thomas McKenzie of Pluscardine the lands and Barony of Alford.

MACKENZIE OF COUL IN ROSS-SHIRE. On 16 October 1673 Kenneth Mackenzie of Coul was created as a Baronet, he died about 1680 when his son Sir Alexander Mackenzie became the 2nd Baronet, he died in 1702 and his son Sir John Mackenzie became the 3rd Baronet, but as he was a Jacobite in 1715 the baronetcy became forfeited.

MACKENZIE OF ROYSTOUN IN MIDLOTHIAN. On 8 February 1704, James Mackenzie of Roystoun, son of the Earl of Cromarty, was created as a Baronet, he died in Edinburgh on 9 November 1744.

MACKENZIE OF GRANDVALE. On 21 April 1704, Kenneth MacKenzie of Grandvale, second son of the Earl of Cromarty, was created as a Baronet.

MACKENZIE OF SCATWELL IN ROSS-SHIRE. On 22 February 1703, Queen Anne created Kenneth Mackenzie MP as Baronet of Scotwell, he died in 1730, and was succeeded by his son Sir Roderick Mackenzie as Baronet of Scotwell until his death on 24 April 1750. [An Anglicised version of the Gaelic *MacCoinich* -son of Coinneach, examples date from the thirteenth century][George McKenzie settled in East New Jersey in 1684, while Dr Alexander McKenzie, died in Kingston, Jamaica, in 1780]

MACKENZIE OF GAIRLOCH IN ROSS-SHIRE. On 22 February 1703, Kenneth Mackenzie was created by Queen Anne as Baronet of Gairloch, when he died on 3 October 1703, he was succeeded by his son Sir Alexander Mackenzie as the 2nd Baronet of Gairloch.

MACKENZIE OF DARIEN IN PANAMA. Alexander Mackenzie was born in Scotland in 1663, participated in the Darien Expedition of 1698-1699, was created Baronet of Darien on 22 February 1703, a Jacobite in 1715, settled in Claredon, Jamaica, and died there on 20 December 1744.

MCLEAN OF DUART IN ARGYLL. On 9 January 1540, King James V granted several properties in Inverness-shire incorporated into the Barony of Duart to Hector McLean, son and heir apparent of Hector McLean of Duart; on 12 November 1542 King James V granted Hector McLean, son and heir apparent of Hector McLean of Duart, the lands and Barony of Duart; on 4 February 1549, Queen Mary granted Hector McLean of Duart the lands and Barony of Ardgour in Inverness-shire; John McLean, alias Makaleer, a merchant in Gothenborg, Sweden, was enobled there in 1649, and later was created a Baronet by King Charles II during his exile, McLean died in Gothenborg when his son Sir John McLean succeeded to the title. Sir Hector McLean, son of Sir John McLean, a Jacobite who fought at the Battles of Killiecrankie and at Sheriffmuir. [an Anglicisation of the Gaelic *Mac Gille Eoin* meaning 'son of the servant of John', examples date from the thirteenth century][John McLean, a rebel, was transported to Jamaica in 1685, while Donald McLean, a merchant, died in St Augustine in 1778.] [The Jacobite Peerage, Edinburgh, 1904]

MCLEAN OF COLL IN ARGYLL. On 25 September 1542, King James V granted John McLean son and heir apparent of John McLean of Coll, the Barony of Coll; on 28 June 1559, King Francis and Queen Mary granted Hector McLean, son and heir apparent of Hector McLean of Coll, the lands and Barony of Coll.

MCLEAN OF MORVERN, ARGYLL. Lachlan McLean was created a Baronet of Nova Scotia on 3 September 1630.

MCLELLAN OF BOMBIE IN KIRKCUDBRIGHTSHIRE. On 5 June 1597, King James VI granted Robert McLellan, eldest son of Thomas McLellan of Bombie, the lands of Bombie and others in Kirkcudbrightshire now united into the Barony of Bombie. [Records of the McClellands of Bombie and Kirkcudbright, Castle Douglas, 1874]

MACLEOD OF GLEN ELG IN INVERNESS-SHIRE. On 20 September 1572, King James VI granted Mary McLeod, niece and heir of Alexander McLeod of Dunvegan, the lands and Barony of Glenelg; on 4 February 1580, King James VI granted Tormid MacLeod of Dunvegan, various lands in Skye and the Isles formed into the lands and Barony of Glen Elg. [The Book of Dunvegan, Aberdeen, 1938]

MACLEOD OF GLENDALE IN SKYE. John MacLeod, born about 1700, son of Alexander MacLeod and his second wife Christina MacLeod, a Jacobite who was created a knight and a baronet by King James VIII, [the 'Old Pretender'] on 5 September 1723, possibly participated in the '45, emigrated to America in 1770, died in North Carolina in 1775. [an Anglicisation of the Gaelic *MacLeoid*, examples date from the thirteenth century] [John McLeod, a prisoner of war, captured at the Siege of Worcester, was transported to Boston in 1652][The Chiefs of Clan MacLeod, Edinburgh, 1988][The Jacobite Peerage, Edinburgh, 1904]

MACLEOD OF LEWIS IN INVERNESS-SHIRE. On 29 June 1511, King James IV granted Malcolm MacLeod, son and heir of Rory MacLeod of Lewis, the land and castle of Lewis and Wattirness, the lands of Assynt in Sutherland, the lands of Coidgeaich in Inverness-shire, with forts, fishing, a mill, with Stornaway Castle as its principal messuage, now incorporated into the Barony and Lordship of Lewis; on 14 February 1572, King James VI granted Torquil McLeod, son and heir apparent of Roderic McLeod of Lewis, the lands and Barony of Assynt; on 10 August 1596, King James VI granted Torquil McLeod of Lewis, the lands and Barony of Assynt, the lands and Barony of Coigach, and the lands, island and Barony of Lewis.

MCLEOD OF GLENELG IN INVERNESS-SHIRE. On 20 September 1572, King James VI granted Mary McLeod, niece and heir of Alexander McLeod of Dunvegan, the lands and Barony of Glenelg.

MCMORANE OF APPLEGARTH IN DUMFRIES-SHIRE. On 10 August 1638, King Charles I granted John McMorane, son of James McMorane a merchant burgess of Edinburgh, the lands and Barony of Applegarth etc. [a surname from the Gaelic *macmugh-ron* meaning 'son of the seal's slave', examples date from the fourteenth century][Edward McMorran, a merchant from Dumfries, emigrated to New York in 1774]

MCNAUGHTON OF LOCH AWE IN ARGYLL. [an Anglicisation of the Gaelic *Mac Neachdainn*, examples date from the thirteenth century; several McNaughtons from Perthshire emigrated to New York in 1775][The Clan McNaughton, Edinburgh, 1977]

MAITLAND OF TYBRIS IN DUMFRIES-SHIRE. King James II confirmed the charter by William Maitland of Thirlstane who had granted his brother-german the following lands Achinbrek, Dumbine, Quhithil, Auchinach, Brauneskevil, Cluachane, Capilrig and Bagraw, now formed into one free Lordship on 10 June 1451. [A surname of French origin usually Maltalent, or Mautalent, examples in Scotland date from the late twelfth century]. [Reverend John Maitland emigrated to Carolina in 1707, while William Maitland was a merchant in Williamsburg in 1771][A Genealogical and Historical Account of the Maitland family, London, 1869]

MAITLAND OF BLYTH IN BERWICKSHIRE. On 20 February 1564, Queen Mary confirmed Richard Maitland of Lethington, in the lands and Barony of Blyth; on 26 March 1581, King James VI confirmed John Maitland, son and heir of Richard Maitland of Lethington, in the lands and Barony of Blyth, which was confirmed on 1 March 1584.

MAITLAND OF THIRLESTOUN IN LANARKSHIRE. On 30 October 1583, King James VI confirmed John Maitland of Thirlestoun in the lands and Barony of Thirlestoun and Biggar; on 28 July 1587, King James VI granted John Maitland of Thirlestoun the Lordship and Barony of Musselburgh, also the lands and Barony of Blyth, etc.; on 9 August 1587, King James VI granted Sir John Maitland of Thirlestoun, the lands and Barony of Stobo in Peeblesshire; on 18 October 1587, King James VI granted John Maitland of Thirestoun the lands and Lordship of Dunbar; on 8 April 1588, King James VI confirmed Margaret Maitland, daughter of John Maitland of Thirlestoun, the lands and Barony of Cesford; on 24 May 1588, King James VI granted Sir John Maitland of Thirlestoun, his Chancelor, the lands and Barony of Stobo; on 21 December 1591, King James VI confirmed John Maitland of Thirlestoun, the Chancellor of Scotland, the Lordship, Barony and Regality of the shire of Musselburgh, this was confirmed on 15 July 1593; on 7 March 1594, King James VI granted John Maitland the Lordship, Barony and Reality of Musselburgh, the lands and Barony of Stobo, the lands and Lordship of Dunbar, the lands and Barony of Braidwood, the Barony of Haddington, the Barony, Lordship and Regality of Thirlestoun, etc; on 20 March 1594, King James VI granted John Maitland of Thirletoun the lands and Barony of Carriden, the lands and Barony of Kettlestoun in West Lothian. [see the line of Scott of Thirlestoun in a History of the Napiers of Merchiston, London, 1921]

MAITLAND OF PITRICHIE AND GIGHT IN ABERDEENSHIRE. On 12 March 1672, Richard Maitland was created Baronet, he was a Senator of the College of Justice, on 6 July 1672 he was granted the Barony of Gight, he died on 22 February 1677, his son Sir Richard Maitland was 2nd Baronet until his death in 1679, the 3rd Baronet of Pitrichie was Sir Charles Maitland from 1679 until 1700, the final Baronet of Pitrichie was his son Sir Charles Maitland.

MAITLAND OF RAVELRIG IN MIDLOTHIAN. On 18 November 1680 John Maitland, son of the Earl of Lauderdale, was created as a Baronet, and died in 1710.

MALCOLM OF LOCHORE IN FIFE. John Malcolm, sometime the Chamberlain of Fife, and Member of Parliament for Kinross, was created 1st Baronet of

Lochore on 25 July 1665, his wife was Emilia, daughter of John Balfour of Burleigh, he died on 30 March 1729 and was succeeded by his son Sir John Malcolm as 2nd Baronet of Lochore, he married Isabel Balfour, and died on 12 August 1753. Their son Sir Michael Malcolm succeeded. He died in Edinburgh on 25 October 1805. [a surname from the Gaelic *Mael Coluimb*; examples date from the thirteenth century][Duncan Malcolm was in Boston by 1694, while Neil Malcolm, a merchant, settled in Jamaica by 1773]

MARSHALL OF MENER IN THE TWEED VALLEY. King Robert I granted Adam Marshall the barony of Mener in Peebles-shire in 13..., which he resigned in favour of Alexander Baddeby. [From the French *Marechal* meaning 'groom', examples date from the twelfth century][John Marshall, a cooper, emigrated to North Carolina in 1775, while Edmund Marshall, from Aberdeen, emigrated to Plymouth Bay colony in 1636]

MAULE OF PANMURE IN ANGUS. Peter de Maule acquired the barony of Panmure before 1215 through his marriage to Christina de Valonis or Vallance, a member of another family with its roots in Normandy. The National Records of Scotland has the barony of Panmure papers from 1346. Sir Thomas Maule of Panmure and his wife Katherine Cramond disposed of the lands of Ballishane in the Barony of Panmure on 12 August 1489; and in 1494 he granted his nephew and heir apparent, Thomas Maule, the lands and Barony of Panmure including Scryne, which was confirmed by King James IV on 2 June 1494; Sir Thomas Maule, was killed at the Battle of Flodden on 9 September 1513. Thomas Maule of Panmure was served heir to his father Robert Maule on 5 June 1560. On 17 March 1541, King James V granted Thomas Maule, son and heir apparent of Robert Maule of Panmure, the lands and Barony of Panmure, with its castle, fort, mills, fishing rights, the mill of Cromby, the lands of Muirdrum, the alehouse at Pitlivie, the lands of Newtoun and Blacklaws, Tofts, Blacate, mill lands at Panmure, the lands of Banven and mill, lads of Balrudderie, lands of Carmyllie and mill, Newtoun, Easterhillis, Midhills, Auchlair and Monquhir, lands of Sechin, Glaster, Carnegie, Pitlivie, Achrennie, Scryne, Craigmill, East Port of Panmure, lands of Balhousie and Ballisshane in Angus, also the lands of Panlathy with mill, and part of Pitcunrane in the Regality of Kirriemuir in Angus, now incorporated into the Barony of Panmure, also the East Port of Panmure was created as a burgh of Barony; on 23 August 1576 King James VI confirmed Patrick Maule, son and heir apparent of Thomas Maule of Panmure, the lands and Barony of Panmure; on 8 January 1639, King Charles I granted Patrick Maule of Panmure the Barony of Balmakellie in Kincardineshire. [The National Records of Scotland have Patrick Maule of Panmure's papers from 1612 until 1666.], Latterly he was 1st Earl of Panmure, he was succeeded by son George, as 2nd Earl, from 1651 until

1674. The 3rd Earl was George Maule from 1665 until 1685, next was James the 4th Earl – he was a Jacobite in 1713 so forfeited his lands and titles. The Earldom of Panmure was created by King Charles I in 1646, The Barony was merged into the new Earldom, though it was recreated in the nineteenth century. [This family has its origins in the department of Seine-et-Oise in France and first appears in Scotland during the reign of King David I, examples of the surname in Scotland date from the twelfth century] [Thomas Maule emigrated to Salem, Massachusetts in 1695; Robert Maule to North America around 1706; James Maull, a minister in Antigua before 1697] [Registrum de Panmure, Edinburgh, 1874]

MAULE OF BAIKIE IN ANGUS. On 17 November 1641, King Charles I confirmed Elizabeth Maule, daughter of Patrick Maule of Panmure, the lands and Barony of Baikie, also the lands and Barony of Belhelvie in Aberdeenshire.

MAXWELL OF CAERLAVEROCK, DUMFRIES-SHIRE. Henry Maxwell of the Barony of Caerlaverock pre1345. [The Book of Caerlaverock, Memoirs of the Maxwells, Edinburgh, 1873]

MAXWELL OF CALDERWOOD. King James II granted John Maxwell of Calderwood the lands and Barony of Finlaystoun and the lands of Stanlee in Renfrewshire, on 4 December 1450 and confirmed on 3 April 1454; on 19 January 1477 King James III granted the lands and Barony of Hiltoun in Berwickshire, also the lands of Auchincloich, Craigtoun, and Drumbuy in Dunbartonshire, to Elizabeth Maxwell the daughter of Sir John Maxwell of Calderwood; On 22 January 1478, King James III granted Sir George Maxwell, son and heir apparent of John Maxwell of Calderwood, the lands and Barony of Finlaystoun in Renfrewshire; on 28 March 1628, Sir John Maxwell of Calderwood was created Baronet of Mauldslie in Nova Scotia with 16000 acres there, He died around 1670 when his son Sir William Maxwell became the Second Baronet and died in 1716. The lands and title were inherited by his cousin Sir William Maxwell as Third Baronet.

MAXWELL OF GREENAN IN KIRKCUDBRIGHTSHIRE. On 22 February 1510, King James IV granted Lord John Maxwell the lands of Gordonstoun, including the lands of Glenkene, Bennahead, Akedenenchu, Knocneman, Strowkawin, and Hottirsduskan, with the grain mill of Bonnahede, Loch Invar, and the lands of Greenan, now incorporated into the Barony of Greenan.

MAXWELL OF CRAWFORDMUIR IN LANARKSHIRE. On 1 January 1530, King James V granted Lord Robert Maxwell the lands and Barony of Crawfordmuir with its house, castle, fort, woods, mills etc, the lands of

Bonnytoun and Hyndford in Lanarkshire, the lands of Halkshaws in Peebles, united into the Barony of Crawfordmuir; also, on 12 June 1541, King James V granted Lord Robert Maxwell the lands and Barony of Buthill in Kirkcudbrightshire.

MAXWELL OF MAXWELL IN ROXBURGHSHIRE. On 28 July 1534, King James V granted Lord Robert Maxwell the Barony of Maxwell, including the lands and Barony of Caerlaverock in Dumfries-shire, the lands and Barony of Sprynkaillie in the Lordship of Annandale, the Stewartship of Annandale and Kirkcudbright, the lands of Garnsallauch and Dursqhen, land in Dumfries, the lands and Barony of Balmacreuchy in Perthshire, the lands of Gordonstoun and Grenane in Kirkcudbrightshire, the lands and Barony of Mearns, also Nether Pollock in Renfrew-shire, castles, towers, forts, mills, fishing rights, pendicles, etc, now incorporated into the Barony and Lordship of Maxwell; Lord Maxwell was killed at the Battle of Flodden on 9 September 1513; on 6 June 1540, King James V confirmed Lord Robert Maxwell in the Barony of Maxwell, as above.

MAXWELL OF MALDISLIE IN LANARKSHIRE. On 30 May 1553, Queen Mary, granted James Maxwell, son and heir of John Maxwell of Calderwood, the lands and Barony of Maldislie.

MAXWELL OF TERRIGLES IN DUMFRIES-SHIRE. On 8 May 1566, King Henry and Queen Mary confirmed John Maxwell in the lands and Barony of Terrigles.

MAXWELL OF LAMINGTOUN IN LANARKSHIRE. On 2 March 1578, King James VI confirmed Edward Maxwell in the lands and Barony of Lamingtoun.

MAXWELL OF FYNDLASTOUN-MAXWELL IN RENFREWSHIRE. On 8 October 1594, King James VI confirmed George Maxwell, son of Patrick Maxwell of Newmark, the lands and Barony of Fyndlastoun-Maxwell.

MAXWELL OF TEALING IN ANGUS. On 19 January 1599, King James VI confirmed David Maxwell of Tealing in the Barony of Tealing which included Tealing with lands in Angus and Perthshire.

MAXWELL OF POLLOCK IN GLASGOW. John Maxwell was created a baronet of Nova Scotia on 25 November 1630; on 12 April 1682, Sir John Maxwell of Pollock was created as a Baronet. [a surname derived from a location in Roxburghshire, examples date from the twelfth century][Dr John Maxwell settled in Port Royal, Jamaica and died in 1673, while David Maxwell emigrated to New York in 1774] ['The Memoirs of the Maxwell of Pollock', W. Fraser, 1863]

MAXWELL OF INNERWEIK IN EAST LOTHIAN. On 13 September 1641, King Charles I confirmed James Maxwell of Innerweik, in the Barony of Innerweik.

MAXWELL OF ORCHARDTOUN IN KIRKCUDBRIGHTSHIRE. On 30 June 1663 King Charles II created Robert Maxwell of Orchardtoun, also of Ballycastle, County Londonderry, as a Baronet, when he died around 1672, he was succeeded as 2nd Baronet by Sir Robert Maxwell who died childless in 1693 when the Barony became extinct.

MAXWELL OF MONREITH IN WIGTONSHIRE. On 8 January 1681 William Maxwell was created as a Baronet, he died in April 1709 when he was succeeded by his son, Sir Alexander Maxwell, as 2nd Baronet of Monreith, he was followed by his son, Sir William Maxwell, on 23 May 1730.

MAXWELL OF SPRINGKELL IN DUMFRIES-SHIRE. On 7 February 1683, Sir Patrick Maxwell was created as a Baronet, he died in April 1723 and was succeeded by his son, Sir William Maxwell, as 2nd Baronet of Springkell, he died on 14 July 1760.

MEIGLE OF MEIGLE IN PERTHSHIRE. In 1378 King Robert II granted John Meigle, son of William Meigle, the barony of Meigle. His descendant William Meigle resigned the barony to David, Earl of Crawford on 24 December 1404. [a surname of territorial origin from Perthshire, examples date from the thirteenth century]

MEIGNERS OF ENACH IN DUMFRIES-SHIRE. On 4 September 1430 King James I granted John Meigners the land and Barony of Enach formerly held by his father Sir David Meigners. [de Meyners is name of Norman origin, examples in Scotland date from the late thirteenth century.]

MELDRUM OF AWNE. King David II granted the Barony of Awne with its forest to Philip Meldrum around 1343. [a territorial surname derived from a location in Aberdeenshire, examples date from the late thirteenth century] [George Meldrum, a Jacobite, was transported to Antigua in 1716, while William Meldrum, a clergyman, emigrated to Virginia in 1756.]

MELDRUM OF FYVIE IN ABERDEENSHIRE. On 21 February 1545, Queen Mary granted William Meldrum, son and heir apparent of George Meldrum of Fyvie, alias Formartine, in Aberdeenshire, with its tower, fort, manor, mill, fishing rights, etc, also the Barony of Auchtirles, etc, also in Aberdeenshire. [Fyvie Castle, London,1928]

MELDRUM OF BARRY IN ANGUS. On 9 October 1587, King James VI granted James Meldrum of Seggy, the lands and Barony of Barry.

MELDRUM OF EDEN IN ABERDEENSHIRE. On 13 February 1599, King James VI confirmed Thomas Meldrum, son and heir apparent of Patrick Meldrum of Eden, in the lands and Barony of Eden.

MELVILLE OF GLENBERVIE IN KINCARDINESHIRE. John Melville was granted the Barony of Glenbervie by King David II on 6 April 1366. [A surname derived from Malaville in Normandy, examples date from the twelfth century][as Melvin it appears in New England by 1684, David Melville, a merchant in Boston by 1690s]

MELVILLE OF CARNBEE IN FIFE. On 11 August 1496, King James IV granted the lands and Barony of Carnbee to John Melville; on 21 February 1509, King James IV granted John Melville of Carnbee, the lands of Grantoun in Midlothian, incorporated into the Barony of Carnbee.

MELVILLE OF DYSART IN ANGUS. On 21 February 1510, King James IV granted John Melville, part of the lands of Baldovy, also the lands of Dysart, with fishing rights on the River South Esk in Angus, now incorporated into the Barony of Dysart. On 18 July 1532, King James V granted Thomas Melville, son and heir of Alexander Melville of Dysart, the lands and Barony of Dysart, Burntoun, etc in Angus; on 20 January 1573, King James VI confirmed James Melville of Liegravin, son and heir apparent of Thomas Melville of Dysart, the lands and Barony of Dysart, Burntoun, etc.

MELVILLE OF WESTER KINGHORN IN FIFE. On 9 January 1588, King James VI granted Robert Melville of Murdocairney, the lands and Barony of Wester Kinghorn, incorporated into the Barony and Regality of Burntisland; on 1 March 1588, King James VI granted Robert Melville, son and heir apparent of Robert Melville of Murdocairney, the lands and Barony of Wester Kinghorn, which was confirmed on 1 February 1592.

MELVILLE OF KILWINNING IN AYRSHIRE. On 17 May 1592, King James VI granted William Melville, the Commendatur of Kilwinning, many lands in Ayrshire incorporated into the Barony and Regality of Kilwinning.

MENTEITH OF PORT OF MENTEITH IN PERTHSHIRE. King Wiliam III granted Malcolm, Earl of Menteith the Port of Menteith as a burgh of barony on 8 February 1467; William Melville of Menteith of Keir was granted the lands and Barony of Alweth on 25 September 1489. [a placename in Perthshire, examples date from the thirteenth century] [Alexander Monteith emigrated to New Jersey in 1684] ['The Red Book of Menteith' by W. Fraser, 1880]

MENTEITH OF WEST KERSE IN STIRLINGSHIRE. On 18 February 1509, King James IV granted Sir William Menteith of Kerse, the lands of Pordovyne with its mill, West Kerse, with its tower, fort, mansion house orchards, fishing rights, the lands of Ochiltree with its mill, the lands of Monguellis and Randiford, now incorporated into the Barony of West Kerse; on 15 March 1541, King James V granted William Menteith of Kerse, the lands and Barony of Tillicoultry, including the lands of Balharty, Drummy, Shannach, Cosnachtoun, Colinsdavach, with grain mill, Carnton and fulling mill, etc in Clackmannanshire; on 26 October 1542, King James V confirmed William Menteith in the lands and Barony of Kerse, the lands of Rannyford, in Stirlingshire, the lands of Ochiltree, the lands of Perdovin, in West Lothian, also the lands and Barony of Alveth, and the lands of Cavirk in Stirlingshire, now incorporated into the Barony of Kerse; on 30 October 1552, Queen Mary granted John Menteith, son and heir apparent of Robert Menteith of Kerse, the lands and Barony of Wester Kerse, also the lands and Barony of Alveth; on 8 July 1565, Queen Mary granted John Menteith, son and heir apparent of Robert Menteith of Kerse, the lands and Barony of Wester Kerse, and the lands and Barony of Alveth, etc. incorporated into the Barony of Wester Kerse; on 13 February 1598, King James VI granted William Menteith, son and heir apparent of Sir William Menteith, was granted the lands and Barony of Kerse.

MENTEITH OF PRESTOUN IN MIDLOTHIAN. On 20 March 1550, Queen Mary confirmed Elizabeth Menteith, daughter of William Menteith of Kerse, in the lands and Barony of Prestoun.

MENZIES OF 'ENATHE'. King David II granted the barony of Enach in the 'Neiche' valley in 13....

MENZIES OF MENZIES IN PERTHSHIRE. On 16 January 1500, King James IV granted land at Eddirule, land at Tolicro also land at Nether Mewan, at Tigirmach, and at Thomtheogle in Appin of Dull, Perthshire, now known as the Barony of Cammysarney, to Robert Menzies of Menzies; on 1 September 1502 King James IV granted to Robert Menzies of that Ilk, the lands of Rannoch in Perthshire, including Downane, Kinlauchter,

Cammysirochtis, Ardlarach, Kilquhonane, Larane, Ardlair, Laragane, the island on Loch Rannoch, the lochs of Rannoch and Erochty now incorporated into the Barony of Rannoch; on 2 October 1510, King James IV granted Sir Robert Menzies of that Ilk, the lands and Barony of Enoch with its mills etc, also the Barony of Culter with its mill, the lands and Barony of Weem, including Aberfeldy, Ardferelemore, Rawire, Dalrawyre, Glassy, Kinnaldy, Glen Golantyne, Comrie, Auchillis, Fernauchty, Merynche, Edromuck, and the lands of the Thanage of Crannick, Auchmore, Duncrosk, Candknok with Roras in Glen Lyon, in Perthshire, formed into the Barony of Weem; on 22 December 1591, King James VI confirmed Alexander Menzies of that Ilk, the lands and Barony of Rannoch; Sir Alexander Menzies, was created Baronet of Castle Menzies on 2 September 1665 by King Charles II on 2 September 1665, he was Member of Parliament for Perthshire, he married Agnes, daughter of Sir John Campbell of Glenorchy, on his death in 1695 the baronetcy went to his grandson Sir Alexander Menzies, his wife was Christian, daughter of Sir Neil Campbell, he died by 1736 and was succeeded by his son Sir Robert Menzies in 3rd Baronet, he married Mary, daughter of the Earl of Bute, Sir Robert died childless on 4 September 1786. [Originally de Meyners a Norman surname, a surname in Scotland since the thirteenth century][Ninian Menzies, from Glasgow, a merchant in Virginia, died on St Eustatia in 1781, while William Menzies, from Weem, settled in Wisconsin around 1820.] [The Red and White book of the Menzies, Glasgow, 1894]

MENZIES OF PITFODELLS IN ABERDEENSHIRE. On 1 May 1517, King James V granted Thomas Menzies, the son and heir apparent of Gilbert Menzies of Findon, the lands of Middleton of Pitfoddells, Easter and Wester Pitfoddell, with fishing on the River Dee, in Aberdeenshire, now incorporated into the Barony of Pitfoddells; on 16 July 1588, King James VI confirmed Gilbert Menzies of Cowlie, son and heir apparent of Thomas Menzies of Pitfodells the Provost of Aberdeen, the lands of Easter, Middle, and Wester Pitfodells, now incorporated into the Barony of Pitfodells.

MENZIES OF RANNOCH IN PERTHSHIRE. On 1 May 1533, King James V granted Alexander Menzies, son and heir apparent of Robert Menzies of Rannoch, the lands and Barony of Rannoch, including Downane, Kinclauchir, Cammyserachtis, Ardlaroche, Kilquhonane, Lairane, Ardlair, the lake of Rannoch and Lochty with their islands.

MENZIES OF CASTLE MENZIES IN PERTHSHIRE. On 2 September 1665, Sir Alexander Menzies of that Ilk was created as a baronet, he was an MP from 1693 until his death in 1695, he was succeeded by his grandson Sir Alexander Menzies as the 2nd Baronet of Castle Menzies, he died in 1730s and his son Sir Robert Menzies became the 3rd Baronet.

MERCER OF MEIKLOUR IN PERTHSHIRE. King James II granted Andrew Mercer the Barony of Meiklour including the lands of Balleyfe, Culcarny, Kynnarde, Mekilloure, Awdese, Dalketh, Tulibagill, Dunbarny, Gilgerstoun and Ledenoch, on 21 March 1443; on 7 May 1511, King James IV granted Henry Mercer the lands and Barony of Meiklour, including the lands of Balleif, Ballachous, Colcarny, Audeys, Dalkeith, Tullibagill, Kinnard, Dunbarnie, Pitcaithly, Gilgistoun, and Lednoch in the counties of Perthshire and Kinross-shire; on 13 July 1527, King James V confirmed Laurence Mercer of Meiklour, in the lands of Meiklour, Tullybaglis with its mill, Windyedge, Dunbarny, Leidnach, Pitcarthly, Kilgraston, Kinnaird, Awdyis with its tower and mill, Balladyis, Ballaif, Cowcarny and Dalkeith in Perthshire, now integrated into the Barony of Meiklour; on 25 April 1545, Queen Mary granted Laurence Mercer the Barony of Meiklour.

MERCER OF BALHOUSIE IN PERTHSHIRE. On 23 May 1478, King James III granted Robert Mercer of Balleffe, the Barony of Balhousie. [The Mercer Family, manuscript, Perth Library]

MERCER OF ALDIE IN PERTHSHIRE. James Mercer of Aldie, was created Baronet of Aldie around 1660. He was son of Sir Lawrence Mercer of Aldie and his wife Cecily Colville, he married Jean Stewart of Grandtully, Perthshire, in 1648. [The surname Mercer is one of occupational origin, initially silk dealer but later merchant. Examples in Scotland date from around 1200 AD] [Early examples in the colonies include Robert Mercer from Ayrshire, bound for Jamaica in 1683; and Hugh Mercer, from Aberdeenshire, a physician and American patriot, who died in Princeton in 1777][An account of the Mercers of Aldie and Meiklour, Perth, 1868]

MIRETOUN OF CAMBO IN FIFE. On 19 April 1506, King James IV granted the lands of Cambo, now a Barony, to David Miretoun of that Ilk; on 16 January 1556, Queen Mary, granted Thomas Miretoun, son and heir apparent, of William Miretoun of Cambo, the lands and Barony of Cambo. [Possibly derived from Myretoun, now Morton, in Kemback, Cambo, Fife]

MITCHELL OF WESTSHORE IN SHETLAND. King George I granted the Baronetcy of Westshore to John Mitchell, Justiciar of the Northern Isles on 19 June 1724, son of John Mitchell and his wife Jean Umphray; their son Sir Andrew Mitchell born 1706, an advocate, became the second baronet of Westshore, he died on 29 June 1764. [the surname is a variant of Michael, examples in Scotland date from the fifteenth century] [John Mitchell, a tobacco factor, settled in Virginia before 1776, while Robert Mitchell, a schoolmaster emigrated to Maryland in 1723][Mitchell family history, Bristol, 1923]

MONCRIEFF OF MONCRIEFF in Perthshire. Matthew Moncrieff obtained a charter from Sir Roger de Mowbray of the lands of Moncreiff and Baconachin which were created into a Barony by King Alexander II in 1248. On 28 December 1464 King James III granted John Moncreiff the lands of Auchindand in Fife, which were merged into the Barony of Moncreiff; King James III confirmed the acquisition of the lands of Gilchristoun in the Barony of Methven in Perthshire on 3 April 1467; on 29 August 1495 King James IV granted John Moncreiff the lands and Barony of Moncreiff. Sir John Moncreiff was killed at the Battle of Flodden on 9 September 1513; on 9 June 1575, King James VI granted William Moncreiff, nephew and heir apparent of William Moncreiff of Moncreiff, the lands and Barony of Moncreiff; on 14 June 1598, King James VI granted William Moncreiff of that Ilk, the lands and Barony of Moncreiff; Sir John Moncreiff, second son of William Moncreiff, was born in 1588, was created Baronet of Moncreiff, in 1626, and died in 1651. On his death the baronetcy was inherited by his son John Moncreiff, born 1635, died around 1686. The third Baronet was Sir David Moncreiff, an officer of the Regiment of Guards who died in 1692 and is buried in Greyfriars, Edinburgh, he was succeeded by his brother Sir James Moncreiff, another army officer who died in 1704; the succession passed to his cousin John Moncreiff of Tippermaloch, born 1628 and died in 1714, when his son Sir Hugh Moncreiff succeeded but died unmarried in 1744. [a surname derived from a place in Perthshire, example date from the thirteenth century][David Moncreiff, a soldier, died at Darien in 1699, while Robert Moncreiff, a clergyman, emigrated to Antigua in1748][The Moncreiffs and the Moncreiffes, Edinburgh, 1929]

MONCRIEFF. Thomas Moncreiff was created as a baronet of New Moncreiff in Nova Scotia on 22 April 1626, a sasine dated 30 June 1626. Thomas Moncrieff of Moncreiff, Perthshire, born 1626, second son of Thomas Moncreiff, a merchant in Kirkwall and his wife Elspeth Baikie, was granted the Barony of Moncreiff, formerly held by Sir John Moncreiff, by King Charles II in 1667, Thomas died in 1715.

MONCUR OF FORDY IN PERTHSHIRE. On 19 November 1541, King James V confirmed Andrew Moncur of that Ilk in the lands of Knap, with its mill, Rashcrook, Forde, Newtoun, in Perthshire, now incorporated in the Barony of Fordy.

MONCUR OF UNTHANK IN PERTHSHIRE. On 26 April 1593, King James VI confirmed Andrew Moncur of Moncur, in the Barony of Unthank. [a surname of Norman-French origin, examples in Scotland date from the thirteenth century][James Moncur emigrated to South Carolina by 1685]

MONEYPENNY OF AIRTH IN STIRLINGSHIRE. On 1 May 1450 King James II created the Halls of Airth a barony for Sir William Monypeny. [Monypenny is a surname derived from Normandy, examples of the surname in Scotland date from around 1200] [Lieutenant Colonel Moneypenny petitioned for land on Cape Breton in 1764]

MONEYPENNY OF BRODLAND IN ABERDEENSHIRE. King James II granted William Moneypeny of Ardweny and Conkirsalte, the lands and Barony of Brodland, Rattray, Rothaquhy and Hillhill and the mill of Creichmount, in Aberdeenshire, also the Barony of Buittle in Kirkcudbrightshire, which included the castle of Buittle, the lands of Kirkennan, Barloghane, Barnahasteris and Donvall, on 7 October 1458.

MONEYPENNY OF FELDY IN PERTHSHIRE. On 25 December 1466 King James III granted the Barony of Feldy to Lord William Moneypenny.; King James III granted the Barony of Torscrachan in Galloway to Lord William Moneypenny on 31 August 1472.

MONEYPENNY OF PITMILLY IN FIFE. On 1 November 1600, King James VI confirmed James Moneypenny of Pitmilly, son of David Moneypenny yhe younger, the Barony of Pitmilly.

MONRO OF FOULIS IN EASTER ROSS. Colonel Hector Monro was created a Baronet of Nova Scotia on 7 June 1634. [Munro is a surname derived from the Gaelic 'Rothach' meaning a man from Ro, examples date from the fourteenth century. [Reverend John Munro, settled in Virginia in 1650, while Donald Munro, a soldier, was transported to Barbados in 1651] [The Monros of Auchinbowie and cognate families, Edinburgh, 1911]

MONTEITH OF CARRIBERS IN WEST LOTHIAN. On 12 February 1642, King Charles I granted William Monteith, a merchant burgess of Edinburgh, the lands and Barony of Carribers. [a surname from a place in Perthshire, examples date from the thirteenth century][Alexander Monteith emigrated to New York in 1684, while Robert Monteith, a sailor, died at Hudson May in 1680]

MONTGOMERY OF EGLINTON IN AYRSHIRE. On 16 November 1528, Hugh Montgomery, the Earl of Eglinton, was granted the lands and Barony of Ardrossan in Ayrshire, the lands and Lordship of Eaglesham, and Eastwood in Renfrewshire, part of Bonnytoun and Poltoun in Midlothian, and at Lochranza on Bute; on 29 November 1545 Queen Mary granted the Earl of Eglintoun the lands and Barony of Tarbortoun in Ayrshire; on 19 May 1546, Queen Mary confirmed Hugh Montgomery, Earl of Eglinton, in the lands and

Lordship of Eaglesham in Renfrewshire, also the lands and Lordship of the lands and Barony of Eaglesham and Robertoun in Ayrshire; on 8 November 1565, King Henry and Queen Mary confirmed Hugh Montgomery, the Earl of Eglintoun, in the lands, Lordship and Barony of Eaglesham; on 22 May 1576, King James VI granted Hugh Montgomery, son and heir apparent of the Earl of Eglinton, [a surname derived from St Foi de Montgomery in Normandy, examples in Scotland date from the twelfth century][Alexander Montgomery, a Covenanter, ws banished to the Carolinas in 1684, while James Montgomery, a planter, died at Darien in 1698. [Memorials of the Montgomeries, Earls of Eglinton, Edinburgh,1859]

MONTGOMERY OF SEYTOUN IN EAST LOTHIAN. On 16 January 1590, King James VI confirmed the grant by Lord Seytoun to Margaret Montgomery his wife, of the lands, Lordships and Baronies of Seytoun, Wintoun, Tranent, Longnidrie, Myldis, Wyndegowleis, and Greendykes.

MONTGOMERIE OF SKELMORLIE IN AYRSHIRE. Sir Robert Montgomerie was created as a baronet of Nova Scotia on 10 January 1628, a sasine dated 29 December 1628, he died in November 1651 when his son Sir Robert became the Second Baronet. [In 1717 Sir Robert Montgomery of Skelmorlie settled in Georgia, while Alexander Montgomery, a Covenanter, was transported to Carolina in 1684]

MONTGOMERY OF BALGRAY IN AYRSHIRE. On 2 August 1601, King James VI granted Nigel Montgomery the younger of Langshaw, various lands in Ayrshire incorporated into the Barony of Balgray.

MORE, WILLIAM, was granted the Barony of Abercorn, formerly held by John Graham, around 1341. [A Middle English surname indicating residence on a moor, or possibly from the Gaelic word *'Mhor'* meaning big, variants include Moore, Muir, examples date from the late thirteenth century]. [William Muir or Moor, from Stirling, was transported to East New Jersey in 1685, while George Muir, a Covenanter, was transported to the colonies in 1685.]

MORESON OF CORSTORPHIN IN MIDLOTHIAN. On 22 October 1599, King James VI confirmed John Moreson, a merchant burgess and baillie of Edinburgh, the lands and Barony of Corstorphine. [a patronymic surname, examples date from the fifteenth century][James Morison was transported to Virginia in 1696, while Norman Morison, a farmer from Lewis, emigrated to Philadelphia in 1774]

MOWAT OF KINBLETHNOT IN ANGUS. [A surname of Norman French origin, originally *Mont Hault*, examples include William Mowat appears in the

Register of Arbroath Abbey in 1219, also as a charter witness between 1198 and 1218. William Mowat signed the Scottish Declaration of Independence in 1320 and was killed at the Siege of Norham Castle in 1327]. A John Mowat was granted lands in the Barony of Ferne, Angus, also lands in the Barony of Kinblackmonth, Angus, by King Robert III, later in 1379 the king granted Richard Mowat, chancellor of the church at Brechin, the barony of Kinblathmont. King Robert II had already granted Barony of Ferne in Angus to Richard Mowat on 3 November 1377. [John Mowat, was transported to Barbados in 1663, while some Mowats emigrated to Georgia in 1774.]

MOWAT OF BROUGHTOUN IN PEEBLES-SHIRE. On 27 January 1507, King James IV granted Alexander Mowat of Stonehouse, the Barony of Broughtoun with its lands and mill; on 28 March 1517, King James V confirmed John Mowat, son and heir apparent of Alexander Mowat of Stonehouse in the lands of Stonehouse, in Lanarkshire, the lands of Brochtoun, Winkistoun and Burofield in Peebles-shire.

MOWAT OF INGLISTOUN IN MIDLOTHIAN. On 2 June 1664, King Charles II created Sir George Mowat of Ingliston, son of Roger Mowat of Dumbruch, a Baronet, he died in September 1666 and was succeeded by his son Sir Roger Mowat the 2nd Baronet of Inglistoun, when he died in 1683 his brother Sir William became the 3rd Baronet of Inglistoun.

MOWBRAY OF BERNBOWGALL IN WEST LOTHIAN. John Mowbray, son and heir apparent of David Mowbray of Bernbowgale, was granted the lands and Barony of Dummanyn in West Lothian by King James III on 23 February 1488; on 27 March 1511 King James IV granted Sir John Mowbray of Bernbowgall, nephew of David Mowbray of Bernbowgall, the lands and Barony of Inverkeithing, including the lands of Kincarny, Pitadro with its mill, the lands of Coldside, Tofts, Balbugy, Caslane, Dalis, Spencerfield, Salweynche, now incorporated into the Barony of Inverkeithing. On 10 March 1539, King James V confirmed Robert Mowbray of Bernbowgall, in the lands and Barony of Dunmany, with the castle, fort and manor, in West Lothian, also fishing rights in the Rivers Cramond and Forth; the lands of Inverkeithing, etc, now incorporated into the Barony of Dunmany; on 12 December 1578, King James VI granted Robert Mowbray, son of John Mowbray of Barnebougall, the lands and Barony of Dunmany with other lands now merged into the Barony of Dunmany. [A surname originating in Calvados, France, examples in Scotland date from around 1200][Thomas Moubray, a Covenanter, was transported to the West Indies in 1678]

MUIR OF ROWALLAN IN AYRSHIRE. Patrick Muir of Rowallan, son of Sir William Muir, was created a Baronet on 4 May 1662 by King Charles II, it became extinct on his death in 1700. [the name means moor, it appears in

Scottish records since the thirteenth century as Muir, Mure, or Moor][James Muir died in Virginia by 1689; while William Muir was transported to East New Jersey in 1685][The History and descent of the House of Rowallan, Glasgow, 1825]

MURE OF WEST NISBET IN BERWICKSHIRE. On 27 December 1639, King Charles I, granted James Mure, a merchant burgess of Edinburgh, the lands and Barony of West Nisbet

MURRAY OF STRATHAVEN IN LANARKSHIRE. King David II granted the Barony of Strathaven to Maurice Murray ca.1341, formerly held by Alexander Stewart, also the Barony of Hawick in Roxburghshire. [A surname of territorial origin derived from Moray, examples date from the early thirteenth century.] [Alexander Murray, was transported to Virginia in 1652, died in Ware, Virginia, by 1703, while Anna Murray, imprisoned in Edinburgh Tolbooth, was transported to Jamaica in 1685.]

MURRAY OF HAWICK AND SPROUSTOUN IN ROXBURGHSHIRE. Thomas Murray was granted the Barony of Hawick and Sproustoun by King David II 1358.

MURRAY OF TULCHADAM IN STIRLINGSHIRE. King James III granted John Murray of Galwamour, the lands and Barony of Tulchadam, the lands of Polmais-Weland, New Park, Schephalch and Wekitshaw, with tenants and tenantries in 1474; on 14 March 1508, King James IV granted William Murray, son and heir of John Murray of Tulchadam, the lands and Barony of Tulchadam, now the Barony of Tulchadam; on 21 March 1569, King James VI confirmed Agnes Cunningham, wife of William Murray of Touchadam, in the lands and Barony of Touchadam. [A genealogical chart 1358-1907, of the Murrays of Touchadam and Polmaise, London, 1907]

MURRAY OF COCKPOOL IN DUMFRIES-SHIRE. On 15 February 1508, King James IV confirmed Sir John Murray in the lands of Cockpool, Ruval, the tower and fort of Cunlungane, Coklakis, Pihyllis, Sclathwait, Runepatrick, Bridechapel, Priestdykes, and Howalside in Annandale, also, the lands of Laik and Ardbigland in Kirkcudbrightshire, now incorporated into the Barony of Cockpool. On 19 July 1625 Master Richard Murray of Cockpuill, was created as a Baronet of Nova Scotia.

MURRAY OF BLACKBARONY IN PEEBLES-SHIRE. On 4 May 1507, King James IV granted John Murray the lands and Barony of Haltoun with its mill and tenantries; then on 9 June 1508, King James IV granted John Murray of

Blackbarony the lands of Overmenzeane in the Barony of Oliver Castle in Peebles-shire, incorporated into the Barony of Haltoun-Murray, alias Blackbarony; on 4 November 1512, King James IV confirmed John Murray of Blackbarony in the King's lands in Peebles now united into the Barony of Haltoun-Murray, alias Blackbarony; on 26 February 1566, King Henry and Queen Mary confirmed John Murray, son and heir apparent of Andrew Murray of Blackbarony, the lands and Barony of Haltoun alias Blackbarony; on 8 March 1593, King James VI granted John Murray of Blackbarony, the lands and Barony of Blackbarony.

MURRAY OF TULLYBARDINE IN PERTHSHIRE. On 26 January 1444, King James II granted David Murray the Barony of Tullibardine, comprising of the lands of Tullibardine, Gask-Murray, Dalreach, Polgoure, Clow, Dundovane-Bordland, Dundovane-Glencoy, Pitver, and Finnach in Strathearn, Perthshire; on 7 November 1542, King James V confirmed William Murray of Tullibardine in the town, Barony, and lands of Tullibardine, with its tower, mill and fort, and other lands now incorporated into the Barony of Tullibardine; on 30 July 1587, King James VI granted John Murray of Tullibardine the lands and Lordship of Balquhidder, which was confirmed on 14 October 1591; on 17 December 1638, King Charles I granted Patrick Murray, Earl of Tullibardine, various lands in Perthshire incorporated into the Barony of Logiealmond; William Murray, the Marquis of Tulibardine, born 1688, a Jacobite in 1715, fought at the Battle of Glenshiel in 1719, and at Culloden in 1746, died in the Tower of London in 1747. [The Clans of Atholl, Blair Atholl, 1997][The Jacobite Peerage, Edinburgh, 1904]

MURRAY OF ARNCORSK IN FIFE. On 21 January 1508, King James IV granted David Murray, son and heir apparent of Sir Andrew Murray, the lands and Baronies of Ancorsk and Kippow, including Pittilloch, Condelane, Heicham, Letham, Forgy, Bene, Catoichill, Balvarde with their manors and mills in the Barony of Ancorsk, also the lands of Kippow, a quarter of Muirtoun of Tentsmuir, Halery, Wilkinstoun, Carlhurly, Lochtoun, plus the mill of Kippow, now incorporated into the Barony of Arncorsk; on 21 January 1572, King James VI granted Andrew Murray, son and heir apparent of Sir Andrew Murray of Arngask, the lands and Baronies of Arncorsk and Kippow; on 26 September 1590, King James VI granted Andrew Murray, son and heir apparent of Andrew Murray of Arngask, the lands and Baronies of Arngask and Kippow etc, now incorporated in Arngask.

MURRAY OF COLLENOWYIS IN PERTHSHIRE. On 10 April 1580, King James VI granted David Murray the lands and Barony of Collenowyis; on 8 October 1584, King James VI granted David Murray, brother german of Andrew Murray of Arngask, the lands and Barony of Collenowyis.

MURRAY OF SEGGY IN FIFE. On 2 March 1601, King James VI granted David Murray of Gosperty, the lands and Barony of Segy.

MURRAY OF CLAIRMONTH. Sir William Murray of Clairmonth was created as a baronet of Nova Scotia on 1 June 1626.

MURRAY OF NOVA SCOTIA. Sir Archibald Murray was created as a Baronet of Nova Scotia on 15 May 1628, also see a sasine dated 10 October 1628.

MURRAY OF ELIBANK. Sir Patrick Murray was created as a baronet of Nova Scotia on 16 May 1628, a sasine dated 23 October 1630.

MURRAY OF NEW DUNEARN. William Murray was created a Baronet of Nova Scotia on 2 October 1630, a sasine dated 30 December 1630.

MURRAY OF LANGNEWTOUN IN ROXBURGHSHIRE. On 5 March 1639, King Charles I granted Captain Walter Murray, brother german of Sir Archibald Murray of Blackbarony, the lands and Barony of Langnewtoun.

MURRAY OF BLEBO IN FIFE. On 17 November 1641, King Charles I confirmed Sir William Murray of Blebo, in the Barony of Blebo.

MURRAY OF ALLOA IN CLACKMANNANSHIRE. On 1 March 1650, King Charles II granted Robert Murray, a merchant burgess of Edinburgh, the lands, Lordship, Barony and Regality of Alloa, also the lands and Barony of Pluscarden in Moray.

MURRAY OF ARBROATH IN ANGUS. On 15 December 1641, King Charles I granted William Murray, the lands and Barony and Regality of Arbroath.

MURRAY OF BROUGHTON. On 13 February 1664 King Charles II created William Murray of Stanhope a Baronet and in 1671 he also had the Barony of Broughton, he died by 1690 and was succeeded by his son Sir David Murray the 2nd Baronet of Stanhope and Broughton on his death on 14 February 1729, the baronies and title went to his son Sir Alexander Murray who sold Broughton to his brother John Murray, the next Baronet was left with Stanhope, He was a Jacobite in 1745 who took refuge in France.

MURRAY OF GLENDOICK IN PERTHSHIRE. On 2 July 1676, Thomas Murray of Glendoick was created as a Baronet, he died in 1684 when his son Sir Thomas Murray became the 2nd Baronet who died in December 1701, next Baronet was his brother, Sir John Murray, the 3rd Baronet until 8 January 1714, followed by Sir Patrick Hepburn-Murray as the 4th Baronet until 1807.

MURRAY OF MELGUND IN ANGUS. On 29 January 1704, Alexander Murray of Melgund was created as a Baronet, on his death in 1713, the title was Melgund inherited by his son Sir Alexander Murray the second Baronet who died in Edinburgh on 7 March 1736.

MYRETON OF GOGAR IN MIDLOTHIAN. On 28 June 1701, Andrew Myreton, a merchant in Edinburgh, was created as a Baronet, on his death in August 1720 his son Sir Robert Myreton became the 2nd Baronet.

NAIRNE OF CROMDALE IN INVERNESS. On 31 July 1535, King James V confirmed Thomas Nairne in the lands and Barony of Cromdale, including Lothinthe, Auchnacrosky, Ballachappill, Runebellie; on 5 March 1554, Queen Mary granted John Nairne, son and heir apparent of Thomas Nairne the Baron of Croimdane, the lands and Barony of Croimdane in Inverness-shire. [a surname from the burgh of Nairn, examples date from the fourteenth century] [James Nairn emigrated to New York in 1774, while William Nairn, a clergyman, settled in Bermuda by 1722] [John Nairne, 1711-1795, London 1931]

NAIRNE OF TULLIGLENNIS IN MORAY. On 14 November 1537, King James V granted Thomas Nairne, the Baron of Cromdale, the lands and Barony of Tulliglennis.

NAIRNE OF SANDFORD IN FIFE. Oliver Cromwell, the Lord Protector granted the Baronies of Sandford and of Innerdovat to Sir Thomas Nairne on 7 July 1657.

NAIRNE OF DUNSINANE IN PERTHSHIRE. On 1 March 1704 Thomas Nairne of Dunsinane was created a Baronet, he died around 1720 and was succeeded as second Baronet by his son Sir William Nairne who died in Scone on 26 June 1754.

NAPIER OF MERCHISTON IN MIDLOTHIAN. On 21 May 1509, King James IV granted Archibald Napier of Merchiston, the lands of Gartness, Dalnare, Blaroure, Gartharne, Ballatis, Douchlas, Badbow, Edinbally, Ballacharne and Thomdaroch, with forests and fishing rights in Loch Lomond, also the mill of Gartnes in Dunbartonshire; the lands of Ardeunan, Tullichannan, Middlethird plus fishing rights on Loch Tay, etc, incorporated into the Barony of Edinballi-Napier; on 21 June 1512, King James IV granted Alexander Napier, son and heir apparent of Archibald Napier of Merchiston, the lands of Edinbally and Ballaucharne in the Barony of Edinbally, also the lands of Gartness, Dalnare, Blairoure, Gartcarne, Douchlas, Badrow, Tomdarrach with forests, fishing rights in Loch Lomond, and others in Dunbartonshire, incorporated into the Barony of Edinbally-Napier; Sir Alexander Napier of Merchiston was killed at the Battle of Flodden on 9 September 1513. Sir Archibald Napier of Merchiston was created as Baronet of Napier in Nova Scotia on 2 May 1627. When he became Lord Napier, the baronetcy merged with the peerage. [a surname of occupational origin meaning an officer in charge of tablecloths and linen, a surname recorded in Scotland since the late thirteenth century][Alexander Napier emigrated to East New Jersey in 1684, while Patrick Napier, from Edinburgh, died in Virginia in 1669][A History of the Napiers of Merchiston, London, 1921]

NAPIER OF WEST NISBET IN BERWICKSHIRE. On 27 December 1639, King Charles I granted Adam Napier, brother german of Lord Archibald Napier of Merchistoun, the lands and Barony of West Nisbet.

NASMYTH OF DAWICK IN PEEBLES-SHIRE. On 31 July 1706, James Nasmyth of Dawick was created a Baronet, he acquired the Barony of Posso by 1709, as second Baronet of Dawick and Posso, he died on 4 February 1779. [A surname from the occupation of knifesmith or nailsmith, examples date from the fifteenth century][John Naysmith settled in East New Jersey by 1688] [The Nasmyth family of painters, Leigh on Sea, 1977]

NEILSOUN OF LEACHT IN WIGTONSHIRE. On 4 April 1649, King Charles II granted Gilbert Neilsoun of Craigcaffie, the Barony of Leacht. [a patronymic surname, examples date from the thirteenth century][William Neilson, a horse thief from Dumfries-shire, was transported to the colonies in 1766, while James Neilson, from Glasgow, emigrated to Antigua in 1722]

NEWTOUN OF NEWTOUN IN EAST LOTHIAN. On 22 April 1581, King James VI confirmed Patrick Newtoun, eldest son of William Newtoun of that Ilk, in the lands and Barony of Newtoun; on 26 January 1599, King James VI confirmed Patrick Newtoun of that Ilk in the lands and Barony of Newtoun. [a surname derived from several locations, examples date from the thirteenth century] [John Newton, was transported to the colonies in 1762, while Jonathan Newton, a Jacobite, was transported to Maryland in 1747]

NICOLSON OF COCKBURNSPATH BERWICKSHIRE. On 17 December 1625, King Charles I created Sir James Nicolson as a Baronet. A patronymic, examples date from the fifteenth century][Isabel Nicolson, an arsonist, was transported to the colonies in 1711, while Katherine Nicolson, from Stornaway, emigrated to Philadelphia in 1774][Clan Nicholson, Edinburgh, 1938]

NICOLSON OF LESWADE IN MIDLOTHIAN. John Nicolson was created as a Baronet of Nova Scotia on 27 June 1629. He died in 1651 and was succeeded by his grandson Sir John Nicolson as second Baronet. He was MP for Edinburgh. When he died around 1680 the Baronetcy went to his son Sir John Nicolson, however he died in 1681 when his brother Sir William Nicolson became the fourth Baronet who died in 1687. When he died the Baronetcy title went to his son Sir John Nicolson the Fifth of Lasswade who died in 1689. The next was his brother Sir Thomas Nicolson as sixth Baronet who died in 1693, then followed his brother Sir James Nicolson who died childness in May 1743.

NICOLSON OF CARNOCK IN STIRLINGSHIRE. Thomas Nicolson, son of John Nicolson of Lasswade, was created as a Baronet of Nova Scotia on 16 January 1637. He was an MP. He died on 8 January 1646. The second Baronet was his son Sir Thomas Nicolson, born 10 June 1628 and died on 23 July 1664. His son succeeded as third Baronet and died on 20 January other 1670. His son Sir Thomas Nicolson was the fourth Baronet.

NICOLSON OF GLENBERVIE IN KINCARDINESHIRE. On 15 April 1700, Thomas Nicolson, an Advocate, was created as a Baronet, he died on 31 August 1728 and was succeeded by his brother Sir William Nicolson, a merchant and Customs Controller who died on 7 June 1766.

NISBET OF DALZELL IN LANARKSHIRE. On12 January 1581, King James VI confirmed Robert Nesbit in the Barony of Dalzell. [a surname derived from a location in Berwickshire, examples date from the twelfth century][Robert Nisbet, a merchant settled in Nevis and St Kitts, died 1740, while Alexander Nisbet, a merchant in Charleston by 1724.] [Nisbet of that Ilk, London, 1941]

NISBET OF NISBET IN ROXBURGHSHIRE. In 1662, King Charles II granted Sir Alexander Nisbet of Nisbet a Baronetcy. [CalSPDom.xxv.46]

OGILVIE OF KETTINS IN ANGUS. Patrick Ogilvie was granted the Barony of Kettins by King Robert Bruce, around 1315. [The surname is of territorial origin and is based on a location in Glamis, Angus] [James Ogilvy was transported from Leith to Virginia in 1666, while some Jacobite Ogilvies were banished to the colonies in 1746] [The House of Airlie, London, 1924]

OGILVIE OF NAVAR IN ANGUS. King Robert III granted Alexander Ogilvie the barony of Navar around 1400.

OGILVIE OF MIDMAR IN ABERDEENSHIRE. Patrick Ogilvy was granted the Barony of Midmar by King James I on 2 August 1428, formerly held by John Brown.

OGILVIE OF OURES IN KINCARDINESHIRE. King James II granted Walter Ogilvie of Beaufort, the lands and Barony of Oures on 26 February 1439.

OGILVIE OF DESKFORD AND FINDLATER IN BANFFSHIRE. On 11 August 1440 King James II granted Sir William Ogilvie the land and Barony of Deskford, also the land and Barony of Findlater; on 22 May 1517, King James V granted Alexander Ogilvie of Deskford, the lands and Baronies of Deskford, Kethmore, the forest of Glen Fiddoch, part of Inverkeroch, Balkery, Drumnaketh, Blairshenoch, Bauchlaw, fishing rights in the River Deveron, the lands of Sandlach with its fishing, the lands of Castlefield, the office of Constable of Culane, with the castles and forts at Findlator and Auchindoune, in Banffshire, also the land and mill of Auchlevin, part of Ardun, fishing rights on the River Ythan in Aberdeenshire, also the land and mill at Balhall, and part of the lands and Barony of Menmuir in Angus, now incorporated into the Barony of Ogilvy;on 23 March 1649, King Charles II granted Patrick Ogilvie, Lord Deskford, the lands and Baronies of Erroll, Bandean, Inchmartin, Pitmidell and Abernyte, the Barony of Glen Dochart, the lands and Barony of Glenloquhey, the lands and Barony of Stalarg, etc

OGILVIE OF FINGASK IN PERTHSHIRE. King James III granted John Ogilvy the lands and Barony of Fingask, formerly held by Ogilvy of Lintrathen in Angus, on 14 October 1472.

OGILVIE OF LINTRATHEN IN ANGUS. On 28 January 1483, King James III granted Sir John Ogilvie the lands of Lintrathen, Airlie, Garloch, Essie, Formale, Fornochty, and Keillor in Angus, also the lands of Wardropertoun in Kincardineshire, and the lands of Calintoy and Fingask in Perthshire, now forming the Barony of Lintrathen; on 24 December 1566, King Henry and Queen Mary granted James Ogilvy, the son of Lord James Ogilvy, the lands and Barony of Lintrathen.

OGILVIE OF OGILVIE IN ANGUS. On 31 March 1496 King James IV nephew and heir apparent of David Ogilvy of that Ilk, was granted the lands and Barony of Ogilvie with its tenantries; on 5 July 1542, King James V granted Gilbert Ogilvy, son and heir apparent of David Ogilvy of that Ilk, the lands and Barony of Ogilvy, with manor and mill, the lands of Powrie in Angus, the lands of Cary with fishing rights on the River Earn in Perthshire; on 12 February 1563 Queen Mary granted James Ogilvy the lands and Baronies of Ogilvy, the land and Barony of Drumnakeith, in Banffshire.

OGILVIE OF BALDAVY IN BANFFSHIRE. On 20 April 1507, King James IV granted William Ogilvie of Geddes, son of Sir Walter Ogilvie of Bone, the lands of Baldavy, also land in Culbirny, in Banffshire, also the lands of Little Goveny in Aberdeenshire now incorporated into the Barony of Baldavy, the king confirmed this on 3 January 1508 when he then granted Inchdrewar, Lodquhagin and Kilpoty, also part of Rothibrisbane in Aberdeenshire, now united into the Barony of Baldavy.

OGILVY OF STRATHEARN IN PERTHSHIRE. On 10 March 1509, King James IV granted to William Ogilvy, the lands and Barony of Strathearn, including Pallouchy, Easter Correbruchty, Wester Correbruchty, Moreclune, Rauchmore, Rauchbeg, Straneune, Banquhary, Invermastreane, Dalquemoch, Dulatir, Badfyn, Cullochquhay, Culmore, Cloanemore, Morelbeg, Moralmore, Thommatyne, Petty, Brauchlie, Flemingtoun, etc.; on 7 March 1517, King James IV confirmed Sir William Ogilvie of Strathearn, in the lands and Barony of Strathearn, including the lands of Petty, Brauchly, Strathearn, the mill of Conynsch, the tower and fort of Hawkhill, in Inverness-shire, now incorporated into the Barony of Strathearn.

OGILVY OF INCHMARTIN IN PERTHSHIRE. On 24 February 1513, King James IV granted James Ogilvy the lands and Barony of Inchmartin, including Easter Inchmartin with its tower and fort, Wester Inchmartin with Skarlatatland, part of Pitmudell, Craigdaily with its mill, King's Inch on the River Tay, the lands of Netherside of Balgally, in Perthshire, now incorporated into the Barony of Inchmartin.

OGILVY OF CLOVA IN ANGUS. On 23 October 1528, King James V granted James Ogilvy, son and heir apparent of Thomas Ogilvy of Clova, the lands and Barony of Cortachy, and Inchewan, in the Barony of Kinyalty, in Angus.

OGILVIE OF CARNOUSIE IN BANFFSHIRE. On 12 June 1530, King James V granted Walter Ogilvie of Monicabock, the lands of Carnousie with its mill, fishing rights on the River Deveron, woods, etc in Banffshire, now incorporated into the Barony of Carnousie; on 9 May 1636, King James V confirmed John Ogilvie of Carnousie with the lands and Barony of Schawquhare, Quhitra, Newtoun, Chapeltoun, Tulloch, Auchlesky, Drum of Pluscardin, the lands and forest of Tulloch, and the office of forester there, in Moray; on 13 December 1538, King James V confirmed Walter Ogilvy in the Barony of Dunlugas in Banffshire; on 28 October 1549, Queen Mary granted Walter Ogilvy, son and heir apparent of Sir Walter Ogilvie of Dunglas, the lands and Barony of Carnousie etc in Banffshire; on 11 July 1583, King James VI confirmed George Ogilvy of Dunlugas, brother german and heir of Walter Ogilvy, the lands and Barony of Carnousie; George Ogilvie of Carnousie was created as a baronet of Nova Scotia on 23 April 1626.

OGILVIE OF KEITHMOR IN BANFFSHIRE. On 31 December 1535, King James V confirmed Alexander Gordon with the lands and Barony of Keith-mor, with the castle and fort of Auchindown, its mill, the forest of Glenfiddich, parts of Auchenstank, Balquhery, Inverquhirrauch, the forest of Blackwater, and part of the River Deveron, in Banffshire

OGILVIE OF DUNLUGUS IN BANFFSHIRE. On 25 August 1536, King James V confirmed Sir Walter Ogilvie in the Barony of Dunlugus in Banffshire; on 28 October 1549, Queen Mary granted Walter Ogilvy the lands and Barony of Carnousies in Banffshire; on 20 March 1576, King James VI granted George Ogilvie the lands and Thanedom of Boyne in Banffshire; on 9 April 1599, King James VI confirmed James Ogilvy, son of George Ogilvy of Dunlugas, the Barony of Bishop's Barns.

OGILVIE OF INVERQUHARITIE IN ANGUS. On 23 February 1542 King James V granted John Ogilvie, son and heir of John Ogilvie of Inverquharitie, the Barony of Inverquharitie, with its castle, fort, fishing rights, grain and fulling mills, the lands of Newtoun, Ednathy, etc, incorporated into the Barony of Inverquharitie. Sir John Ogilvie of Innerquharitie was created as a Baronet of Nova Scotia on 29 September 1626. He was succeeded by his son Sir David Ogilvie as Second Baronet around 1660, he died by 1679 when his son Sir John Ogilvy became the Third Baronet, he was dead by 1735 when his son Sir John Ogilvy became the Fourth Baronet of Inverquharity, he died at Kinnordy in Angus in 1748.

OGILVY OF INCHMARTINE IN PERTHSHIRE. On 10 March 1539, King James V granted Patrick Ogilvy the lands and Barony of Inchmartine, including Balgall with its orchards and manor in the Barony of Inchture; on 18 April 1593, King James VI confirmed Patrick Ogilvie of Inchmartine, in the lands and Barony of Inchmartine.

OGILVY OF BARCLAY IN ABERDEENSHIRE. On 27 June 1551, Queen Mary confirmed Margaret Ogilvy, relict of John Stewart of Boquhane, in the Barony of Barclay.

OGILVIE OF FINDLATER IN BANFFSHIRE. On 26 July 1594, King James VI granted Walter Ogilvie of Findlater the lands and Barony of Keithmore and Auchindoun in Banffshire.

OGILVIE OF BOYNE IN BANFFSHIRE. On 4 August 1595, King James VI granted Andrew Ogilvy, son of Alexander Ogilvy of Boyne, the lands, Barony and Thanage of Boyne.

OGILVIE OF BANFF. George Ogilvie of Banff was created as a Baronet of Nova Scotia on 20 July 1627, a sasine dated 30 June 1626.

OGILVIE OF BARRAS IN KINCARDINESHIRE. George Ogilvie was Governor of Dunnottar Castle during the siege by Cromwell's army, was created as a Baronet around 1662, when he died in 1680 the title went to his son Sir William Ogilvie, he died in 1707, when Sir David Ogilvie, his son, succeeded to the barony, around 1740 his son Sir William Ogilvie became the 4th Baronet of Barras.

OGILVY OF FORGLEN IN BANFFSHIRE. On 24 June 1701, Alexander Ogilvy son of Lord Banff, was created as a Baronet, an MP and a Senator of the College of Justice, he died on 30 March 1727.

OLIPHANT OF KELLIE IN FIFE. Walter Oliphant was granted the Barony of Kellie by King David II in 1320s. [A surname possibly of Anglo-Norman origins recorded in Scotland since the late twelfth century]. [William Oliphant, a Covenanter, was transported to East New Jersey in 1685, while Dr David Oliphant settled in South Carolina by 1772] [The Oliphants of Gask, London, 1910]

OLIPHANT OF TURING IN ANGUS. On 1 March 1504, King James IV granted Colin Oliphant, son and heir of Lord John Oliphant, the lands and Barony of Gallowrow with land in Over Turing, also land in the Barony of Aberdelgie in Perthshire. Lord Oliphant was killed at the Battle of Flodden on 9 September 1513.

OLIPHANT OF STRABROCK IN WEST LOTHIAN. On 27 December 1507, King James IV granted William Oliphant of Berriedale, the lands and Barony of Strabrock.

OLIPHANT OF KELLY IN FIFE. On 20 July 1511, King James IV granted Sir John Oliphant the lands and Barony of Kelly, including Over Kelly, Kellyside, Baldutho, Bellistoun, Kellymills, Arncroach, and Greenside, Easter Pitcorthy, and the lands of Pitkery in Fife, now incorporated into the Barony of Kelly. On 2 October 1542 King James V confirmed Sir Alexander Oliphant of Kelly, in the lands and Barony of Kelly.

OLIPHANT OF NEWTOUN. James Oliphant was created a Baronet of Nova Scotia on 28 July 1629, a sasine dated 28 August 1629.

OLIPHANT OF ERROLL IN PERTHSHIRE. On 19 July 1638, King Charles I granted John Oliphant of Bachiltoun, the lands and Lordship of Erroll, the lands and Barony of Caputh, also the lands and Barony of Cowie in Kincardineshire.

OLIPHANT OF GASK IN PERTHSHIRE. James Oliphant of Gask, born 1692, a Jacobite who fought at Sheriffmuir in 1715, he succeeded his father James Oliphant of Gask in 1732, he fought as a Jacobite at Falkirk and Culloden, moved to France where he was created by King James VIII as Baron Oliphant on 14 July 1760, he died in 1767. [The Jacobite Peerage, Edinburgh, 1904]

ORMISTOUN OF ORMISTOUN IN ROXBURGHSHIRE. King James II granted George Ormistoun, son of James Ormistoun of that Ilk, the lands of Ormistoun and Semanstoun now united into the Barony of Ormistoun on 20 June 1452. [a surname derived from a place in East Lothian or in Roxburghshire, examples date from around 1200][Joseph Ormiston was in East New Jersey by 1699, while Thomas Ormiston, a merchant from Edinburgh, settled in Savannah in 1736][The Ormistons of Teviotdale, Exeter, 1951]

ORWELL OF SANQUHAR IN MORAY. King James III granted the lands and Barony of Sanquhar to James Orwell on 10 Sir 1478; on 22 March 1511, King James IV granted Robert Orwell, the lands and Barony of Sanquhar, Whitera, Newtoun, Chapeltoun, Tulloch, Auchinlesk, Drum of Pluscardin with its lands and forest, and alehouse in Forres. [a territorial surname from a location in Kinross, examples date from the thirteenth century]

PARKER OF EASSIE IN ANGUS. On 10 March 1369, King David II confirmed Andrew Parker in the lands of Kingennie, Carntona, and Omachy, incorporated into the Barony of Eassie. [from the occupation of 'park-keeper', examples date from the thirteenth century][James Parker, a Glasgow merchant, settled in Jamaica by 1754, while William Parker, guilty of forgery, was transported to Boston in 1751]

PATTERSON OF BANNOCKBURN IN STIRLINGSHIRE. On 16 March 1656 Hugh Patterson was created as a Baronet, on his death his son Sir Hugh Patterson became the 2nd Baronet, but the baronetcy was forfeited in 1746 resulting from his Jacobitism. [It signifies 'son of Peter or Patrick', examples date from the fifteenth century] [Ninian Paterson was transported to East New Jersey in 1684, while Jean Paterson, from Aberdeen, guilty of assault, was transported to Virginia in 1772

PENICUIK OF PENICUIK IN MIDLOTHIAN. On 10 January 1508, King James IV granted John Penicuik, son and heir apparent of Sir John Penicuik of that Ilk, the lands and Barony of Penicuik including the lands of Newbigging and Lufness with its tower; on 22 March 1596, King James VI confirmed Andrew Penicuik, son and heir of John Penicuik, the lands and Barony of Penicuik.

[a territorial surname from a place in Midlothian, examples date from the thirteenth century] [Robert Penicuik was master of the St Andrew to Darien in 1698]

PIGGOTT OF GLEN CLOVA IN ANGUS. Olver Cromwell, Lord Protector, granted the lands and Barony of Clova, with its castle and manor-place, to Alexander Piggott the minister of Kinnettles, Angus, formerly held by David Ogilvie of Clova, on 31 July 1657. [a name of Norman-French origin, examples date from the thirteenth century] [Alexander Piggott, a Jacobite from Kingoldrum, was transported to Jamaica in 1747]

PITCAIRN ON MONEYTHIN IN KINCARDINESHIRE. King David II granted the Barony of Moneythin around 1369. [a surname based on the lands of Pitcairn in Fife, as a surname it is recorded from the mid-thirteenth century] Pitcairn of Pitcairn was killed at the Battle of Flodden on 9 September 1513. [Robert Pitcairn, a tavern-keeper from Fife, settled in Spanish Town, Jamaica, by 1780; Major John Pitcairn, was killed at Bunker Hill in 1775] [History of the Fife Pitcairns, Edinburgh, 1905]

PITSCOTTY OF LUNCARTY IN PERTHSHIRE. On 11 December 1543, Queen Mary, granted David Pitscotty of Luncarty, with the Barony of Luncarty. [A territorial surname from Fife, examples date from the thirteenth century] [Colin Pitscottie, a sailor aboard the Rising Sun bound for Darien in 1699]

POLLOCK OF POLLOCK IN RENFREWSHIRE. On 30 November 1703, Robert century Pollock was created as a Baronet, he died on 22 August 1735, succeeded by his grandson Sir Robert Pollock who died on 26 October 1783 when the Baronetcy became extinct. [a surname of territorial origin, from Pollock or Pook in Renfrewshire, examples date from the twelfth century][John Pollock, a Covenanter, was banished to East New Jersey in 1685, while Colonel Thomas Pollock, settled in North Carolina in the 1690s] [The Pollock Pedigree, 1080-1950, London, 1950]

PRESTOUN OF GOUIRTOUN IN AYRSHIRE. King David II granted the Barony of Gouirtoun to John Preston in 1320s

PRESTON OF GOURTOUN IN MIDLOTHIAN. King James III granted to William Prestoun of Craigmillar, the lands of Auldistoun, Langhald and Swinhop in Berwickshire, how forming the Barony of Gourtoun on 14 October 1472;

PRESTON OF CRAIGMILLAR IN MIDLOTHIAN. On 10 August 1511, King James IV granted Sir Simon Preston of that Ilk, the lands of Craigmillar with its castle, fort, and mill, now incorporated into the Barony of Craigmillar; Queen Mary granted Simon Preston, son and heir apparent of George Preston of that Ilk, the lands and Barony of Balgavie in Angus, also confirmed Simon in the lands and Barony of Craigmillar, and the lands of Aldinstoun, Langhald, and Swynhope in Berwickshire; on 2 June 1569, King James VI granted David Prestoun, son and heir apparent the lands and Barony of Craigmillar also lands in Berwickshire, now united into the Barony of Craigmillar; on 27 March 1576, David Prestoun of Craigmillar, was granted the lands and Barony of Prestoun by King James VI; on 2 February 1641, King Charles I granted George Prestoun the lands and Barony of Prestoun also the lands and Barony of Craigmillar.

PRESTON OF VALLEYFIELD IN PERTHSHIRE. On 13 March 1642, King Charles I granted George Prestoun, son of Sir John Prestoun of Valleyfield, the Barony of Valleyfield; and George Preston was created as a Baronet of Nova Scotia on 13 March 1637, he died on 26 November 1679. The second Baronet was his son Sir William Preston, who died about 1703. Next came Sir George Preston as third Baronet of Valleyfield who died in September 1741 aged about 70. The fourth Baronet was Sir George Preston who died at Valleyfield on 2 March 1779. [a surname derived from Preston near Edinburgh, examples date from the thirteenth century] [James Preston, from Stirling, was bound for Canada in 1815]

PRESTON OF AIRDRIE IN LANARKSHIRE. Sir John Preston, was created as a baronet of Nova Scotia on 22 February 1628 by King Charles I.

PRIMROSE OF CARRINGTON IN WEST LOTHIAN. Sir Archibald Primrose of Carrington, born 16 May 1616, was created as a Baronet in 1651, died on 27 November 1679, was succeeded by his son Sir William Primrose as 2nd Baronet, when he died on 23 September 1687 the Barony went to his brother Sir James Primrose. In 1703 he was created Viscount Primrose when the baronage was merged with the peerage. [History of the Primrose-Roseberry family, 1500-1900, London, 1907]

PRIMROSE/FOULIS OF RAVELSTON. Sir John Foulis of Ravelston, son of George Foulis of Ravelston and his wife Jane Sinclair, was created a baronet in October 1661, he married four times, his first wife was Margaret Primrose, daughter of Archibald Primrose and Elizabeth Keith. Archibald Primrose of Carrington became Viscount Primrose in 1700 and Earl of Roseberry in 1703. Sir George Foulis changed his surname to Primrose on inheriting the estate of Dunipace and his grandson became the 2nd Baronet of Ravelston. He was found guilty of high treason, being a Jacobite, and was executed in Carlisle and his land and titles forfeited to the Crown. [a territorial surname from a place near Dunfermline, examples date from the fourteenth century][John Primrose was naturalised in North Carolina in 1821]

PRINGLE OF STITCHELL IN ROXBURGHSHIRE. On 8 August 1655, Oliver Cromwell, the Lord Protector, granted the lands and baronies of Home and those of Duns, plus various lands in the barony of Coldingham, and others, formerly held by the Earl of Home, Home of Plendergaist, and George Home of Durington, to Robert Pringle now of the barony of Stitchill. The first Baronet Pringle of Stitchill was Robert as from 1655, son of Robert Pringle the laird of Stitchill. On his death the lands ant titles went to his son, Sir John Pringle, who was created a baronet in 1683. He married Margaret Elliot of Stobs, they had four sons, including Sir John Pringle MD a famous physician, and three daughters. The early baronets of this branch of the Pringles were Sir Robert Pringle the 1st baronet who died in 1700, who fathered nineteen children, then Sir John James Pringle born 1662, died in 1721, the 3rd baronet was Sir Robert Pringle, who was born in 1690 and died in 1779. [Pringle is a surname of territorial origin and is based on 'Hoppringle' a location in the parish of Stow in Roxburghshire. [Robert Pringle, a physician, died in Philadelphia in 1775, while Walter Pringle was Governor of Dominica before 1768][Records of the Pringles or Hoppringles Edinburgh, 1933

PURVES, Sir WILLIAM, OF PURVES HALL, Berwickshire, son of Robert Purves a burgess of Edinburgh and his wife Anne Douglas, was created as a baronet in July 1665, he married Margery Stewart, he died in 1684. The second Baronet was their son Sir Alexander Purves of Purves Hall, he was Solicitor General of Scotland, husband of ….Hume, he died in 1701. The 3rd Baronet of Purves, was Sir William Purves, his son born 1700, who married Elizabeth Deans, on his death in 1730 the baronetcy went to Sir William Purves, born 14 January 1701, his wife was Anne, daughter of the Earl of Marchmont, he died on 18 June 1762. [a surname recorded in Berwickshire since the 13th century][John Purvis of that Ilk, HM Consul in Florida, died in Pensacola in 1827][The Purvis Family, 1694-1988]

RAIT OF DRUMNAGAR IN KINCARDINESHIRE. On 11 June 1512, King James IV granted David Rait, son and heir apparent of William Rair of Drumnagar, the lands of Drumnagar, and land in Inverbervie, now incorporated into the Barony of Drumnagar. [the place name is probably derived from a place in Morayshire, examples of the surname date from the thirteenth century] [Margaret Raitt, from Montrose, died in Virginia in 1714, while John Rait from Inverkeilor, died on Nevis in 1675][The Scottish Raits, Florida, 1988]

RAMSAY OF CARNOCK IN FIFE. King David II granted the barony of Carnock to Alexander Ramsay in 13… [The surname if probably from a place in Huntingdonshire, England, examples date from the twelfth century]

[William Ramsay, was skipper of the *Eagle* bound for Nova Scotia in 1627, while Gilbert Ramsay, was an Episcopalian minister in the West Indies from 1686 until 1727].

RAMSAY OF DALHOUSIE IN MIDLOTHIAN. King James II granted Sir Alexander Ramsay the baronies of Dalhousie and of Carrington, both in Midlothian, also the Barony of Foulden in Berwickshire, which were confirmed by King James III on 20 March 1473; Sir Alexander Ramsay of Dalhousie was killed at the Battle of Flodden on 9 September 1513; on 20 May 1528, King James V granted George Ramsay, son and heir apparent of Nicholas Ramsay of Dalhousie, the lands and Barony of Dalhousie, with its castle, fort, mill, etc, also the Barony of Carrington with its mill in Midlothian, and the lands and Barony of Foulden, with its tower, fort, mill, etc, in Berwickshire; on 23 October 1589, King James VI confirmed John Ramsay of Dalhousie, the lands and Barony of Dalhousie, also the lands and Barony of Foulden in Berwickshire, now incorporated into the Barony of Dalhousie.

RAMSAY OF BALMAYNE IN KINCARDINESHIRE. On 13 May 1510, King James IV granted John Ramsay of Terrenzeane, the lands and Barony of Balmayne, including Esly, Wester Strath, the mill of Fettercairn, lands of Maurtis, Pitnenan, the mill of Kincarde, the fulling mill of Pitnamone, Dorynch Myre, Whitfield, Fresky, now incorporated into the Barony of Balmayne; On 12 August 1588, King James VI confirmed David Ramsay of Balmain in the lands and Barony of Balmain etc; on 24 August 1590, King James VI confirmed David Ramsay, son and heir apparent of David Ramsay of Balmain, land in that Barony.

RAMSAY OF LEUCHARS-RAMSAY IN FIFE. On 5 March 1540, King James V granted Henry Ramsay, son of heir apparent of David Ramsay of Collessie in Fife, the lands and Barony of Leuchars-Ramsay, including part of Raschmyre, Seggypark, the Kirktoun of Leuchars, lands of Balbeuchlie, fishing rights on the River Eden, the grain mills at Scheilinghauch, Wester Fotheris and its castle also the fort at Leuchars, etc, in Fife, now in the Barony of Leuchars.

RAMSAY OF CANTERLAND IN KINCARDINESHIRE. On 19 December 1511, King James IV granted John Ramsay the lands of Canterland, Kinnaird, and Cumystoun now incorporated into the Barony of Canterland.

RAMSAY OF BALMAIN IN KINCARDINESHIRE. On 12 August 1588, King James VI confirmed David Ramsay of Balmain in the lands and Barony of Balmain etc; on 24 August 1590, King James VI confirmed David Ramsay, son and heir apparent of David Ramsay of Balmain, land in that Barony.

RAMSAY OF NOVA SCOTIA. On 3 September 1625, King Charles I created Gilbert Ramsay as a Baronet of Nova Scotia, a sasine dated 8 November 1625.

RAMSAY OF WEST NISBET IN BERWICKSHIRE. On 27 December 1639, King Charles I granted Andrew Ramsay a minister in Edinburgh, the lands and Barony oF West Nisbet.

RAMSAY OF BOTHANES IN EAST LOTHIAN. On 27 March 1650, King Charles II granted Dr Alexander Ramsay, the royal physician, the lands and Barony of Bothanes.

RAMSAY OF DRONLEY IN ANGUS. Oliver Cromwell, the Lord Protector, granted Dr Alexander Ramsay, the former Royal Physician, the lands and Barony of Dronley, and the barony of Garden, the Barony of Redcastle, Cowhills and Inverkeillour, with all castles, towers, fortalices, manor places, corn and waulk mills, fishings, salmon and others, dove-cots, feu duties, and the services of free tenants, also some properties in Arbroath; plus lands in the Baronies of Finavon, Rescobie, Restenneth, Turing, Balgavies, Greenmyes, and Carss, on 19 February 1658.

RAMSAY OF WHITEHILL IN EDINBURGH, John Ramsay, born 1624, son of Simon Ramsay and his wife Elizabeth Stevenson, an advocate, was created a baronet on 2 June 1665 by King Charles II, He married Anne Baird, daughter of advocate James Baird of Newbyth, he died 5 June 1674, their son Sir John Ramsay succeeded to the Baronetcy, he married Anne Carstairs in 1671, he died on 14 April 1715, and was succeeded by his son Sir John Ramsay. Sir John Ramsay 3rd Baronet married Marjory Deans and died on 5 October 1717. He was succeeded by his brother Sir Andrew Ramsay as 4th Baronet of Whitehill. Sir Andrew was born on 26 June 1678, was an advocate and Sheriff Depute of Edinburgh, he married Elizabeth Learmonth, and died on 24 December 1721. Their son Sir John Ramsay, born 1720, became the 5th and last Baronet of Whitehill, he died, unmarried, on 22 October 1744 when the Baronetcy became extinct.

RAMSAY OF BAMFF IN PERTHSHIRE. On 17 May 1595, King James VI granted George Ramsay of Bamff, the lands of Bamff and other lands incorporated into the Barony of Bamff. On 3 December 1666, Sir Gilbert Ramsay of Bamff was created as a Baronet, he died around 1686 and was succeeded as 2nd Baronet of Bamff by his son Sir James Ramsay, a Member of Parliament, on his death in 1730, the Baronetcy went to his son Sir James Ramsay as 3rd Baronet, and in 1738 his son Sir James Ramsay became the 4th Baronet. [Bamff Charters, 1232-1703, Oxford, 1915]

RAMSAY, ANDREW MICHAEL, was created by King James VIII as a Baronet on 23 March 1735. [The Jacobite Peerage, Edinburgh, 1904]

RANDOLPH OF MORTHINGTON AND LONGFORMACUS, ALSO THE BARONY OF ABERDOUR IN FIFE, around 1320. [RGS.I.App.A.214/Index B.6] [A rare surname in Scotland, examples date from the thirteenth century] [Richard Randolfe was a merchant in Barbados in 1659, while Robert Randal, a printer from Edinburgh, emigrated to Maryland in 1774.]

RATTRAY OF BALUNIE IN ANGUS. King James III granted Silvester Rattray of that Ilk, the lands and Barony of Balunie on 18 May 1481. [a territorial surname from Perthshire, examples date from the thirteenth century] [John Rattray, a judge, died 1761 in Charleston, while Ann Rattray, was transported to Maryland in 1728]

RATTRAY OF SALTOUN IN EAST LOTHIAN. On 23 January 1640, King Charles I granted David Rattray of Craighall, the lands and Barony of Saltoun.

REDPATH OF GREENLAW-REDPATH IN BERWICKSHIRE. On 20 January 1509, King James IV granted William Redpath of Greenlaw the mansion, lands and Lordship now incorporated into the Barony of Greenlaw-Redpath; on 10 August 1511, King James IV granted Andrew Redpath, son and heir apparent of William Redpath, the lands and Barony of Greenlaw-Redpath. [a name derived from a place in Berwickshire, examples date from the thirteenth century]

REIDHEUGH OF TULLOCHEDILL IN PERTHSHIRE. On 8 April 1513, King James IV granted James Reidheugh the lands of Tullochedill with its mill, Malar-Rannoch, Dalquhorn, Malar-MacNab, Dunduf, part of Megour, and the lands of Drumcorse in Glen Lochy with its mill, now incorporated into the Barony of Tullichedill. [a surname from one of several places, examples date from the thirteenth century]

RENTOUN OF LAMBERTOUN IN BERWICKSHIRE. On 10 October 1639, King Charles I granted John Rentoun of Lambertoun, the lands and Barony of Lambertoun. [a territorial surname from Berwickshire, examples date from the thirteenth century][Alexander Renton, a surveyor, settled in Bostonby 1729, while James Renton, a Jacobite, was transported to Virginia in 1716]

RICHARDSON OF SIMONSTOUN IN LANARKSHIRE. Around 1318, King Robert I granted the Barony of Simonstoun to Thomas Richardson, son of Richard Richardson. [The surname means 'son of Richardson, examples date from the thirteenth century.] [William Richardson was transported to the colonies in 1679, while William Richardson, a printer from Edinburgh, emigrated to Maryland in 1774]]

RICHARDSON OF PENCAITLAND. Robert Richardson was created a baronet of Nova Scotia on 13 November 1630.

RIDDELL OF RIDDELL. John Riddell was created as a baronet of Nova Scotia on 14 May 1628. [a surname derived from Rydale in Yorkshire, England, examples date from the twelfth century] [Hugh Riddell, a Covenanter, was transported to New York in 1683] [for writs since 1506 see NRS.GD1.35.1.1-28]

RIDDELL OF ARDNAMURCHAN IN ARGYLL. On 2 September 1778, James Riddell of Ardnamurchan and Sunart , was created as a Baronet, he died on 2 November 1797. [Riddell Papers 1638 to 1899, NRS.GD1.395]

ROBERTSON OF FASCALLY IN PERTHSHIRE. Alexander Robertson of Fascally, was created a baronet by King James VIII on 18 May 1725, he died in 1732; he was succeeded by his son George Robertson of Fascally as 2nd Baronet, he was a Jacobite in 1745. [Robertson is a patronymic surname meaning 'son of Robert'. It is one of the most common surnames in Scotland with examples dating from the fourteenth century] [Dr William Robertson, from Fife, settled in East New Jersey in 1684, wile Reverend George Robertson settled in Virginia by 1693][The Clans of Atholl, Blair Atholl, 1997][The Jacobite Peerage, Edinburgh, 1904]

ROBERTSON OR COLYEAR. Alexander Robertson alias Colyear, in Holland, son of Major David Colyear or Robertson, was created as a Baronet on 20 February 1677, he died before 1691, he was succeeded by his son Sir David Colyear an officer of the Scotch Brigade in Dutch service, as the second Baronet, however being made Lord Portmore in 1699 the baronetcy was merged with his other titles.

ROBERTSON OF STRUAN IN PERTHSHIRE. King James II granted the lands and Barony of Struan to Alexander Robertson on 1 April 1460; on 10 November 1546, Queen Mary confirmed a charter of Robert Robertson of Struan appointed William Robertson as his heir to the Barony of Struan. Alexander Robertson of Struan, 13th Chief of Clan Robertson, was born around 1668 son of Alexander Robertson and his wife Marion Baillie, educated at the University of St Andrews, fought for the Jacobites in 1689 at Killicrankie, was attainted in 1690, fled to France but was pardoned by Queen Anne in 1703 and returned to Scotland, fought for the Jacobites at

Sheriffmuir in 1715 and again escaped to France, was created a Baronet by King James VIII in 1725, returned to fight for the Jacobites at Prestonpans in 1745, died on 18 April 1749. [Robertson is a patronymic surname meaning 'son of Robert'. It is one of the most common surnames in Scotland with examples dating from the fourteenth, century][George Robertson of Struan, settled as a schoolmaster in Virginia by 1693, while Janet Robertson, from Edinburgh, was transported to Maryland in 1704][The Jacobite Peerage, Edinburgh, 1904][The Robertson Heartland, Pitlochry, 1992]

ROCHEID OF INVERLEITH IN MIDLOTHIAN. On 4 June 1704, James Rocheid of Inverleith was created Baronet of Rocheid, when he died on 1 May 1737 he was succeeded by his cousin, Sir John Rocheid as second Baronet of Inverleith. [examples date from the fifteenth century] possibly a descrptive surname meaning 'Rough Head', examples date from the thirteenth century] [John Rockhed emigrated to East New Jersey, died in Monmouth County in 1737]

ROLLOCK OF DUNCRUB IN PERTHSHIRE. On 26 August 1511, King James IV granted William Rollock the lands of Duncrub, Laidcaty, Pittenskeich, Kirktoun of Dunning, also Findony with its grain mill and fulling mill in Perthshire, now incorporated into the Barony of Duncrub; William Rollo of Duncrub was killed at the Battle of Flodden on 9 September 1513; on 21 May 1540, King James V granted George Rollock, son and heir apparent of Andrew Rollock the lands and Barony of Duncrub, Laidcaty, Pittenskeich, the Kirktoun of Dunning and Findony, with grain mill and fulling mill in Perthshire, now incorporated in the Barony of Duncrub; on 18 July 1547, Queen Mary confirmed Andrew Rollock of Duncrub, in the lands and Barony of Edindunning in Perthshire. On 10 January 1651 King Charles II created Andrew Rollock of Duncrub, Lord Rollo of Duncrub. [the surname appears as Rollock or Rollo, examples exist from the fourteenth century][Andrew Rollock settled in Barbados by 1679, while William Rollo from Edinburgh was in Boston in 1766] [Rollo Family History, Glasgow, 1993]

ROLLOCK OF GARDYNE IN ANGUS. On 19 September 1601, King James VI granted Sir Walter Rollock of Lawtoun, the lands and Barony of Gardyne.

ROLLO OF BANNOCKBURN IN STIRLINGSHIRE. Sir John Rollo second son of Lord Rollo of Duncrub and Catherine Murray, was created Knight Baronet of Bannockburn on 25 July 1636.

ROME OF KIRKGUNZEON IN KIRKCUDBRIGHTSHIRE. On 14 July 1638, King Charles I granted George Rome of Kirkpatrick-Irongray, the lands and Barony of Kirkgunzeon, etc; on 31 July 1638, King Charles I granted George Rome of

Kirkpatrick-Irongray, the lands and Barony of Amisfield in Dumfries-shire. [examples date from the seventeenth century] [George Rome, a Covenanter, was transported to Carolina in 1684]

ROSE OF KILRAVOCK IN NAIRNSHIRE. On 11 March 1475, King James III granted the lands and Barony of Kilravock and the lands of Geddes, to Hugh Ross; on 7 July 1485, King James III granted Hugh Rose of Kilravock, the lands of Culmore in Inverness-shire. On 31 January 1528, King James V granted Hugh Rose of Kilraverock, the lands and Barony of Shanquhar, Whitera, Newtoun, Chapeltoun, Auchinlesk, the Drum of Pluscardine, the lands and forests of Drummynd and Tulloch, etc; on 8 March 1600, King James VI confirmed William Ross of Kilravock in the lands and Barony of Kilravock; [the surname is possibly a variant of Ross, examples date from the fourteenth century][Dermot Rose, a prisoner of war captured at Dunbar in 1650, was transported to New England, while John Rose, a pewterer from Inverness, emigrated to Jamaica in 1730]   [Family of Rose of Kilravock, Edinburgh,1848]

ROSS OF KILFAUNS IN PERTHSHIRE. King Robert III granted Hugh Ross the Barony of Kilfauns, Craigie and Maler, with its mill in 1370s. [The surname Ross may have been brought from Yorkshire in the twelfth century, another source is Ross in the Northern Highlands, examples of both variants date from the twelfth century][David Ross, a distiller settled in Jamaica in 1736] [The Great Clan Ross, Canada, 1972]

ROSS OF KIPPANEROS IN PERTHSHIRE. On 7 March 1507, King James IV granted John Ross of Kippaneros the lands of Kippanerait, Auchlochy, Culinnis with its grain mill and fulling mill, and the lands of Lettyr in Strathearn, Perthshire, now incorporated into the Barony of Kippaneros.

ROSS OF AUCHLOSSIN IN ABERDEENSHIRE. On 4 February 1508, King James IV confirmed the incorporation of part of the lands of Auchlossin with its mill, and the lands of Carnbaddy in Oneill, Aberdeenshire, into the Barony of Auchlossin; on 30 April 1517, King James V confirmed the grant by John Ross of Auchlossin of the lands and Barony of Auchlossin, including most of the lands of Auchlossin, the lands of Carnboddye, and the mill of Auchlossin, in Aberdeenshire, to his son Nicholas Ross.

ROSS OF MELVILLE IN MIDLOTHIAN. On 21 February 1509, King James IV granted Lord John Ross of Halkhead the house and lands of Melville with its mill, the lands of Stonehouse with its mill, in Midlothian, also, the lands of Tortrevin, Prestoun with mills, and Walterstoun, in West Lothian, the lands of Morowingside with its mill in Stirlingshire, also the lands of Mosshouse in

Midlothian, now incorporated into the Barony of Melville. Lord Ross was killed at the Battle of Flodden on 9 September 1513. On 13 September 1548, Queen Mary granted James Ross, son and heir of Ninian Ross of Halkhead, the lands, Barony, and Lordship of Melville.

ROSS OF CRAIGIE IN PERTHSHIRE. On 16 December 1511, King James IV granted John Ross, son and heir apparent of John Ross of Craigie, the lands and Barony of Craigie, Wester Malare, Pithelvis, with the mill of Craigie, the lands of Auchinleskane, Tullochlembar, Lakenscredan with its mill, Kirkton, Auchtowis, Cowill and Drumness in Perthshire, incorporated into the Barony of Craigie; on 14 September 1537, King James V granted John Ross of Craigie, the lands and Barony of Craigie and Wester Malar in Perthshire; on 5 April 1538, King James V granted John Ross of Craigie the lands of Kirktoun of Kilfauns now incorporated into the Barony of Craigie. On 24 November 1538, King James V confirmed John Ross in the lands of Craigie with its mill, lands of Pithelvis, Wester Malar with mansion house, mill, loch, fishery, woods in Perthshire, incorporated into the Barony of Craigie-Malar; on 13 September 1541, King James V granted the lands and Barony of Craigie to Thomas Ross, son and heir apparent of John Ross of Craigie; on 10 February 1598, King James VI confirmed Robert Ross in the lands and Barony of Craigie.

ROSS OF FARR IN SUTHERLAND. On 18 June 1565, Queen Mary granted Henry Ross, Earl of Ross, many lands in Sutherland now incorporated into the Barony of Farr.

ROSS OF STRATHOYKELL IN SUTHERLAND. On 15 June 1582, King James VI granted George Ross of Balgowan the lands and Barony of Strathoykell

ROSSIE OF ROSSIE IN ANGUS. King Robert III granted the barony of Rossie to Bernard Rossie around 1400. [A surname derived from the lands of Rossie in Fife, examples date from the early thirteenth century] [Reverend John Rosse settled in Maryland in 1754]

RUTHERFORD OF EDGARSTOUN IN ROXBURGHSHIRE. King James IV confirmed James Rutherford of that Ilk in the lands and Lordship of Edgarstoun, also properties of Swyneside, Capehope, Fillogir and Cunyartoun in the Barony of Hownam, plus the lands and Barony of Broundoun namely Elphinshope and Eddillisschede, also land and the house Maxtoun in the Barony of Cavers on 15 January 1493; he also obtained lands in Rutherford, and in Wellis in the Barony of Cavers on the same date. [a surname derived from a location in Roxburghshire, examples date from the thirteenth century][Richard Rudderford settled in Virginia by 1635, while John Rutherford died in Jamaica in 1692]

RUTHERFORD OF SCRAISBURGH IN ROXBURGHSHIRE. On 18 April 1537, King James V confirmed the grant by Ninian Gleninning of that Ilk to John Rutherford of Hunthill the lands and Barony of Scraisburgh.

RUTHVEN OF RUTHVEN IN PERTHSHIRE. On 2 July 1480, King James II granted William Ruthven and John Ruthven, sons of William Ruthven of that Ilk, the lands and Barony of Ruthven, and its tenantries and tenants, also the lands of Cowgask in Strathearn, the lands and baronies of Balernoch and Newton with tenants and tenantries, in Midlothian, which was confirmed on 12 July 1480; On 17 January 1503 King James IV granted Lord William Ruthven the lands and Barony of Glen Cuthill in Aberdeenshire; on 1 August 1507, King James IV granted John Ruthven, alias John Lindsay, brother of William Ruthven his son and heir apparent, the lands of Cullltirany and Drumdrane with part of the mill of Auchtergavin in the Barony of Ruthven; on 2 June 1509, King James IV granted William Ruthven of that Ilk, son of Lord William Ruthven, the lands of Torsoppy, Auchtergavin, Wallacetoun, and Rait in Perthshire now included in the Barony of Ruthven; on 24 April 1510, King James IV granted William Ruthven superiority of the lands of Few, in the Barony of Balhousie now in the Barony of Ruthven; William Ruthven, master of Ruthven, was killed at the Battle of Flodden on 9 September 1513; on 20 October 1581, King James VI granted Lord William Ruthven the lands and Barony of Gowrie in Perthshire.   [Ruthven is a location in Angus, examples of the surname date from the thirteenth century] [David Ruthven, a farmer, settled in the Carolinas around 1820, while Robert Ruthven emigrated to Ontario in 1821] [The Ruthven Family Papers, London, 1912]

RUTHVEN OF BALVANY IN BANFFSHIRE. On 9 September 1580, King James VI confirmed Mary Ruthven, eldest daughter of William Ruthven, the Royal treasurer, was confirmed in the lands and Barony of Tullymat, the lands and Barony of Logierait, the lands and Barony of Rattray, in Perthshire, also the Lordship of Balvany in Banffshire

RUTHVEN OF REDCASTLE IN ANGUS. On 11 July 1666, Francis Ruthven of Redcastle was created as a Baronet, as he died in 1700 without children the Baronetcy became extinct.

SANDILANDS OF CALDER IN MIDLOTHIAN. On 14 July 1489, King James IV granted Sir James Sandilands of Calder the lands and Barony of Airthbissate, also the lands of Slamannan, and part of the lands of Bannockburn; On 23 August 1510, Sir James Sandilands of Calder, nephew of Sir James Sandilands of Calder, was granted the lands and Barony of Slamannan with its mill, also the lands and Barony of Airthbissate and Bannockburn and its mill, also Tibermasko, in Stirlingshire, incorporated into the Barony of Airthbissate; on 12 May 1567, Queen Mary confirmed James Sandilands, son and heir apparent of John Sandiland of Calder, the lands and Barony of Calder . [a territorial name derived from Sandilands in Lanarkshire, examples date from the fourteenth century][James Sandiland participated on the Swedish expedition to [New Sweden] Delaware in 1638, while James Sandeland was in Boston around 1687][The Barony Court Book of Calder, 1584-1601, NLS.ms3724-5]

SANDILANDS OF PITLAIR IN FIFE. On 9 June 1540, King James V, granted James Sandilands of Cruvy, son of James Sandilands, deceased, and his wife Katherine Scott, the Barony of Pitlair, including Newtoun of Collessie, Gadwell, Schelis, the lands of Kirktoun of Collessie, Mylnehill, and Pitlochy, Collessie, etc, now incorporated into the Barony of Pitlair.

SANDILANDS OF AIRTH-BISSETT IN STIRLINGSHIRE. On 29 November 1553, Queen Mary granted John Sandilands the lands and Barony of Airth-Bissett.

SANDILANDS OF TORPICHEN IN WEST LOTHIAN. On 24 January 1564, Queen Mary granted Lord James Sandilands of St John's, several baronies incorporated into the Barony of Torpichen. [Barony of Torpichen papers 1563-1649. NRS.RH9.4.3.47]

SCHAW OF SAUCHY IN CLACKMANNANSHIRE. On 11 September 1529, King James V granted Alexander Schaw of Sauchy, the lands and Barony of Sauchy; on 4 August 1578, King James VI granted James Schaw, son and heir of James Schaw of Sauchy, the lands and Barony of Sauchy. [a name of territorial origin probably in Renfrewshire, examples date from the thirteenth century] [John Shaw, a cabinetmaker, settled in Annapolis in 1772, while John Shaw emigrated from Jura to North Carolina in 1754] [A History of Clan Shaw, Chichester, 1983]

SCOTT OF BRANXHOLM IN ROXBURGHSHIRE. King James III granted the lands of Branxholm now created into a Barony with the lands of Langtoun, Lempetlau, Elrig, Rankilburn, and the lads and Barony of Kirkurde in Peebles-shire, also, the lands of Eckford and the lands of Whitchester in Roxburghshire, all united into the Barony of Branxholm, on 7 December 1463, on 28 October 1528, King James V confirmed a grant by Sir Walter Scott of Branxholm, to his son David Scott the lands and Barony of Branxholm and Eckford in Roxburghshire, the land and Barony of Kirkurd in Peebles-shire, and the lands of the Lordship of Buccleugh, Rankilburn and Lampitlaw in Roxburghshire; on 1 October 1594, King James VI granted Sir Walter Scott of Branxholm, the lands, Lordship and Barony of Hailes, also the lands and Barony of Crichtoun, the lands and Barony of Woltoun, the lands and Barony of Chalmerlane-Newtoun, the land and Barony of Dryvisdale and Carruthers, the lands and Barony of Kirkmichael, the lands and Lordship of Bothwell, the lands and Baronies of Elgarigill, Wolstoun, and Dolphintoun, the lands and Barony of Dunsyre, the lands and Barony of Liddesdale, etc; on 16 August 1599, King James VI granted Branxholm and other baronies incorporated into the Barony of Branxholm; [A surname associated with the Borders, examples date from the early thirteenth century][Alexander Scott emigrated to East New Jersey in 1684, while Christian Scott, a Covenanter, was transported there in 1685]

SCOTT OF GLENDOICK IN PERTHSHIRE. King James III granted William Scott of Balwearie, the lands and Barony of Glendoick with its mill on 16 October 1484; On 26 May 1510, King James IV granted William Scott of Balwearie the lands and Barony of Glen Doick with its mill, the lands of Fingask, Flawcraig with its mill, Craighall, Tullycurren with its mill, and Dalgarno, also, the lands and forest of Glenhaitnyth, now incorporated into the Barony of Glen Doick.

SCOTT OF FINGASK IN PERTHSHIRE. King James IV granted William Scott of Flawcrag, the lands and Barony of Fingask on 18 August 1493.

SCOTT OF STRATHMIGLO IN FIFE. On 27 February 1510, King James IV granted Sir William Scott of Balwearie, the lands of Strathmiglo, Eglismartin with manor house, fort, mills, etc., Pitlour, Auchnary, Carncatt, Kilgour, Hairhope, Drumduff, Rauchmakggallyn, with its mill, Dury, Pitscotty with its mill, part of Pitferran, part of the Barony of Ceres ie Craghall, Balqyhy, Baltuly, Kingarrat, Burnshiels, Dempstertoun, Kilboisland, Scolloland, Drumreichlak, Langsland, united into the barony of Strathmiglo on 27 February 1510; on 9 March 1511, King James IV granted Sir William Scott of Balwearie the lands of Mugrum with fishing rights now merged into the Barony of Strathmiglo; on 5 March 1529, King James V confirmed a grant by William Scott of Balwearie to his son and heir apparent Sir William Scott of Inverteil with is manor-house, Brigland, Mairland, part of Inverkeithing, Pittencreiff, lands in the Barony of Strathmiglo with fishing rights on the River Tay, part of Ceres with its mill, Craighall, Balquhy, Baltuly, Kingarrat, Callynch, Pitscotty with its mill, Dury, Ramgally, Burntisland, Cairns, . Pitfirran, Cash, land at Falkland and Ballinbla, land at Wemyss, the lands and Barony of Glendoick, Abbavele, Fuddois, Gallowhill and Myreflat in Perthshire, etc., on 25 April 1548, Queen Mary granted William Scott son and heir apparent of William Scott of Balwearie the lands and Barony of Invertail in Fife and the lands and Barony of Strathmiglo, the lands and Barony of Glendoick in Perthshire; on 18 May 1550 Queen Mary confirmed William Scott, son of William Scott of Balwearie, in the lands and Barony of Inverteill; on 4 December 1553, Queen Mary granted William Scott of Balwearie, the Barony of Strathmiglo. ['The Scotts of Buccleuch', W. Fraser, 1878]

SCOTT OF DOWNIE IN PERTHSHIRE. On 25 April 1510, King James IV granted Sir William Scott of Balwearie, the lands and Barony of Downie, including Downie, Bordland, Edirarnochty, Cultolony, Stroneymuk, Faynyeand, Invereddre with its mill, Bynnanmore, Bynnanbeg, Rundeweyoch, Kerauch, Couthill, and Balmonge and parts of Pitbrane, Glengaisnot, and Glenbeg in Perthshire. On 23 September 1538 King James V granted Thomas Scott the lands and Barony of Downy with the above etc; on 17 August 1537, King James V granted Thomas Scott, Clerk of the Judiciary, the lands and Barony of Downy, with its mills, fishing rights, etc.

SCOTT OF ARDROS IN FIFE. On 6 May 1590, King James VI confirmed William Scott, of the College of Justice, the lands and Barony of Ardros and Carmurie; on 14 August 1595, King James VI confirmed William Scott, Chancellor of the College of Justice, the lands and Barony of Ardros and Carmurie.

SCOTT OF ROSSIE IN FIFE. On 20 October 1639, King Charles I granted Colonel James Scott of Rossie, the lands and Barony of Rossie.

SCOTT OF MERTOUN IN BERWICKSHIRE. On 22 September 1641, King Charles I granted Sir William Scott of Harden, the Barony of Mertoun.

SCOTT OF WEST BARNS IN FIFE. On 20 March 1649, King Charles I granted Sir James Scott of Scottstarvit the lands and Barony of West Barns.

SCOTT OF THIRLESTANE IN SELKIRKSHIRE. On 22 August 1666, Francis Scott of Thirlestane, was created as Baronet of Thirlestane, he was a Member of Parliament and Master of the Works, he died in Edinburgh on 7 March 1712, his son Sir William Scott then succeeded to the Baronetcy and died on 8 October 1725, the last Baronet of Thirlestane as it merged when he became Lord Napier.

SCOTT OF ANCRUM IN ROXBURGHSHIRE. On 27 October 1671, John Scott of Ancrum was created as a Baronet, he died in 1712, when he was succeeded by his son Sir Patrick Scott as the 2nd Baronet of Ancrum, he died in 1734 to be followed by his son Sir John Scott as 3rd Baronet.

SCRYMGEOUR OF GLASSARY IN ARGYLL. On 12 July 1491, King James IV confirmed the grant by James Scrymgeour, the Constable of Dundee, of the lands and Barony of Glassary to his brother John Scrymgeour; On 1 March 1513, King James IV confirmed John Scrymgeour with the lands of Balmullo in Fife. John Scrymgeour of Glassary was killed at the Battle of Flodden on 9 September 1513. On 2 March 1542, King James [a surname derived from the Old French word *eskermisor* meaning a fencer; examples in Scotland date from the thirteenth century][James Scrymgeour emigrated to East New Jersey in 1685, while H.Y. Scrymgeour emigrated to Jamaica in 1774] [The Scrymgeours, Edinburgh, 1980][Scrymgeour of Glasswell, Dundee, 2006]

SCRYMGEOUR OF PANBRIDE IN ANGUS. On 26 October 1511, King James IV granted John Scrymgeour of Glaster, the lands and Barony of Panbride with its mill, port and fishing rights; on 1 March 1513, King James IV granted John Scrymgeour of Glaster the lands of Balmullo in Fife.

SCRIMGEOUR OF FARDILL IN PERTHSHIRE. On 15 June 1512, King James IV granted David Scrimgeour, the heir apparent of James Scrymgeour of Fardill, the lands of Fardill with mills, the lands of Ard, Drumadderty and Little Gourdie, with fishing rights on the Tay, now incorporated into the Barony of Fardill.

SCRYMGEOUR OF DUDHOPE IN ANGUS. On 2 March 1542, King James V granted James Scrymgeour, the lands and Barony of Dudhope, with tower, fort, mills, the lands of Castlehill, the lands of Kirktoun of Earlsstrathdichty in Angus, also, land at Inverkeithing, with mills, in Fife, lands in Perthshire, and Sonahard in Aberdeenshire, incorporated into the Barony of Dudhope; on 30 June 1565, Queen Mary granted James Scrymgeour, son and heir apparent of John Scrymgeour of Dudhope, the Constable of Dundee, the lands and Barony of Dudhope etc.; on 15 November 1587, King James VI granted James Scrymgeour of Dudhope the lands and Barony of Dundee, also the lands and Barony of Glassary in Argyll, etc

SEATON OF TRANENT IN MIDLOTHIAN. King Robert I granted Alexander Seaton the Barony of Tranent by 1320; also the Barony of Seatoun, plus the town and Burgh of Barony of Setoun in Midlothian; on 16 April 1425, King James I, granted John Seaton the Barony of Winchburgh formerly held by James Dundas. [originally 'de Say's toun' , Seiher de Say, of Norman-French origin, was granted land in East Lothian by David II, examples date from the twelfth century][John Seaton from Fife, emigrated to Virginia in 1635, while John Seton emigrated to East New Jersey in 1685]

SEATOUN OF TULLIBODY IN CLACKMANNANSHIRE. King James I granted the Barony of Tullibody, also the Barony of Kilsaurle in Banffshire, to Alexander Seatoun of Gordoun on 8 January 1426; on 14 January 1535, King James IV granted Walter Seaton, son and heir apparent Sir Ninian Seaton of Tullibody the lands and Barony of Touch-Fraser with its fort and manor house, also the lands and Barony of Tullibody; on 2 July 1563, Queen Mary granted James Seatoun, son and heir apparent of Walter Seatoun of Tullibody; the lands and Barony of Touch-Fraser also the lands and Barony of Tullibody.

SEATOUN OF TULCHFRASER IN STIRLINGSHIRE. On 4 November 1510, King James IV granted the lands and Barony of Touch-Fraser to Sir Alexander Seatoun, now incorporated into the Barony of Touch-Fraser; Sir Alexander Seton was killed at the Battle of Flodden on 9 September 1513.

SEATOUN OF BERNS IN EAST LOTHIAN. On 1 February 1512, King James IV confirmed Lord George Seatoun in the lands and Barony of Berns; Lord Seatoun was killed at the Battle of Flodden on 9 September 1513, on 12 March 1541, King James V confirmed Lord George Seatoun in the lands and Barony of Winchburgh, the lands of Cragy and Dundas, with castles, towers, forts, mills, fsing rights, collieries etc in West Lothian now incorporated into the Barony of West Niddry.

SETON OF PARBROATH IN FIFE. On 28 July 1512, King James IV granted John Seton, nephew and heir apparent of Alexander of Parbroath, the lands and Barony of Parbroath, with its land and manor-house, the lands of Laudisfern with its mill, land at Ramsay-Forthir, the lands of Urquhart, in Fife, also te lands of Haystoun and Scrogarfield in Angus, now incorporated into thhe Barony of Parbroath; on 29 November 1592, King James VI confirmed David Setoun of Parbroath in the lands and Barony of Parbroath. [John Seton, son of Robert Seaton and his wife Margaret Newtoun, in Parbroath, emigrated to Virginia on the <u>Globe</u> in 1635]

SETON OF GARGUNNOCK IN STIRLINGSHIRE. On 19 January 1535, King James V granted John Seton, son and heir apparent of John Seton the lands Barony and mill of Gargunnock.

SETON OF MELDRUM IN ABERDEENSHIRE. On 8 February 1535, King James V confirmed William Seton in the Mains of Meldrum, with tower and fort, the house and lands of Old Meldrum, the mill of Crumlee, lands of Parcak with alehouse, house and lands of Ardconan and Balcarne with mill, house and lands of Gonir, Fosterhill, Caute, Cardru, Tullach, house and lands of Belhelvie, the house and lands of Ardquhork, the house and lands of Kilblane in Aberdeenshire, incorporated into the Barony of Meldrum; on 24

August 1578, King James VI confirmed Alexander Seton, son and heir apparent of William Seton of Meldrum, the lands and Barony of Meldrum.

SETON OF WEST NIDDRY IN WEST LOTHIAN. On 2 August 1539, King James V confirmed Lord George Seton in the lands and Barony of Wynchburgh, the lands of Up Craigie, with castle, towers, forts, mills, fishing, collieries, etc in West Lothian now incorporated into the Barony of West Niddry, this was confirmed on 12 March 1541; on 25 May 1552, Queen Mary confirmed Lord George Seton, in the lands and Barony of West Niddry; on 6 August 1554, Queen Mary granted George Seton, son and heir apparent of Lord George Seton, the lands and Barony of West Niddry, also the lands and Barony of Setoun and Wintoun in East Lothian; on 24 December 1638, King Charles I granted George Seton the Earl of Wintoun, the Barony of Broxburn.

SEYTOUN OF BARRACH IN ABERDEENSHIRE. On 26 January 1599, King James VI granted George Seytoun of Meldrum, the Barony of Barrach.

SETON OF ABERCORN IN WEST LOTHIAN. Walter Seton, son and heir of Alexander Seton of Kilcreuch, was created Baronet of Abercorn on 3 June 1663, however he sold Abercorn and acquired Northbank which became his Barony, he died on 20 February 1692 when his son, Sir Walter Seton, became the Baronet of Northbank, the 3rd Baronet was Sir Henry Seton who died in 1751.

SETON OF GARLETOUN IN EAST LOTHIAN. On 9 December 1664, King Charles II created John Seton of Garletoun, born 1639 in East Lothian, as a Baronet, on his death in February 1686, his son Sir George Seton became the 2nd Baronet, however as he was a Jacobite in 1715 the land and titles were forfeited to the Crown,

SETON OF PITMEDDAN IN ABERDEENSHIRE. On 15 January 1684 Sir Alexander Seton of Pitmeddan was created as a Baronet, he died in 1719, when he was succeeded by his son Sir William Seton as 2nd Baronet of Pitmeddan, he died in 1744.

SETON OF WINDYGOUL IN EAST LOTHIAN. On 24 January 1671, Robert Seton, son of the Earl of Winton, was created as a Baronet, however he died childless in November 1671 when the baronetcy became extinct.

SEMPLE OF RENFREWSHIRE. On 21 September 1505, King James IV granted Lord John Semple the lands of Catletoun with its park and loch, the lands of Elliotstoun, Schuterflat, Nether Pennell, Halstentoun, Fernynes, Rayflat, Bar in Kilbarchan, Brandiscroft, Wetlands, Harry's Pennaldis, Borlands, Mecheltoun, and Cragynfeach in the Barony of Renfrew, also, the lands of Suthanane, Padzouchredding, in Cunningham, Ayrshire, and the lands of Glasford in Lanarkshire, now incorporated into the Barony of Semple. This was confirmed by King James IV on 16 February 1506; on 4 July 1508, King James IV granted Lord John Semple the lands of Southinane in Ayrshire, with its tower, fort, and mill of Cunningham, also the grain mill and fulling mill of Auchindonan, etc in Renfrewshire now incorporated into the Barony of Semple; on 2 June 1512, King James IV granted Lord John Semple the lands of Paidyeaucheriding and Haly in Ayrshire, to be merged into the Barony of Sempill; Lord Sempill was killed at the Battle of Flodden on 9 September 1513; on 17 March 1540, King James V confirmed Lord William Semple in several lands in Renfrewshire also some in Ayrshire, incorporated into the Barony of Craginfeauch, also on 17 March 1540, lands in Renfrewshire and in Lanarkshire incorporated into the Barony of Semple; etc on 10 February 1544, Queen Mary confirmed Robert Semple, eldest son and heir apparent of Lord William Semple in the Barony of Semple and other Baronies in Renfrewshire, Ayrshire and Lanarkshire; on 7 March 1545, Queen Mary confirmed John Sempill, second son and heir of Gabriel Sempill of Cathcart, the Barony of Cathcart. [a surname possibly a corruption of St Paul, examples date from the thirteenth century] [John Semple, a merchant from Glasgow, in Virginia and Maryland around 1765, while Robert Semple was Governor in Chief of Rupert's Land at Hudson Bay, before 1816]

SEWARD OF KELLIE IN FIFE. King Robert I granted William Seward the Barony of Kellie in Fife around 1320. [from a Scandinavian or Anglian name, commonly appears as Sword, examples date from the fourteenth century] [Humphrey Sword, a Jacobite, was transported to Virginia in 1716, while John Sword, also a Jacobite, was transported to St Kitts in 1716]

SHARP OF SCOTSCRAIG IN FIFE. On 21 April 1683 William Sharp, son of Archbishop James Sharp, was created as a Baronet, on his death on 27 January 1712 his son, Sir James Sharp, succeeded to the Baronetcy, until he died on 25 April 1738, the next baronet was his son Sir James Sharp who died in 1748. [examples date from the fourteenth century][John Sharp, from Aberdeen, emigrated to Virginia in 1699; while William Sharp emigrated to East New Jersey in 1685][Sharp Family History, Fife, 2006]

SIBBALD OF RANKEILLOUR IN FIFE. On 8 June 1540, King James V granted Alexander Sibbald, son and heir apparent of Sir James Sibbald of Over Rankeillor the lands of Rankeillour with its tower, manor, fort, mill,etc, Edensmuir, part of Auchindowny, part of Pitcullo, in Fife now incorporated into the Barony of Rankeillour. James Sibbald was created a baronet of Nova

Scotia on 24 July 1630. [A surname of Old English origin, examples date from around 1200.][Peter Sibbet died in Virginia before 1678; while David Sibbald settled as a planter in Jamaica before 1772]

SINCLAIR OF CESSWORTH. King Robert II granted Walter Sinclair the Barony of Cessworth, with its mill, on 8 March 1376.

SINCLAIR OF ROSLYN IN MIDLOTHIAN. King James IV granted Edward Sinclair, son and heir apparent of Sir William Sinclair of Roslin, the lands and Barony of Roslyn, together with many lands in the Lothians, also the lands and Barony of Harbertshire in Stirlingshire, which Sir William Sinclair had resigned; King James IV granted George Sinclair, son and heir apparent of Oliver Sinclair, the lands and Barony of Roslin, also the lands and Barony of Harbertshire on 5 January 1492; also granted were the lands and Barony of Pentland with the lands of Pentlandmuir – Kirktoun, Whithalch, Loganhouse, Earncraig and Sunnonyshope, incorporated into the Barony of Pentland; on 9 May 1506, King James IV granted George Sinclair, son and heir apparent of Sir Oliver Sinclair of Roslyn, the lands and Barony of Herbertshire; on 11 April 1510 King James IV granted Sir Oliver Sinclair of Roslin, the lands and Barony of Herbertshire, including the lands of Stonehouse, Weyndis, Dunipace, Heydis, Cuthilltoun, Fivakers, Meikle Dunovan, and others, now incorporated into the Barony of Herbertshire; on 17 December 1527, King James V granted Sir William Sinclair of Roslyn, the lands and Barony of Roslyn, including its castle and town, Otislee, the fulling mill and grain mill of Dryden, Dryden Wester, Caikmuir, Nettleflat, Cowbyrehill, Catcune, Baxterland of Leith, lands of Halderstoun, Ravensneuk, Carnehill, in Midlothian, the lands and Barony of Herbertshire, namely lands of Stonehouse, Weynds, Dunipace, Helds, Cuthilltoun, Lilliesleaf, Barnego, Fiveacres, Meikle Donavan, Biris, Bords, Quarter, Broomhill, Torsaukk, Garlios, Blairs, Bukkesyde, Mains, Offers, Little Dany, and Green with its fulling mill and granary, etc, now incorporated into the Barony of Roslyn. On 14 November 1533 King James V granted Sir William Sinclair the lands of Roslyn formerly held by Sir Henry Sinclair the Earl of Orkney. On 25 August 1542, King James V confirmed Sir William Sinclair in the lands and Barony of Roslyn, also in various lands in Midlothian now incorporated in the Barony of Pentland. [The Sinclairs had their origin in Normandy, specifically in St Clare in the Pont d'Eveque arrondissement, examples date from the twelfth century, the family was well represented in Caithness.] [Robert Sinclair, born 1669 in Kirkwall, settled in New York in 1680; while Robert Sinclair emigrated to Pennsylvania in 1697]

SINCLAIR OF PENTLAND IN MIDLOTHIAN. On 10 December 1476, King James III granted Oliver Sinclair the lands and Barony of Pentland, also including Kirktoun, Quhithalch, Loganhouse, Erncrag, Sunnemishope, Moretoun and Mortonhall, in Midlothian; this was confirmed by King James III on 1 November 1486.

SINCLAIR OF DYSART AND RAVENSCRAIG IN FIFE. King James IV granted Lord Henry Sinclair the lands and Barony of Dysart and Ravenscraig with its castle, on 9 January 1494; on 24 November 1549, Queen Mary, granted Henry Sinclair, son and heir apparent of Lord William Sinclair, the lands and Barony of Dysart also the Barony of Ravenscraig in Fife, and the lands and Barony of Newburgh in Aberdeenshire; on 24 July 1577, King James VI granted James Sinclair, son and heir apparent of Lord Henry Sinclair, the lands and Barony of Ravenscraig, the lands and Barony of Dysart in Fife, also the lands and Barony of Newburgh in Aberdeenshire; on 5 July 1592, King James VI confirmed James Sinclair, son and heir apparent of Lord Henry Sinclair, the lands and Barony of Dysart.

SINCLAIR OF DUNBEITH IN INVERNESS-SHIRE. On 2 November 1529, King James V granted Alexander Sinclair of Stamster, the lands of Dunbeath, Raa, and Sandside in Inverness-shire, now incorporated into the Barony of Dunbeith, this was confirmed on 11 January 1530.

SINCLAIR OF ROSLYN IN MIDLOTHIAN. On 14 November 1533, King James V granted Sir William Sinclair the lands of Roslyn formerly held by Sir Henry Sinclair the Earl of Orkney; on 5 June 1574, King James VI granted Edward Sinclair, son and heir of Sir William Sinclair of Roslyn, the lands and Barony of Roslyn including many lands in Midlothian; on 28 October 1583, King James VI confirmed William Sinclair, his brother german in the lands and Barony of Roslyn, etc. incorporated into the Barony of Pentland. [The Sinclairs of Roslin, Caithness and Goshen, Charlottetown, 1901]

SINCLAIR OF PITCAIRN IN PERTHSHIRE. On 12 January 1537, King James V granted Oliver Sinclair the lands of Pitcairn now formed into a Barony.

SINCLAIR OF COCKBURNSPATH IN BERWICKSHIRE. On 5 April 1541, King James V granted Alexander Sinclair, brother german of Sir William Sinclair of Roslin, the lands, Lordship and Barony of Cockburnspath, with its tower, fort, house, the lands of Mains, woods, mills, fishing rights, etc, also the lands of Bowshiel, Paddocleuch, Rauchenside, Tourlie, etc.

SINCLAIR OF PENTLAND IN MIDLOTHIAN. On 10 December 1476, King James III granted Sir Oliver Sinclair, son of William Sinclair the Earl of Caithness, the lands and Barony of Pentland etc incorporated into the

Barony of Pentland; on 5 June 1574, King James VI granted Edward Sinclair, son and heir apparent of Sir William Sinclair of Roslyn, the lands and Baronies of Pentland and of Roslyn in Midlothian.

SINCLAIR OF PLAIDIS IN EASTER ROSS. On 18 December 1591, King James VI confirmed George Sinclair of May, in the lands and Barony of Plaidis.

SINCLAIR OF CANISBY IN CAITHNESS. King Charles I created James Sinclair, as a Baronet of Nova Scotia on 2 June 1631.

SINCLAIR OF STEVENSTOUN. John Sinclair was created as a Baronet of Nova Scotia on 18 June 1636.

SINCLAIR OF LONGFORMACUS IN BERWICKSHIRE. On 10 December 1664, Sir Robert Sinclair, son of James Sinclair of Longformacus, was created a Baronet by King Charles II on 10 December 1664, he died in 1678 and was succeeded by his son Sir John Sinclair as 2nd Baronet, he died by 1698 when his son Sir Robert Sinclair became the 3rd Baronet until his death on 5 December 1764.

SINCLAIR OF DUNBEATH IN CAITHNESS. On 12 October 1704, James Sinclair of Dunbeath was created Baronet of Dunbeath, when he died on 28 September 1742, he was succeeded by his son Sir William Sinclair as second Baronet of Dunbeath.

SKENE OF SKENE IN ABERDEENSHIRE. King Robert I granted the Barony of Skene to Robert Skene on 1 June 1317. Alexander Skene of Skene was killed at the Battle of Flodden on 9 September 1513. [a territorial name derived from a place in Aberdeenshire, examples date from the late thirteenth century] [A. Skene, was a secretary in Barbados before 1705, while James Skene, a physician from Aberdeen, settled in Charleston before 1766] [Court Book of Skene, 1613-1655, NRS.GD1.299][Memorials of the family of Skene of Skene, Aberdeen, 1887]

SKENE OF CURRIEHILL. Sir James Skene of Curriehill, was created as a Baronet on 22 February 1628 by King Charles I, he died in Edinburgh on 10 October 1633, and was succeeded by his son Sir John Skene as second Baronet, he was a soldier who died in Germany, having no heir the Baronetcy became extinct. [he Family of Skene of Skene, Aberdeen, 1887]

SKENE OF LIBERTOUN IN MIDLOTHIAN. On 22 January 1640, King Charles I granted John Skene, a clerk of the Supreme Senate, the lands and Barony of Libertoun, and the Barony of Halyards.

SOMERVILLE OF CAMBUSNETHAN IN LANARKSHIRE. The barony was granted by King Robert III in 1391 to Thomas Somerville. King James II created the town of Carnwath into a burgh of barony on 2 June 1451; on 29 April 1477, King James III granted William Somerville the lands and Barony of Carnwath in Lanarkshire, the lands and Barony of Linton in Roxburghshire with tenants and tenantries, also those of the lands of Gilmerton near Edinburgh; King James IV granted the Barony of Cambusnethan to John Somerville on 20 July 1488; on 13 March 1508, King James IV granted the lands and Barony of Carnwath, including Cawl, Carlyyndean, Muirhall, Torbrekks, Black Castle, Greenfield, Auchingray, Moyshat and Crofthill, Sydwood, Cleuch and Hyewood, in Lanarkshire to Lord John Somerville of Cambusnethan; on 13 March 1512. Sir John Somerville was killed at the Battle of Flodden on 9 September 1513. King James IV confirmed the charter of Sir John Somerville of Cambusnethan who granted his son John Somerville the lands of Gilmertoun and Gutters in Midlothian; on 4 October 1539, King James V confirmed John Somerville in the lands and Barony of Cambusnethan, with tower, fort, mill, fishing rights etc.; on 19 January 1581, King James VI confirmed John Somerville, son and heir of John Somerville of Cambusnethan, the lands and Barony of Cambusnethan. [Somerville is another surname of Norman origin which is derived from a town of that name near Caen in Normandy; examples of the surname date from the thirteenth century] [Reverend James Somerville settled in Antigua in 1768, while Andrew Somerville settled in Upper Canada in 1821][The Baronial House of Somerville, Glasgow, 1920]

SOMERVILLE OF BRAXFIELD IN LANARKSHIRE. On 26 March 1500, King James IV confirmed a charter of Thomas Somerville of Braxfield granting to his son and heir apparent Alexander Somerville the lands and Barony of Braxfield.

SOMERVILLE OF LINTOUN IN ROXBURGHSHIRE. On 10 April 1538, King James V granted Lord Hugh Somerville the lands and Barony of Lintoun.

SOMERVILLE OF PLANE IN STIRLINGSHIRE. On 15 May 1542, King James V granted Thomas Somerville the Barony of Plane.

SOULLIS OF THORTHORWALD IN DUMFRIES-SHIRE. Sir John Soullis was granted the Barony of Thortorwald by King Robert I, and the Barony of Kirkandrews, also in Dumfries-shire ca.1320. [RGS.I.App.Bb.B.33; B91]

SPALDING OF ASHINTULLY IN STRATHARDLE, PERTHSHIRE. King James VI granted David Spalding the lands of Ashintully, the houses and lands of Over and Nether Werei, with the mill, the houses and lands of Spital with its mill, and crofts, Glenbeg, the houses and lands of Cammis, Tomezecharaw, Dathhangaine, Over and Nether Soilzereis, Tomenamowin, Tomephin and Ballachragane, lands of Pitvirren, the houses and lands of Easter Downie, Ballinald, Balinkilyie and Glengeynit, Dalreach, Wester and Middle Inverchroskeis and Kirkton, all incorporated into the Barony of Ashintully on 10 January 1615. [The surname is derived from Spalding in Lincolnshire, England; examples date from the early thirteenth century] [James Spalding, a merchant from Bonnington Mills, settled in East Florida before 1772, while William Spalding settled in Upper Canada in 1818] [NB. the Spalding papers of the eighteenth century, are in the National Library of Scotland, NLS.17579-86.]

SPENCE OF ARDROIS IN FIFE. Oliver Cromwell, the Lord Protector, granted Marion Spence, daughter of James Spence in Alveth, the lands and barony of Ardrois including the town, port and harbour at Elie; plus, the lands, Barony and Mains of Dairsie with its mansion, manor place, mills, mill-lands, and others, on 15 December 1654. [An occupational surname based on the office of dispenser; examples date from the thirteenth century] [Helen Spence was transported to Virginia in 1696, while George Spence, a judge, died in Jamaica in 1780.]

STEWART OF FENDRAUGHT IN ABERDEENSHIRE. Margaret Stewart, daughter of the Earl of Lennox, was granted the land and Baronies of Biggar and Thankerton, in Lanarkshire, on 12…..; King Robert Bruce granted John Stewart, the lands and Barony of Fendraught in 1320s.[see Earls of Lennox in The History of the Napiers of Merchiston, London, 1921]

STEWART OF NISBET. King Robert I granted Robert Stewart, son of Walter Stewart, the baronies of Nisbet, Langnewton and Maxton, also the Barony of Caverton in Roxburghshire by King Robert I by about 1318.

STEWART OF METHVEN IN PERTHSHIRE. Robert Stewart was granted the Barony of Methven, and Kellie in Angus by King Robert I around 1320. [an occupational surname, from 'steward', examples in Scotland date from the twelfth century] [Agnes Stewart, emigrated to East New Jersey in 1685, while Charles Stewart, a prisoner of war after the Siege of Worcester, was transported to Boston in 1652]

STEWART OF ETHIEBEATOUN IN ANGUS. King Robert I granted Alexander Stewart the lands and Barony of Ethiebeatoun around 1320.

STEWART OF URQUHART IN INVERNESS-SHIRE. On 19 June 1372 King Robert II granted David Stewart, the Earl of Strathearn, the Barony of Urquhart.

STEWART OF INVERLUNAN IN ANGUS. On 4 January 1378, King Robert II granted Alexander Stewart the Barony of Inverlunan.

STEWART OF COULL AND O'NEILL IN ABERDEENSHIRE. King Robert III granted the Barony of Coull and O'Neill to John Stewart, son of the Duke of Albany, around 1400.

STEWART OF KILBRIDE IN LANARKSHIRE. King Robert III granted James Stewart, his natural son, the Barony of Kilbride, around 1400.

STEWART OF KINEDWART IN ABERDEENSHIRE. On 15 June 1415, Robert, Duke of Albany, the Regent of Scotland, granted John Stewart the Earl of Buchan, the Barony of Kinedwart; the lands and Barony of Kinedwart were granted to James Stewart by King James IV on 27 July 1490; on 20 June 1515, King James IV granted the Earl of Buchan the lands and Barony of Glen Cuthill in Aberdeenshire.

STEWART OF TILLICOUTRY IN CLACKMANNANSHIRE. On 25 February 1425, King James I granted John Stewart, the Earl of Buchan, the lands and Barony of Tillicoutry; on 24 April 1707 Robert Stewart, 2nd son of Sir James Stewart of Bute, was created Baronet of Tillicoutry, on his death on 1 October 1710 his son Sir Robert Stewart became the second baronet, he died on 4 March 1767, childless, so the barony became dormant.

STEWART OF TARBOLTOUN IN AYRSHIRE. King James I granted Sir Henry Stewart of Darnley the Barony of Tarbolton on 17 July 1428; on 2 February 1512, King James IV granted John Stewart, son and heir apparent of Matthew Stewart, the Earl of Lennox, the land and Barony of Tarbolton, also the lands of Galton with its tower, fort, manor house, mill, etc, and the lands of Dreghorn, now incorporated into the Barony of Tarboltoun. The Earl of Lennox was killed at the Battle of Flodden on 9 September 1513. [The Stewarts, Adam to Adam, USA, 1998]

STEWART OF ROSYTH IN FIFE. King James I granted the Barony of Rosyth to Sir David Stewart on 24 August 1428; on 5 January 1459, King James II granted Sir David Stewart, son and heir of Henry Stewart of Rosyth, the land and Barony of Rosyth; King James IV granted lands and Barony of Rosyth, and the Barony of Schandbody in Clackmannanshire, on 22 November 1490; on 6 May 1513, King James IV granted David Stewart, son and heir apparent of William Stewart, the lands and Barony of Rosyth, the lands of Craigie, Gerpot, part of Fordell, Culbaky and Straubirn, the lands of Luchelde, Pitrivie, Wester Cleish, Dunduf, Colstoun, Balnamule and Montqwn in Fife, the lands of Corb, Bouchondy and Laidgreen in Perthshire, and the Barony of Durisdeer in Dumfries-shire, now united into the Barony of Rosyth, also the Barony of Schandbothy in Clackmannanshire; on 14 July 1514, King James V granted Henry Stewart, son and heir apparent of David Stewart of Rosyth, the lands and Barony of Rosyth; on 7 September 1550, Queen Mary granted Robert Stewart, son and heir apparent of Henry Stewart of Rosyth, the lands and Barony of Rosyth, the lands and Barony of Crags in Fife, the lands and Barony of Durrisdeer in Dumfries-shire, also the lands and Barony of Schambody in Clackmannanshire; on 30 May 1593, King James VI confirmed James Stewart, son and heir apparent of Henry Stewart of Rosyth, the lands and Barony of Rosyth and the lands and Barony of Schambody.

STEWART OF MINTO IN ROXBURGHSHIRE. Alexander Stewart, son and heir of William Stewart of Dalswinton in Dumfries-shire, was granted the lands and Barony of Minto, Hewpaslot, and Long Newton in Roxburghshire, the lands of Glassartou in Wigtounshire, the lands of Dalswinton in Dumfries-shire, also the lands of Galwidie in Kirkcudbrightshire, and the lands of Morebattle on 13 January 1459; Sir John Stewart of Minto was killed at the Battle of Flodden on 9 September 1513; on 7 January 1530, King James V confirmed Robert Stewart of Minto, in the lands and Barony of Minto.

STEWART OF MANUEL IN STIRLINGSHIRE. King James II granted Mary his Queen, the lands and Barony of Manuel on 15 April 1459, formerly held by Lord John Somerville, also the land of Kirkandris, and of Plunctoun in Dumfries-shire formed into the Barony of Kirkandris.

STEWART OF STRATHALVA IN BANFFSHIRE. On 1 March 1467, King James III granted the lands and Barony of Strathalva and Downe, also the castle of Banff, and fishing rights on the River Deveron in Banffshire to James Stewart.

STEWART OF AUCHTERHOUSE IN ANGUS. On 22 September 1478 King James III granted the lands, lordship and barony of Auchterhouse with its castle and manor-house, tenants and tenandries, the lands and Barony Nevay, the lands and Barony of Essie, Kinnalty, and Kettins, the lands and Barony of Glen Dooquhy with castle and manor-house in Banffshire with fishing rights in Banff and the River Deveron, the lands and Barony of Strathalway and Montblary in Banffshire, the lands and Baronies of Glenuchtill, Grandoun and Midmar in Aberdeenshire, the lands of Glaskego, Cartralezane and Belistoune and some land in Dyce, Aberdeenshire , also the lands of Rylands, Culburnie and Inchdewar in Banffshire to James Stewart the Earl of Buchan; on 27 June 1489 King James IV granted James Stewart the Earl of Buchan, lands in Bacormo, Argaith, and Ladencreif, also the lands of Keith, Pitlyall and Bowhouses with their mills, in Angus; on 20

May 1491 King James IV confirmed the grant by James Stewart, Earl of Buchan, to his son Alexander Stewart of the Barony of Kettie, the lads of Leoucht in the Barony of Auchterhouse in Angus, on 20 May 1491; on 19 May 1492 King James IV granted Alexander Stewart, son of James Stewart the Earl of Buchan, the lands, lordship and Barony of Auchterhouse with its castle and manor house, also the lands and Baronies of Nevay and Kettins in Angus, and the Baronies of Strathalva and Montblary in Banffshire; on 12 July 1528, King James V confirmed John, Earl of Buchan, in the lands Barony and Lordship of Auchterhouse with its castle, fort, mills, the Barony of Eassie, including Castletoun, Ailhouse, Brewland, Newmylne, Balkery with its mill, Glenquharites, Bakgrange, Derraland, the lands and Barony of Nevay, the lands of Pitdinnie in the Barony of Kettins, in Angus; the lands and Barony of Montblary, with fishing rights, woods and mill, the lands of Westrin, the lands of Newton with its mill and manor-house, Todlaw, Whitfield, Smedytoun, Achinbaddy with its mill and fishing rights, the lands of Stanelie, Ryland with its mill, Tulloch and its mill, the lands and Barony of Glendowoquhay alias Doune with mill, fishing and brewhouse, the lands of Meilris with mill and fishing rights, Montblatoun with salmon fishing on the River Deveron, in Banffshire, Banff castle, the lands of Pitgar with its mill, Mynone and Cartrilzeare, Colane in Banffshire, the lands and Barony of Glencuthill, the lands of Achmeddan with fishing, Inchbrek, Salcots, Towie and Pitmacaldar, land in the Barony of Cartrilzeare, lands of Balmaddie in the Barony of Grandoun, the lands of Glascofores, and the lands and Barony of Cartrilzeare, in Aberdeenshire, now formed into the Barony and Lordship of Glendowoquhy; on 4 August 1547, Queen Mary granted John Stewart, son and heir apparent of the Earl of Buchan, the lands, Barony and Lordship of Glendowequhey; on 13 February 1574, King James VI granted Robert Stewart the lands, Barony and Lordship of Glendowoqhy, , the lands, Barony and Lordship of Auchterhouse, the lands and Barony of Essie, the lands and Barony of Nevay, the lands and Barony of Montblary, the lands and Barony of Glencuthill, the lands and Barony of Cartrilzaree, the lands and Barony of Kinyawtie, etc

STEWART OF BRAIDWOOD IN LANARKSHIRE. King James III granted Alexander Stewart, son of James Stewart of Craigiehale, the lands and Barony of Braidwood, with the land of Hewades in Lanarkshire, also the patronage of the hospital of St Laurence in the burgh of Lanark, on 13 December 1482.

STEWART OF AVONDALE IN LANARKSHIRE. King James III granted Alexander Stewart, son and heir apparent of Walter Stewart of Morphy, the lands and Barony of Avondale on 4 January 1486; King James IV granted Alexander

Stewart of Avondale the lands and barony of Feldy in Perthshire on 4 February 1488; on 25 July 1531, King James V, granted Andrew Stewart, son and heir apparent of Lord Andrew Avendale, the lands, Barony and Lordship of Avendale, with its forts, mills, fishing, etc.; on 4 February 1500 King James IV granted Lord Andrew Avondale the lands and Barony of Morphy-Frissell with fishing rights on the North Water of the River Esk in Kincardineshire; Lord Avondale was killed at the Battle of Flodden on 9 September 1513.

STEWART OF TRAQUAIR IN PEEBLES-SHIRE. On 3 February 1479, King James III granted James Stewart, the Earl of Buchan, the lands of Traquair with its tenants and tenantries of Quylteth, lands of Grebistoun, as a free Barony; James Stewart, son of the Earl of Buchan, was granted the lands and Barony of Traquair by King James IV on 23 January 1493; on 11 August 1512, King James IV granted William Stewart, son and heir apparent of James Stewart of Traquair, the lands and Barony of Traquair, Schelyn with its grain mill and fulling mill, and the lands of Innerleithen, in Peebles-shire, now incorporated into the Barony of Traquair; on 29 March 1538, King James V granted William Stewart, son and heir apparent of James Stewart of Traquair the lands and Barony of Traquair, including tower, fort, grain mill, fulling mill, lands of Schelinlaw, Innerleithan, and part of the Glen, Peebles-shire; on 12 February 1639, King Charles I granted John Stewart the Earl of Traquair the lands and Barony of Maner in Peebles-shire. [History of the Stuarts, Earls of Traquair, London, 1840]

STEWART OF INNERMETH IN PERTHSHIRE. King James II granted John Stewart, Lord Lorne, the Barony of Innermeith, and the Barony of Redcastle in Angus on 20 June 1452; on 12 July 1481 King James III granted Walter Stewart the Barony of Redcastle and its mill. Lord Lorne was killed at the Battle of Flodden on 9 September 1513. On 23 June 1542, King James V confirmed John Stewart, Lord Innermeith, in the Barony of Redcastle including Inverkeillor. [Clan Stewart of Appin, 1463-1752, Argyll, 1997]

STEWART OF AUCHTERHOUSE IN ANGUS. On 22 September 1478 King James III granted the lands, lordship and barony of Auchterhouse with its castle and manor-house, tenants and tenandries, the lands and Barony Nevay, the lands and Barony of Essie, Kinnalty, and Kettins, the lands and Barony of Glen Dooquhy with castle and manor-house in Banffshire with fishing rights in Banff and the River Deveron, the lands and Barony of Strathalway and Montblary in Banffshire, the lands and Baronies of Glenuchtill, Grandoun and Midmar in Aberdeenshire, the lands of Glaskego, Cartralezane an Belistoune and some land in Dyce, Aberdeenshire, also the lands of Rylands, Culburnie and Inchdewar in Banffshire to James Stewart the Earl of Buchan; on 27 June 1489 King James IV granted James Stewart the Earl of Buchan, lands in Bacormo, Argaith, and Ladencreif, also the lands of Keith, Pitlyall and Bowhouses with their mills, in Angus; on 20 May 1491 King James IV confirmed the grant by James Stewart, Earl of Buchan, to his son Alexander Stewart of the Barony of Kettie, the lads of Leoucht in the Barony of Auchterhouse in Angus, on 20 May 1491; on 19 May 1492 King James IV granted Alexander Stewart, son of James Stewart the Earl of Buchan, the lands, lordship and Barony of Auchterhouse with its castle and manor house, also the lands and Baronies of Nevay and Kettins in Angus, and the Baronies of Strathalva and Montblary in Banffshire; on 12 July 1528, King James V confirmed John, Earl of Buchan, in the lands Barony and Lordship of Auchterhouse with its castle, fort, mills, the Barony of Eassie, including Castletoun, Ailhouse, Brewland, Newmylne, Balkery with its mill, Glenquharites, Bakgrange, Derraland, the lands and Barony of Nevay, the lands of Pitdinnie in the Barony of Kettins, in Angus; the lands and Barony of Montblary, with fishing rights, woods and mill, the lands of Westrin, the lands of Newton with its mill and manor-house, Todlaw, Whcalderitfield, Smedytoun, Achinbaddy with its mill and fishing rights, the lands of Stanelie, Ryland with its mill, Tulloch and its mill, the lands and Barony of Glendowoquhay alias Doune with mill, fishing and brewhouse, the lands of Meilris with mill and fishing rights, Montblatoun with salmon fishing on the River Deveron, in Banffshire, Banff castle, the lands of Pitgar with its mill, Mynone and Cartrilzeare, Colane in Banffshire, the lands and Barony of Glencuthill, the lands of Achmeddan with fishing, Inchbrek, Salcots, Towie and Pitmacaldar, land in the Barony of Cartrilzeare, lands of Balmaddie in the Barony of Grandoun, the lands of Glascofores, and the lands and Barony of Cartrilzeare, in Aberdeenshire, now formed into the Barony and Lordship of Glendowoquhy; on 13 February 1574, King James VI granted Robert Stewart the lands, Barony and Lordship of Glendowoqhy, , the lands, Barony and Lordship of Auchterhouse, the lands and Barony of Essie, the lands and Barony of Nevay, the lands and Barony of Montblary, the lands and Barony of Glencuthill, the lands and Barony of Cartrilzaree, the lands and Barony of Kinyawtie, etc .

STEWART OF INNERMETH IN PERTHSHIRE. King James II granted John Stewart, Lord Lorne, the Barony of Innermeith, and the Barony of Redcastle in Angus on 20 June 1452; on 12 July 1481 King James III granted Walter Stewart the Barony of Redcastle and its mill. Lord Lorne was killed at the Battle of Flodden on 9 September 1513. On 23 June 1542, King James V confirmed John Stewart, Lord Innermeith , in the Barony of Redcastle including Inverkeillor. [Clan Stewart of Appin, 1463-1752, Argyll, 1997]

STEWART OF GLENTILT IN ATHOLL IN PERTHSHIRE. On 2 July 1502, King James IV granted John Stewart, son and heir apparent of John Stewart the Earl of Atholl, the Thanage of Glen Tilt, including Blairwauchtir, and Inverslane.

STEWART OF BRECHIN IN ANGUS. On 24 September 1511, King James IV granted Sir Cristiarno Stewart, the lands and Lordship of Brechin and Navaar, with forts, mills, in Angus, now incorporated into the Barony of Brechin.

STEWART OF CRICHTOUN IN MIDLOTHIAN. On 28 August 1511, King James IV granted Agnes Stewart, daughter of the Earl of Buchan, the lands, Lordship and Barony of Crichtoun, with its castle, woods, parks, orchards, etc., the lands of Pitcocks in East Lothian, also the lands and Barony of Earlstoun with mills in Galloway.

STEWART OF UPSETLINGTON IN BERWICKSHIRE. On 5 November 1516, King James V granted Alan Stewart, the lands and Barony of Upsetlington

STEWART OF METHVEN IN PERTHSHIRE. On 17 July 1528, King James V granted Henry Stewart, brother german of Andrew, Lord Avondale, the lands and Lordship of Methven, with its castle, mill, fishing rights, etc, also the lands, and Lordship of Balquhidder, with mills, fishing rights, forests, etc. in Perthshire, now incorporated as the Lordship and Barony of Methven, this was confirmed on 3 October 1530; on 18 February 1548, Queen Mary, confirmed Henry Stewart, Lord Methven, the lands and Lordship of Methven; on 10 October 1551, Queen Mary granted Henry Stewart, Lord Methven, the lands and Lordship of Methven.

STEWART OF AVENDALE IN LANARKSHIRE. On 25 July 1531, King James V, granted Andrew Stewart, son and heir apparent of Lord Andrew Avendale, the lands, Barony and Lordship of Avendale, with its forts, mills, fishing, etc.

STEWART OF STRATHERNE IN INVERNESS-SHIRE. On 13 May 1532, King James V granted his brother James Stewart, the Earl of Moray the lands and Barony of Stratherne including the lands of Petty, Brauchlie and Stratherne, also the mill of Conysche, and the tower and fort of Halhill.

STEWART OF PITCAIRN IN PERTHSHIRE. On 16 October 1532, King James V granted Alexander Stewart the lands of Pitcairn with its mill in Perthshire, now incorporated in the Barony of Pitcairn.

STEWART OF DOUGLAS IN LANARKSHIRE. On 28 October 1534, James Stewart, the eldest natural son of the king, was granted by King James V, the lands and Barony of Douglas, with fort, mill, fishing rights, etc, the lands and Baronies of Dunsire, Crawfordjohn, and Bothwell, with forts, mills, fishing rights, etc, in Lanarkshire, the lands and Barony of Jedburgh-forest with mills, fishing rights, etc, the lands and Barony of Buncle in Berwickshire, with fort, mills, fishing rights, etc; the lands and Barony of Tantallon in Midlothian, with fort, castle, mills, fishing rights, etc.

STEWART OF GLENLOCHAY IN PERTHSHIRE. On 15 July 1536, John Stewart, Earl of Atholl, was granted the Barony of Glenlochy.

STEWART OF GRANTULLY IN PERTHSHIRE. On 14 March 1540, King James V granted Thomas Stewart, son and heir apparent of Alexander Stewart of Grantully, the lands of Grantully, Kiltulie, Tullochcrosk, Pitoquharne, incorporated into the Barony of Grantully.

STEWART OF GARRULES IN KIRKCUDBRIGHTSHIRE. On 23 October 1542, King James V granted Andrew Stewart, son and heir apparent of Alexander Stewart of Garrules the Barony of Garrlules, also the Barony of Dalswinton in Dumfries-shire.

STEWART OF RATTRAY IN PERTHSHIRE. On 8 May 1564, Queen Mary granted John Stewart, the Earl of Atholl, the lands and Barony of Rattray.

STEWART OF TARBOLTOUN IN AYRSHIRE. On 18 April 1572, Queen Mary granted Charles Stewart the lands and Barony of Tarboltoun; on 5 March 1580, King James VI granted Esmo Stewart, Lord Aubignie, the lands and Barony of Tarboltoun.

STEWART OF INCHECHYNNAN IN RENFREWSHIRE. On 25 May 1579, King James VI confirmed Elizabeth Stewart, Lady Lovat, in the lands and Barony of Inchechynnan in Renfrewshire.

STEWART OF BOTHWELLMUIR IN LANARKSHIRE. On 24 August 1580, King James VI granted James Stewart, son and heir of Andrew, Lord Ochiltree, the lands of Bothwellmuir and other lands in Lanarkshire merged into a Barony and a Lordship; on 22 April 1581, King James VI granted Captain James Stewart of Bothwellmuir the Barony of Arran, also the lands and Barony of Hamiltoun, the Barony of Cumnock, the lands and Barony of Mauchlin, the lands and Barony of Drumsargatt, the lands and Bariny of Kirkkinner, the lands and Barony of Kinneill, also the lands and Barony of Carriden, etc.

STEWART OF DALKEITH IN MID LOTHIAN. On 5 June 1581, King James VI granted Esmo Stewart, Lord Darnley, the lands, Lordship, Regality and Barony of Dalkeith, the lands and Barony of Garmiltoun Dunning, the lands and Barony of Caldercleirr in Midlothian, the lands and Barony of Whittingham in East Lothian, the lands and Barony of Aberdour in Fife, the lands and Barony of Mordington in Berwickshire, etc now united into the Barony of Dalkeith.

STEWART OF BRAIDWOOD IN LANARKSHIRE. On 15 November 1581, King James VI granted Henry Stewart of Gogar, brother german of the Earl of Arran, the lands and Barony of Braidwood.

STEWART of KELSO IN ROXBURGHSHIRE. Francis Stewart, Commandator of Kelso, on 16 June 1581, was granted by King James VI the Lordship and Barony of Hailes, the lands and Barony of Oldhamstocks, the lands and Barony of Morham, the lands and Lordship of Crichtoun, the lands and Barony of Whitsum, the lands and Barony of Yetholm, the lands and Barony of Weltoun, the lands and Barony of Chalmerlan Newtoun, in Roxburghshire, the lands and Barony of Dryfesdale and Carruthers, in Dumfries-shire, the lands and Barony of Kirkmichael in Dumfries-shire, the lands and Barony of Earlstoun in Kirkcudbrightshire, the Lordship of Bothwell, the lands and Baronies of Elgarsgill, Wolstoun and Dolphintoun, the lands and Barony of Dunsyre, in Lanarkshire.

STEWART OF INVERMAY IN PERTHSHIRE. On 4 November 1587, King James VI confirmed John Stewart in the lands, Lordship and Barony of Invermay; on 16 June 1589, King James VI granted James Stewart son and heir of John Stewart of Invermay the lands and Barony of Redcastle and Inverkeillour etc in Angus, also the lands, Lordship, and Barony of Invermay.

STEWART OF KINNEILL AND CARRIDEN IN WEST LOTHIAN. On 28 May 1582, King James VI granted James Stewart, son of the Earl of Arran, the lands, Lordship, and Baronies of Kinneill and Carriden.

STEWART OF LENNOX IN STIRLINGSHIRE/DUNBARTONSHIRE. On 31 July 1583, King James VI granted Ludovic Stewart, son of Esmo Stewart the Duke of Lennox etc, the Dukedom, Lordship, Barony and Regality of Lennox; on 24 March 1586, King James VI granted Ludovic the Duke of Lennox, the lands and Lordship of Methven in Perthshire; on 26 June 1591, King James VI granted Ludovic, the Duke of Lennox, the Lordship and Barony of Hailes and the lands and Lordship of Liddesdale; on 6 December 1594, King James VI granted Ludovic the Duke of Lennox, the lands, Lordship, Barony and Regality of Kirriemuir in Angus, also the lands and Lordship of Abernethy in

Perthshire, the lands, Lordship and Barony of Selkirk, the lands, Lordship and Barony of Jedburgh Forest, the lands Lordship and Baronies of Bunkle and Prestoun, the lands, Lordship, Barony and Regality of Bothwell, the lands, Lordship and Barony of Douglas, the lands, Lordship and Barony of Crawford-Lindsay; the lands, Lordship and Barony of Cockburnspath, the lands and Barony of Barres, etc.

STEWART OF KELLIE IN ABERDEENSHIRE. On 24 August 1584, King James VI granted Margaret Stewart of Saltoun, the lands and Barony of Kellie.

STEWART OF DOUGLAS IN LANARKSHIRE. On 20 October 1584, King James VI granted the lands, Lordship and Barony of Douglas to William Stewart of Monktoun.

STEWART OF NEWTOUN IN AYRSHIRE. On 27 May 1587, King James VI granted James Stewart, son of Lord James Stewart, the lands and Barony of Newtoun, also the lands and Barony of Colville-Barnwell and Symington.

STEWART OF CARSTAIRS IN LANARKSHIRE. On 1 November 1587, King James VI granted Sir William Stewart, son of Andrew Stewart of Ochiltree, the lands and Barony of Carstairs.

STEWART OF HAMILTON IN LANARKSHIRE. On 24 June 1589, King James VI confirmed James Stewart, Lord Hamilton, Earl of Arran, in the lands and Barony of Hamilton; on 19 November 1639, King Charles I granted James the Marquis of Hamilton, Earl of Arran, the lands and Barony of Monkland in Lanarkshire.

STEWART OF OCHILTREE IN AYRSHIRE. On 26 August 1589, King James VI granted Andrew Stewart of Ochiltree, the lands and Lordship of Ochiltree; on 2 August 1691, King James VI granted Andrew Stewart of Ochiltree, the lands and Barony of Earlston in Kirkcudbrightshire.

STEWART OF CLUNY IN PERTHSHIRE. On 3 December 1593, King James VI confirmed James Stewart of Stuiks, in the lands and Barony of Cluny.

STEWART OF FERME IN LANARKSHIRE. On 21 July 1599, King James VI confirmed Walter Stewart, eldest son and heir apparent of Sir Matthew Stewart of Minto, in the lands and Lordship of Ferme.

STEWART OF NOVA SCOTIA. James Stewart, son of the Earl of Galloway, was created as a Baronet of Nova Scotia on 18 April 1627. [an occupational surname, from 'steward'] [examples in Scotland date from the twelfth century]

STEWART OF STRATHBRAAN IN PERTHSHIRE. On 31 July 1638, King Charles I granted Sir Thomas Stewart of Gairntullie, various lands in Perthshire incorporated into the Barony of Strathbraan.

STEWART OF DALMAHOY IN MIDLOTHIAN. On 18 November 1657, Oliver Cromwell, the Lord Protector, granted Lewis Stewart the town, lands, and Barony of Dalmahoy in Stirlingshire.

STEWART OF BLACKHALL IN RENFREWSHIRE. On 27 March 1667, Archibald Stewart of Blackhall was created as a Baronet until his death around 1722, when his grandson, Sir Archibald Stewart, a Member of Parliament, became the 2nd Baronet of Blackhall, when he died in April 1724, the Baronetcy was inherited by his brother Sir Michael Stewart, an advocate.

STEWART OF ETHIEBEATON IN ANGUS. Alexander Stewart was granted the lands and barony of Ethiebeaton, he died in 1701.

STEWART OF BLAIR AND BALCASKIE IN FIFE. On 2 June 1683 Thomas Stewart was created as a Baronet, on his death he was succeeded by his son Sir George Stewart as 2nd Baronet, he died on 1 November 1759.

STEWART OF GOODTREES IN MIDLOTHIAN. On 22 December 1705, James Stewart of Goodtrees was created as a Baronet, on his death on 9 August 1727, the baronetcy went to his son Sir James Stewart, who died on 12 June 1773.

STEWART OF TILLICOULTRY IN CLACKMANNANSHIRE. On 24 April 1707, John Stewart, son of Sir James Stewart of Bute, was created 1st Baronet, on his death on 1 October 1710, the baronetcy was inherited by his son Sir Robert Stewart, as he died without children on 4 March 1767 the Baronetcy became dormant.

STIRLING OF KEIR IN STIRLINGSHIRE. On 10 September 1503, King James IV granted Sir John Stirling, son and heir apparent of Willima Stirling of Keir, the lands of Keir with its tower, manor house, fulling mill and granary, also Lupnow with its fishing rights, Strowe with its mill, Davochlowan, Reterne-Stirling alias Coygis of Strathallan, Classingallis, Schanrow, Wester Coig, Welcoyg, Bereholm, Little Coyg, West Poffil with Coygis mill, and Glenty, in Perthshire, incorporated into the Barony of Keir; on 14 May 1513, King James IV granted Sir John Stirling of Keir, the lands of Lupno, Dauchlewan, and Reterne-Stirling, and the Coigs of Strathallan, which were united into the Barony of Keir; King James VI granted Sir John Stirling of Keir, the lands of Lupno, Dauchlewan, and Reterne-Stirling, and the Coigs of Strathallan, which were united into the Barony of Keir, on 16 September 1579, King James VI confirmed Archibald Stirling, son and heir of Sir James Stirling of Keir, the lands and Barony of Keir. [a surname of territorial origin, derived from the town of that name, examples date from the twelfth century] [David and John Stirling were captured at the Siege of Worcester then transported to Boston in 1652, while Thomas Stirling died in Maryland by 1685][The Stirlings of Keir, Edinburgh, 1858]

STIRLING OF GLORAT IN STIRLING. On 30 April 1666, Charles Stirling of Glorat, was created a Baronet by King Charles II, George Stirling died about 1680 and was succeeded by his son Sir Mungo Stirling as second Baronet of Glorat. He died on 21 April 1712 when the title went to his eldest son and heir Sir James Stirling, who was a Lord of Session known as Lord Alva, he died at Glorat, childless, on 30 April 1771.

STIRLING OF ARDOCH. Sir William Stirling, son of Henry Stirling of Ardoch, was created Baronet of Ardoch on 2 May 1666 by King Charles II.

STRACHAN OF MONYABBOK, TULLIMADDIN AND CRAIG IN ABERDEENSHIRE. King David II granted the Barony of Monyabbok, Tullimaddin, and Craig to Donald Strachan, around 1345. [a surname derived from Strachan in Kincardineshire, recorded in Scotland since 1200] [Alexander Strachan was bound for Nova Scotia in 1627, while Margaret Strachan was transported to Virginia in 1667]

STRACHAN OF THORNTOUN IN KINCARDINESHIRE. On 4 January 1475, King James III granted John Strachan the lands and Barony of Thorntoun, the lands of Muirtoun, Wismantoun, Pitgarvy and the castle of Kincardine, in Kincardineshire; on 5 March 1488, King James III granted David Strachan, son of John Strachan of Thorntoun, the lands and Barony of Thorntoun, which was confirmed by King James IV on 6 January 1504; on 2 May 1521, King James V granted Alexander Strachan, the lands and Barony of Thorntoun with its mill, also the lands of Pitgarvy, Muirtoun, Wismanstoun, and Kincardin's mill, in Kincardineshire; on 30 August 1588, King James VI confirmed Alexander Strachan of Thorntoun in the lands and Barony of Thorntoun; on 12 February 1601, King James VI confirmed Alexander Strachan of Thorntoun, in the lands and Barony of Strachan. [Memorials of the Strachans, Baronets of Thornton, London, 1873]

STRACHAN OF STRACHAN IN NOVA SCOTIA. On 28 May 1625 Sir Alexander Strachan, son of Robert Strachan, husband of Sarah Douglas, was created by King Charles I as the First Baronet of Strachan with 16000 acres in Nova

Scotia, a sasine dated 14 July 1625. Sir Alexander married twice, firstly to Margaret Lindsay daughter of Lord Menmuir, and secondly to Jean Ogilvy, daughter of Lord Airlie. During the Wars of the Three Kingdoms, he was a Royalist and lived in exile in Bruges, Flanders, where he died in 1659. He had no obvious heir but the baronetcy was claimed by a distant relative which was disputed. [a surname derived from the lands of Strachan in Kincardineshire, examples of the surname date from 1200] Alexander Strachan emigrated to Nova Scotia in 1627, while Robert Strachan, a shipwright, died on St Vincent in 1805]

STRACHAN OF KINNETTLES IN ANGUS. On 6 February 1516, King James V granted Alexander Strachan, nephew and heir apparent of Alexander Strachan of Brigtoun the lands and Barony of Kinnettles.

STRACHAN OF LENTURKS IN ABERDEENSHIRE. On 13 April 1548, Queen Mary granted John Strachan the lands, house, mill and woods of Lenturks now incorporated into the Barony of Lenturks.

STRACHAN OF BRIGTOUN OF KINNETLES IN ANGUS. On 29 December 1561, Queen Mary, granted Alexander Strachan, nephew and heir apparent of Alexander Strachan of Brigtoun, the lands and Barony of Brigtoun of Kinnettles.

STRATOUN OF STRATOUN IN KINCARDINESHIRE. On 28 November 1509, King James IV granted Alexander Stratoun of Laurencetoun, the lands and Barony of Stratoun, also the lands of Little Futhes in Kincardineshire, and the lands of Southouse in Midlothian, the Close of Peebles in Peebles-shire, Seybeggis, Castlecary and Skaithmuir. [a surname derived from a places in Ayrshire or Fife, a surname since the thirteenth century][Effie Stratton emigrated to East New Jersey in 1684, while Janet Straton was transported to Virginia in 1696]

STRATOUN OF DISCLUNE IN KINCARDINESHIRE. On 3 February 1534, King James V granted Andrew Stratoun, son of the deceased Alexander Stratoun of that Ilk, and Katherine Menzies, the lands and Barony of Disclune; on 16 July 1541, King James V granted Andrew Stratoun of that Ilk the lands of Wester Kinneff, castle and fort, etc, now formed into the Barony of Kinneff. [The Stratons of Lauriston, Exmouth, 1939]

SUTHERLAND OF DOWNIE IN ANGUS. King David II granted the Barony of Downie, also, the Baronies of Kincardine, Aberlethnott and Fettercairn, to William the Earl of Sutherland on 28 September 1343.

SUTHERLAND OF THORBOLL IN SUTHERLAND. Nicoll Sutherland was granted the Barony of Sutherland by King Robert III in 1363.

SUTHERLAND OF URQUHART IN INVERNESS-SHIRE, King David II granted the Barony of Urquhart to the Earl of Sutherland before 1358. [derived from Sutherland – the southern land of the Vikings, a surname in Scotland since the fourteenth century] [William Sutherland, a soldier during the French and Indian Wars, settled near Fort Ticonderoga in 1764, while Ansell Sutherland, a prisoner of war, was transported to Boston in 1651] ['The Sutherland Book', Sir William Fraser, 1892]

SUTHERLAND OF DUFFUS IN MORAY. On 22 July 1527, King James V granted William Sutherland, son and heir apparent of William Sutherland of Duffus, the lands and Barony of Duffus, with its castle, fort, mills, fishing rights, etc, the lands of Brychtmont and Kinstary with mill, in Nairnshire, united as the Barony of Duffus; on 3 August 1588, King James VI confirmed William Sutherland of Duffus in the lands and Barony of Duffus, etc.

SUTTIE OF BALGOUN IN EAST LOTHIAN On 5 May 1702, Queen Anne created George Suttie as Baronet of Balgoun, he was a magistrate of Edinburgh and died around 1710. [examples date from the seventeenth century][David Suttie, a mariner from Kirkcaldy, died on the Darien Expedition in 1698]

SWINTOUN OF SWINTOUN IN BERWICKSHIRE. On 26 June 1598, King James VI confirmed Robert Swintoun of that Ilk, in the Lordship and lands of Swintoun Magna, and the Barony of Cranshaws. [Swintons of that Ilk, Edinburgh,1883]

SWINTOUN OF BOWN IN BERWICKSHIRE. On 22 May 1558, Queen Mary confirmed Elizabeth Swintoun, wife of John Cranstoun of Corsby, in the lands and Barony of Bown. [probably of Danish origin, Swin = Svein, Swinton a place in Berwickshire, examples date from the thirteenth century] [Alexander Swinton, died in Darien, Panama, in 1699, while Douglas Swinton, a Jacobite, was transported to Jamaica in 1747]

TAYLOR OF WEST BARNS IN FIFE. On 20 March 1649, King Charles II granted James Taylor a merchant in St Andrews, the lands and Barony of West Barns. [an occupational surname, examples date from the thirteenth century] Alexander Taylor, a mason and rioter from Aberdeen, was transported to the colonies in 1767, while John Taylor, a goldsmith, died on St Eustatia in 1783]

THANE OF EDINDUNNING IN PERTHSHIRE. On 26 October 1530, King James V granted Alexander Thane, nephew of John Thane of Edindunning, the lands of Edindunning, Cults, and Common Dunning, now integrated into the Barony of Edindunning. [originally a rank similar to baron, examples date from the twelfth century][Daniel Thain, a clergyman from Aberdeen, died in New Jersey in 1763]

THOMSON OF DUDDINGSTON IN MIDLOTHIAN. Thomas Thomson was created a baronet of Nova Scotia on 20 February 1636. [A patronymic surname meaning 'son of Thom', very common in Scotland, examples date from the late fourteenth century.][George Thomson, a prisoner of war, was transported to New England in 1650, while Margery Thomson, emigrated to East New Jersey in 1685][John Thomson of Duddingstone, a memoir, Edinburgh,1895]

TILLIEDAFF OF TILLIEDAFF IN ABERDEENSHIRE. On 28 March 1533 King James V confirmed Andrew Tilliedaff of that Ilk in the lands and Tillidaff, including the lands of Logieruif, and of Orchardtoun of Tillieduff.

TOSHACH OF MONIVAIRD IN PERTHSHIRE. On 7 May 1509, King James IV confirmed Andrew Toshach of Monivaird, the lands of Monivaird with its mill, Glen Turret, and Makvene in Perthshire, now incorporated into the Barony of Monivaird; on 11 February 1587, King James VI confirmed Duncan Toshach, son of Edward Toshach of Monyvaird, the lands and Barony of Monyvaird. [A surname from the Early Gaelic meaning 'leader'; examples date from the early thirteenth century][David Toshach of Monivaird emigrated to East New Jersey in 1684, while Katherine Toshach, from Perthshire, was transported to the colonies in 1728]

TOWERS OF INNERLEITH IN EAST LOTHIAN. King James IV granted the lands of Innerleith and Dalry with their mills, also the lands of Garmiltoun-Noble now forming the Barony of Innerleith to Sir John Tours on 26 November 1489. On 19 February 1642, King Charles I confirmed Alexander Towers, son of Sir Alexander Towers of Garmiltoun, the lands and Barony of Inverleith. [The family is said to be descended from Walter Towers, a French merchant in Edinburgh during the reign of King David II; examples of the surname date from the thirteenth century. [Patrick Tower, a prisoner of was captured at the Siege of Worcester in 1651, was transported to Boston, while James Towers a physician from Aberdeen, settled in St Thomas in the West Indies after 1775]

TULLOCH OF CRAIGNESTOUN IN KINCARDINESHIRE. On 22 June 1512, King James IV granted John Tulloch the lands of Craignestoun, including

Netherset and Inchgray, also the lands of Oldmanstoun, now incorporated into the Barony of Craignestoun; on 18 February 1547, Queen Mary, granted William Tulloch, son and heir apparent of Andrew Tullloch of Craignestoun, the lands and Barony of Craignestoun; Alexander Tulloch, son and heir apparent of William Tulloch of Craigneston, was confirmed in the lands and Barony of Craigneston, on 22 February 1576 by King James VI. [a name derived from a place, meaning Green Hill in Gaelic, in Easter Ross, examples of the surname date from the fourteenth century][Robert Tulloch, a physician in Jamaica, around 1799, while David Tulloch, from Edinburgh, applied to settle in Canada in 1827]

TURING OF FOVERAN IN ABERDEENSHIRE. On 17 May 1514, King James V granted William Turing, brother-german of Gilbert Turing of Foveran, the lands and Barony of Foveran, with its mill, Miltoun, the manor-house of Foveran, the lands of Balgirshaw, Drummys, Ardoch, Aikenshill, Pitmulan, part of Little Auchnakoy, the lands of Over Tibberlaw, and the lands of Waltersmuir in Aberdeenshire; On 29 March 1527, King James V granted William Turing, son and heir apparent of Gilbert Turing of Foverane, the lands and Barony of Foverane with its mill and manor-house, the lands of Balgarshaw, Drums, Ardach, Sauchak, Atkinshill, Pitmulan, parts of Little Auchnakoy, the lands of Tibbertaw, and Waltersmuir in Aberdeenshire, on 18 February 1541, King James V confirmed Wiliam Turing in the lands and Barony of Foveran. Sir John Turing was created Baronet of Foveran by King Charles I around 1642, he fought at the Siege of Worcester as a Royalist in 1651, he died in 1662. He was succeeded by his grandson John Turing as the second Baronet, he died in Edinburgh in February 1682 with no children to succeed him casing the barony to become extinct. [A surname based on Turin in Angus, examples date from the fourteenth century][Sir Irving Turing of Foveran, died in Jamaica in 1791][The lay of the Turings, 1316-1849, 1850]

TURNBULL OF BEDRULE IN ROXBURGHSHIRE. On 20 January 1571, King James VI granted William Turnbull, son and heir apparent of Thomas Turnbull of Bedrule, the lands and Barony of Bedrule. [possibly derived from the Old English *Trumbald* meaning bold, examples date from the fourteenth century] [Thomas Turnbull, a Covenanter, was transported to Jamaica in 1685, while ....Turnbull, from Roxburghshire, was transported to Virginia in 1665][Turnbulls of Bedrule, Hawick, 1955]

TWEEDY OF DRUMELZIER IN PEEBLES-SHIRE. On 30 April 1511, King James IV granted John Tweedy the lands of Horne Hunter's land in Innerleithen, Peebles-shire, now united into the Barony of Drumelzier; on 5 June 1540, King James V granted James Tweedy the Barony of Drumelzier. [a surname derived from the lands of Tweedie in Lanarkshire, examples of the surname date from the thirteenth century][Janet Tweedie from Roxburghshire was transported to the American colonies in 1764, while James Tweedie, from Dumfries-shire, died in New Brunswick in 1860][A history of the Tweedie family, London, 1902]

URQUHART OF CULBO IN MORAY. On 24 November 1600, King James VI granted John Urquhart the tutor of Cromarty, the lands and Barony of Craigie-Fintry in Aberdeenshire. [a surname derived from a settlemeny by Loch Ness in Invrness-shire, examples date from the fourteenth century] [Thomas Urquhart, a planter in Barbados in 1678, while Reverend Urquhart was a minister on Prince Edward Island around 1800. [History of the Family of Urquhart, Aberdeen, 1946]

VACHE, [VEITCH?], OF DAWICK IN PEEBLES-SHIRE. On 20 May 1536, King James V granted James Vache, son and heir apparent of William Vache of Dawick, the lands and Barony of Dawick, also North Sintoun in Roxburghshire. [Genealogical fragments re Veitch, Berwick, 1855]

VAUS OF MENNY IN ABERDEENSHIRE. On 3 January 1530, King James V confirmed John Vaus of Menny, in the lands of Findon, Portlethan, Boquharn, Auchorthy and Cookstoun in Kincardineshire, also the lands of Mennie, Cookbyrn, and fishing on the River Dee, in Aberdeenshire, now incorporated in the Barony of Menny. On 3 November 1534, King James V granted John Vaus of Mannie the lands of Easter and Wester Ruthven, with mills, incorporated into the Barony of Mennie. [a name of French origin, examples in Scotland date from the twelfth century][Charles Vass, a sailor, was bound for Darien in Panama in 1698, while Jane Vaus emigrated to South Carolina in 1767]

VAUS OF MYRETOUN IN WIGTONSHIRE. On 16 January 1697, King James VI confirmed Patrick Vaus of Barnbarroch in the lands and Barony of Myretoun.

VIPONT OF CARRIDEN IN MIDLOTHIAN. On 16 April 1369, King David II granted William Veteri Pont the Barony of Carriden, also those of Bolton and Langtoun. [the surname originated in France but became Vipont in Scotland]

WALLACE OF CRAIGIE-WALLACE IN AYRSHIRE. William Wallace of Craigie was killed at the Battle of Flodden on 9 September 1513. On 12 July 1588, King James VI appointed John Wallace of Craigie the baillie of the lands, Lordship and Barony of Monkton in Ayrshire. In 1638 King Charles I created

Sir Hugh Wallace as Baronet of Craigie Wallace and Newton in Ayrshire, he resigned the Baronetcy, and died by 1660. [Wallace may be an old Celtic name meaning a Strathclyde Briton, examples date from the twelfth century] [Archibald Wallace died in Jamaica in 1779, while George Wallace, a Jacobite, was transported to Maryland in 1747][The Book of Wallace, Edinburgh, 1889]

WARDLAW OF PITREAVIE IN FIFE. Henry Wardlaw was granted the Barony of Wilton in Roxburghshire by King Robert I around 1318; on 18 May1562, Queen Mary, granted Andrew Wardlaw, son and heir apparent of Henry Wardlaw of Torry, the lands and Barony of Easter Lochore; Sir Henry Wardlaw, was created a baronet of Nova Scotia on 5 March 1631. [Wardlaw is derived from a placename in Scotland, examples of the surname date from the early thirteenth century][Harry Wardlaw, a lawyer from Edinburgh, settled in Jamaica after 1746][The Wardlaws in Scotland, Edinburgh, 1912][A genealogical account of the Wardlaw family of Pitreavie, 1811]

WARRENDER OF LOCHEND IN EAST LOTHIAN. George Warrander, born 1648 son of George Warrender and his wife Margaret Cunningham, was created Baronet of Lochend on 2 June 1715, was Lord Provost of Edinburgh in 1707 and 1714, later MP for Edinburgh until his death on 4 March 1722; he was succeeded by his son Sir John Warrender as second baronet of Lochend, he too was Lord Provost of Edinburgh and a Member of Parliament and died on 13 January 1772. [The surname is of occupational origin, that is the keeper of a rabbit warren, examples date from the thirteenth century]. [William Warrender, a foremastman, was bound from Leith to Darien in Panama in 1698, while ... Warren, a soldier, settled in Quebec after 1762]

WEDDERBURN OF BLACKNESS IN ANGUS. On August 9, 1704, John Wedderburn of Blackness was created as a Baronet, when he died in 1706, the title was inherited by his son Sir Alexander Wedderburn as second Baronet of Blackness, he died in February 1710, next came his brother Sir John Wedderburn, an army officer, who died unmarried in 1723, the title of fourth Baronet of Blackness went to his cousin Sir Alexander Wedderburn, who died on 21 September 1744. [a territorial surname from Berwickshire, examples date from the thirteenth century] [George Wedderburn in New York in 1689, while James Wedderburn, an attorney, died in Jamaica in 1797][The Wedderburn Book, 1898]

WEMYSS OF LEUCHARS IN FIFE. On 10 September 1473 King James III granted Sir Thomas Wemyss of Reras, the lands and Barony of Leuchars, also the lands of Bordland, Miltoun, lands of Pursk, Baltony, Brigend, the tofts of Muris, the lands of Logymurtho, Wester Casoy, Brighous of

Logymurtho, in Fife. [The surname is derived from a place of that name in Fife, examples of the surname date from the early thirteenth century] [Alexander Wemyss died in New York in 1782, while James Wemyss, an Ensign, died at Darien in Panama in 1699,]

WEMYSS OF WEMYSS IN FIFE. On 28 August 1511, King James IV granted Sir David Wemyss of that Ilk, the lands of Wemyss-shire, Little Lune, Tullibrek, the mill at Cameron, Halch, Doniface, Pitconnochy, Wester Tarbet, Wester Dron, and Hilldron, in Fife, also the lands of Elchok and Balabraham, parts of Strathardle and Ardargy, the lands of Kinard in Perthshire, and Balhalwell in Angus, with mills, now incorporated into the Barony of Wemyss; Sir David Wemyss was killed at the Battle of Flodden on 9 September 1513; on 24 June 1530, King James V confirmed David Wemyss of that Ilk, in the lands of Wemyss, Little Lun, Tullibrek, Cameron mill, Halch, Donipace, Tarbet, Dron, Hilldron, in Fife, and Elcho, Balabraham, part of Strathardle in Perthshire, and the lands of Balhalwell in Angus, now incorporated into the Barony of Wemyss; on 10 May 1589, King James VI granted John Wemyss, son and heir apparent of David Wemyss of that Ilk, the lands of Wemyss with other lands in Fife, Perthshire, and Angus now incorporated into the Barony of Wemyss. [Memorials of the family of Wemyss of Wemyss, Edinburgh, 1888]

WEMYSS OF PITTENCREIFF IN FIFE. On 16 September 1538, King James V granted Patrick Wemyss as Baron of Pittencreiff.

WEMYSS OF MAIRCAIRNY IN FIFE. On 27 March 1595, King James VI granted Andrew Wemyss of Maircairny, the lands and Barony of Maircairny.

WEMYSS OF NOVA SCOTIA. Sir David Wemyss was created baronet of New Wemyss with 16,000 acres in Nova Scotia by King Charles I on 30 September 1626. He married Jean Gray, daughter of Lord Patrick Gray. When he became Lord Wemyss in 1679, the Baronetcy merged with his peerage.

WEMYSS OF BOGIE IN FIFE. On 12 October 1704, James Wemyss of Bogie was created Baronet of Bogie, when he died about 1706, he was succeeded by his son Sir John Wemyss as second Baronet, who died about 1750.

WHITEFOORD OF BLAIRQUHAN IN AYRSHIRE. On 29 January 1642, King Charles I granted John Whiteford in Maybole, the lands, and Barony of Blairquhan; On 30 December 1701, Adam Whitefoord was created as a Baronet, he died in November 1727, when his son Sir John Whitefoord, a soldier and eventually a Lieutenant General, became the 2nd Baronet.

[a place near Paisley, examples date from the thirteenth century][James Whiteford emigrated to Maryland in 1730]

WILSON OF CUMNOCK IN AYRSHIRE. Oliver Cromwell, the Lord Protector, granted the lands and Barony of Cumnock, together with the burgh of Barony of Cumnock with its weekly markets and annual fair to Anthony Wilson, treasurer to the Commissioners for Forfeited Estates in Scotland. [a patronymic surname 'son of Will', very common in Scotland, examples date from the sixteenth century] [Andrew Wilson, a founder from Aberfoyle, was transported to Maryland in 1771, and Peter Wilson, born in Aberdeenshire in 1766, the Professor of Classics at Columbia, died in 1825][The Wilsons, a Banffshire family, Edinburgh 1936]

WINTON OF BALGAVIE IN ANGUS. On 18 September 1559, King Francis and Queen Mary confirmed John Winton, son and heir apparent of Alexander Winton, in the lands and Barony of Balgavy. [the surname comes from a location in East Lothian, examples date from the late twelfth century] [David Winton, aboard the Olive Branch bound for Darien in 1699]

WISEMAN OF DUNE IN ANGUS. King David II granted William Wiseman the Barony of Dune around 1340 formerly held by David Strathbogie. [an old surname in Angus and Moray, examples date from 1232]

WISHART OF PITARROW IN KINCARDINESHIRE. On 30 April 1512, King James IV granted James Wishart the lands of Pitarrow with its tower and messuage, the lands of Woodtoun, the lands of Carnbeggs, now incorporated into the Barony of Pitarrow. [a surname of Old French origin, examples in Scotland date from 1200] [James Wishart, from Kincardineshire, died in Jamaica before 1755, while Margaret Wishart, a spinner, emigrated to Quebec in 1774][Genealogical history of the Wisharts of Pitarrow and Logie Wishart, Perth,1914]

WISHART OF CLIFTONHALL IN MIDLOTHIAN. On 17 June 1706 George Wishart of Cliftonhall was created a Baronet, on his death around 1722, the title was inherited by his grandson Sir William Stuart who died in Paris on 6 December 1777.

WOOD OF LARGO IN FIFE. On 21 August 1513, King James IV granted Sir Andrew Wood of Largo, the lands of Largo and Coitlands with its mill and brewery, the lands of Fawfields and Frostleys in the Barony of Reres, also Brown Islands with tofts and crofts in Fife, now incorporated into the Barony of Largo; on 4 December 1541, King James V granted Andrew Wood of Largo, the lands of Fawfield and Frostleyis now part of the Barony of Largo;

on 8 October 1594, King James VI confirmed Andrew Wood of Largo in the Barony of Largo, etc; on 25 February 1597, King James IV confirmed Andrew Wood of Largo in the lands and Barony of Largo. [possibly a residential surname indicating a residence, examples date from the thirteenth century][William Wood from Glasgow, applied to settle in Canada in 1818, while John Wood was transported to Barbados in 1665][Memorials of the family of Wood of Largo, 1863]

WOOD OF HILTOUN IN KINCARDINESHIRE. On 6 January 1542, King James V granted David Wood of Craig, the lands of Easter Dunnone, with tower, fort, mill, the lands of Whitfield, Drumgeith, Balkello, and Fullerton, in Angus, also the lands of Hiltoun, with harbour and fishing rights, in Kincardine, now united in the Barony of Hiltoun.

WOOD OF FETTERCAIRN IN KINCARDINESHIRE. On 4 February 1555, Queen Mary granted Walter Wood, son and heir apparent of John Wood of Fettercairn, the lands and Thaneage of Fettercairn and Aberlethnott in Kincardineshire; on 31 January 1596, King James VI granted Walter Wood, son of Walter Wood of Balbegyenoth, the lands and Thanage of Fettercairn and Aberlethnot and other lands now incorporated in the Barony and Thanage of Aberlethnot.

WOOD OF LETHAM IN ANGUS. On 12 July 1601, King James VI granted Patrick Wood of Bonyngtoun, the Barony of Letham also the lands and Barony of Birnes in Aberdeenshire

WOOD OF BONYNGTOUN IN ANGUS. On 11 May 1666, John Wood of Bonyngtoun was created as a Baronet, he died in January 1693, his son and heir Sir James Wood, an officer in the Dutch Army and later the British Army, then became the 2nd Baronet until his death on 3 May 1738

SOME SCOTS—IRISH BARONETS

ACHESON OF GLEN CAIRNEY IN COUNTY ARMAGH. Sir Archibald Acheson, born in Edinburgh, was denised in Ireland on 12 February 1618, he was created as a Baronet of Nova Scotia by King Charles I on 1 January 1628, he died in Donegal on 9 September 1634.

BINGHAM OF COUNTY MAYO. On 7 June, 1636, KinDonegal on 9 September 1634g Charles I created Captain Henry Bingham of Castlewar in County Mayo, a Baronet of Nova Scotia.

BROWNE OF COUNTY MAYO. On 17 June 1636, King Charles I created John Browne of Neale in County Mayo, a Baronet of Nova Scotia.

CALDWELL OF COUNTY FERMANAGH. On 23 June 1683, James Caldwell of Wellskillen was created as a Baronet.

CORSBIE OF WICKLOW. On 24 April 1630, King Charles I created Walter Corsbie of Corsbie Park in County Wicklow, a Baronet of Nova Scotia.

ECHLIN OF RUSH HOUSE. King George I created Sir Henry Echlin, born 1652 as Baronet of Rush House in County Dublin, on 7 October 1721, died on 29 November 1725. He was descended from Henry Echlin, from Scotland, Bishop of Down and Connor. On his death the baronetcy passed to his grand son and heir Sir Robert Echlin, born 13 November 1699, died on 13 May 1757, as he had no children the baronetcy went to his nephew Sir Henry Echlin. Sir Henry Echlin, the third baronet, was born on 22 December 1740, and died in 1799. [The surname comes from a place in West Lothian, examples date from the thirteenth century][Thomas Ecklin, a former soldier settled in Ontario in 1817]

FORBES OF COUNTY LONGFORD. On 29 September 1628, King Charles I created Captain Arthur Forbes of Castle Forbes in County Longford, a Baronet of Nova Scotia.

HAMILTON OF COUNTY DOWN. On 29 September 1628, King Charles I created Francis Hamilton of Killach in County Down, as a Baronet of Nova Scotia.

HAMILTON OF COUNTY TYRONE. George Hamilton of Donalong, County Tyrone, son of the Earl of Abercorn, was created as a Baronet in 1664, he died in 1679 and was succeeded by his son James Hamilton as the 2nd Baronet but as he succeeded as Earl of Abercorn in 1701, the baronetcy merged into the peerage.

HAMILTON OF COUNTY ARMAGH. On 6 April 1662 King Charles II created Hans Hamilton as a Baronet on 6 April 1662, he died childless on 14 February 1682 when the barony became extinct.

HAMILTON OF MANOR CUNNINGHAM IN COUNTY DONEGAL. On 23 January 1775 Henry Hamilton, son and heir of Reverend Andrew Hamilton, was created a Baronet on 23 January 1775, as he died childless on 26 June 1782 the baronetcy became extinct.

HUME OF ARDGORTE IN COUNTY FERMANAGH. George Home, son of Sir John Home of North Berwick in Scotland, was created a Baronet of Castle Home in Ireland by Charles I in 1638, he died in Edinburgh around 1657. The next Baronet was his son Sir John Hume, a supporter of King William, he died on 10 January 1685. He was succeeded as third Baronet by Sir Gustavus Hume who died childless on 25 October 1731, when the title went to his cousin Sir Charles Hume who died in April 1747 again with no children when the baronetcy became extinct.

HAMILTON OF COUNTY ARMAGH. On 19 February 1683, Sir Robert Hamilton of Mount Hamilton was created as a Baronet.

IRVINE OF COUNTY FERMANAGH. On 31 July 1677 Gerard Irvine of Lowtherstown, was created as a Baronet.

JOHNSTON, OF GILFORD IN COUNTY DOWN. Richard Johnston, son and heir of Richard Johnston, was born on 1 August 1743, was created a Baronet on 27 July 1772, died 22 April 1795.

KENNEDY, ROBERT, of Ballygarvey in County Wicklow, was created as a Baronet on 25 January 1665

SLOANE OF KILLILEAGH IN COUNTY DOWN. Hans Sloane, born 10 April 1660, son of Alexander Sloane of Killileagh, was created as a Baronet on 3 April 1716, a physician and President of the Royal Society, died in Chelsea, London, on 11 January 1753, and as childless the baronetcy became extinct. [The surname is one of Gaelic origin, examples, in Scotland date from around 1500][John Sloan, settled in Maryland in 1674, while John Sloan, from Dumfres-shire, settled in New Brunswick in 1821]

SOMERVILLE OF ATHULNEY. Sir James Somerville, son of Thomas Somerville a merchant in Dublin, was created as Baronet of Athulney by King George I on 17 June 1748, and died on 16 August 1748. , The second Baronet of Athulney was Sir Quaile Somerville, born 1714, died in Brownstown in County Meath on 5 December 1772.

STEWART OF COUNTY TYRONE. On 2 October 1628, King Charles I created Andrew Stewart of Castle Stewart in County Tyrone, a Baronet of Nova Scotia.

www.ingramcontent.com/pod-product-compliance
Lightning Source LLC
Chambersburg PA
CBHW070401240426
43661CB00056B/2492